VOICES

FROM THE

WARHAWK AIR MUSEUM

"Veterans Day"[i]

---

[i] Joseph Ambrose, an 86-year-old World War I veteran, attends the dedication day parade for the Vietnam Veterans Memorial in 1982. He is holding the flag that covered the casket of his son, who was killed in the Korean War – photo by Mickey Sanborn, Department of Defense, Defense Audiovisual Agency, National Archives and Records.

VOICES

FROM THE

WARHAWK AIR MUSEUM

VETERANS HISTORY PROJECT

Warhawk Air Museum,
Nampa, Idaho

ISBN – 13: 9781508956440
ISBN – 10: 1508956448

FRONT COVER–Photo titled "Gung Ho!" by Joseph J. Rosenthal, U.S. Marines on Mt. Suribachi, Iwo Jima, February 23, 1945. Design by Kaycee Porter.

BACK COVER–Photos of VHP veterans. Crew members of a US Army BlackHawk helicopter holding an American flag as they posed with five returning Wounded Warriors at Camp Korean Village, Iraq, December 29, 2009–USO Photo by Mike Theiler. Design by Kaycee Porter.

PHOTOGRAPHS–All veterans' photos in this book were provided by the Warhawk Air Museum Veterans History Project. Other photographs included were taken from the internet "public domain," unless otherwise cited.

INTRODUCTION

In 2002, the Warhawk Air Museum, a 501(c)(3) nonprofit museum located in Nampa, Idaho, was honored to become a part of the national effort (under the direction of the Library of Congress) to collect, preserve and make accessible the personal accounts of American wartime veterans and civilians. The purpose of the project was so future generations of Americans, and the world at large, would understand the realities of war. This endeavor is called the "Veterans History Project."

Because of the dedicated Warhawk Air Museum volunteer team who has been willing to spend thousands of hours interviewing, filming and editing, we have preserved over 900 filmed stories. We have submitted them for perpetual keeping to the Library of Congress, the Warhawk Air Museum archival files, and most importantly, as a gift to each veteran for their families to have forever. These stories are compelling, many times emotional, and at all times revealing about how truly personal war is to each person who serves his or her country. The stories are extremely powerful in that the experiences the veterans lived through are told as they remembered them in their own words and emotions, with little editing. Many veterans had harrowing, life-threatening, experiences overseas; while others never left the United States. But all their stories are important, because these men and women served our country during times of war and were able to describe in their own words and their own memories what it was like on the home-front and military environments. Many veterans had never before told their stories, and their families are indebted to this project for giving them a chance to share in a loved one's war experience.

I would like to thank Bob Sobba for his vision in preserving these stories in book form and donating so much of his time and financial support to this project. I would also like to thank the dedicated team of volunteers who spent countless hours transcribing these stories. I hope the sixty-one stories included in this book will provide you with an opportunity to learn about some of the unforgettable experiences from the people who lived them. This is not Hollywood, and these stories are not fiction. They are real, and we honor the people who served our country and are grateful for their willingness to share their war stories.

It has been an honor to be a part of the Veterans History Project.

Sue Paul
Executive Director
Warhawk Air Museum

Warhawk Air Museum Executive Director Sue Paul (center) and Warhawk Air Museum VHP Director Barry Hill (left), presenting the 500th VHP film to Bob Patrick, National Director of the Veterans History Project, Washington, D.C.

ACKNOWLEDGMENTS

Special thanks should be extended to John and Sue Paul, co-founders of the Warhawk Air Museum, for their longtime commitment to military veterans and their histories. The Warhawk Air Museum started the Veterans History Project (VHP) over twelve years ago, and since that time approximately 900 veterans' oral histories have been recorded and preserved for future generations.

During one of our training sessions, I suggested putting some of these stories in a book and using the proceeds from its sale to support the VHP at the Warhawk Air Museum. The idea was met with enthusiasm from Sue and other volunteers. Soon we had a committee assembled and all members have worked diligently on this book, preparing for the publication of sixty-one of the stories gleaned from the VHP interviews.

We had no specific criteria for deciding which interviews were selected, other than wanting a broad overview of all the veterans we had interviewed. We made sure we covered the major wars and conflicts of the last seventy-five years, as well as peacetime military service.

Our dedicated team of authors consisted of Ali and Barry Hill (Barry also helped collate digital photos and assisted with research), Susan Hill (who also helped edit), Stan Hobson, Judy Menger, Jan Peterson and myself.

Our chief editors, Bob and Kathy Christensen, did a commendable job, not only editing the individual stories, but also preparing the book for final publication.

Recognition should also be given to Kaycee Porter for her artistic expertise in designing the book's covers.

Available space does not allow us to name all the volunteers who have contributed to the success of the VHP at the Warhawk Air Museum, but their efforts are appreciated by our team and the hundreds of veterans who have been interviewed.

Lastly, Heather Mullins, who despite her expanding workload as the museum's administrative assistant, spent considerable time with editing, computer work, and a variety of other tasks that arose as the book took shape.

We hope the reader will enjoy these compelling stories of our heroic veterans.

Bob Sobba
Veterans History Project
Book Coordinator

TABLE OF CONTENTS

...If they want to call us heroes we can live with that. As for us who lived in these times, and still survived, let us prayerfully reflect on our experiences, reverently remember our lost comrades, and tell our war stories one more time. And, in those times of celebration and commemoration, let us enjoy a moment of pride. Then let us fold our tents and quietly move on, for there are others behind us from other wars waiting for their day of glory. Heroes, too!

Thomas R. Young
U.S. Army Air Corps
WWII - POW

Hubert L. Andrew
U.S. Army
WWII
1944–1945

Ike shouted, "Just do it!"

Hubert was born in Missouri in November of 1925. He finished the third grade in Missouri and then moved with his parents to Kansas. The family later made a move to Paul, Idaho. Before finishing high school, Hubert went to work and was later drafted into the Army on May 2, 1944. He and other draftees went by train from Rupert, Idaho, to Fort Douglas, Utah. Because of his good eyesight, physical condition and marksmanship, he was singled out as a prospective Army scout. His training at Fort Knox, Kentucky, was in weaponry and included the Thompson submachine gun, carbine, and M-1 rifle, as well as flare pistols. Hubert also gained additional training in scouting and river-crossing techniques at Fort Meade, Maryland, and in New York State.

In November of 1944 Hubert and 3,000 other replacement troops boarded the *USS General Brooks,* bound for England and France. Fifty-one ships in the convoy made the fourteen-day trans-Atlantic crossing. They zigzagged across the Atlantic to evade German U-boats and landed in Le Havre, France, in early December. They then boarded a train for Brussels, Belgium, where they slept in tents and ate K-rations. Finally, Hubert and another scout were put into a half-track (a truck with regular wheels at the front and continuous tracks at the back) and sent north.

Hubert was designated as first scout in a three-man scout unit. The third scout in the unit was known as the "get-away man." In

1

the event the other two encountered trouble or wanted to get a message back to headquarters, this man's responsibility was to head back. Typically there were three scouts afoot, moving in front of Allied lines with the intent of finding the enemy's location and strength. Occasionally they would participate in larger scouting parties–from squad-size up to thirteen men. Each man had to be adept at map reading and possess good night vision. As first scout, Hubert carried a Thompson submachine gun with a muzzle suppressor to lessen the flash.

Hubert and his team were then assigned to the 7th Armored Division, 87th Mechanized Cavalry and were called "troopers." They scouted in front of their division continuously for about eight months, but most often returned to their command post daily. They worked their way forward by following lines of timber, ditches or other cover and then scouted out towns, working their way into the town center from its outskirts. The scouts knew that the Germans often hid tanks in old bombed-out buildings. So, many times they would wait for Belgium locals to come out of their houses. They would then quiz the older people about German armament locations. Children were also free-talkers and many of them spoke some English. Hubert commented that in his opinion the "Belgian folks" were nice to the GIs and would cooperate with them. For example, a Belgian lady asked Hubert to come into her home to help with some chores. She was alone because her son had been conscripted into the German army. After Hubert finished, she invited him and his team to come inside and sleep in real beds for the night. That was a special treat!

Hubert was always mindful that once exposed, a scout's life was in danger. They carried no radios and were instructed if they wrote anything down and were in danger, they should throw the message away. The scouts could signal the Allied lines with flares, but once a scout sent up a flare, he needed to remain hidden for several hours. Scouts did not wear helmets, because they were too reflective, so they wore wool caps instead.

At Leinsdorf in the Ruhr Valley, Hubert entered a wine shop, and when he came out a German captain was waiting for him, pointing a burp-gun at him. The captain explained that he had 400 German troops who hadn't eaten in several days, and he wanted the people of the village to feed them. The German promised to release Hubert, but only after the troops were fed. Four hours later he was released and the Germans disappeared.

During the Battle of the Bulge, Hubert's unit scouted alongside Patton's Army. Scouts had passwords and color codes, as well as other devices, to assure their safe return to their command post. They didn't want to be mistaken for Germans, who often dressed in dead GI uniforms in order to infiltrate Allied units. If the scouts ended up being out more than one day, it was essential that they knew the next two days' passwords as well.

The Bulge was seventy-five miles wide and 140 miles long. During the conflict, 319 GIs in his division were shot and killed by the Germans. It was up to Hubert and his team to investigate and recover each man's dog tags. He was in the Bulge campaign until it ended and was then sent to scout the area near Bastogne. He remembered advancing on the city by way of a World War I trench, while German V-1 buzz bombs attacked Bastogne.

If the scouts knew they would be out overnight, they sometimes took mummy sleeping bags with them. They often went many days without showers. At one point Hubert remembered he hadn't changed his fatigues in six weeks. What a relief it was when they finally were able to bathe in the Rhine River. The locals ate a diet that mainly consisted of potatoes and cabbages. Both Belgian and German civilians ate these same staples. Hubert witnessed children whom the SS had murdered and left hanging on power poles–their throats had been cut. Hubert

3

and his unit also scouted the Arnhem River, Netherlands, for General Montgomery. During their travels they were also surprised when they encountered advancing Russian troops and a unit of Spanish soldiers.

Hubert's unit drove across the Remagen Bridge shortly after it was taken, and he witnessed the first ME-162 German jet take out another bridge in the same area. American P-38 and P-47 fighters gave chase, but the jet outran them both. Near the close of the war, Hubert and his men scouted out two Nazi concentration camps. At Buchenwald he crawled up to the outer fence. Under the machine gun tower he discovered a prisoner who had been electrocuted on the perimeter fence and was still hanging there. In the morning, he also saw about 500 dead prisoners in the camp. That afternoon Generals Patton and Eisenhower arrived to inspect the area. Eisenhower was adamant that they get local villagers to come bury the dead. Thousands of villagers were brought in to bury the bodies, and when many objected to touching the dead, Ike (General Eisenhower) shouted, "Just do it!" Hubert and his scout team were also instrumental in releasing 200 Canadians from another campsite which was about eight kilometers from the Allied lines.

With the war winding down, Hubert and another scout were sent on to Hamburg and from there were allowed to start back home. They took a train to Camp Lucky Strike in Le Havre, France, and boarded a ship. Hubert remembered, after going onto the ship, that four GIs came aboard carrying an extra duffle bag that seemed to be wiggling. They had smuggled an orphan aboard and were taking him back to the U.S. with them. Because the ship sailed straight across the Atlantic without zigzagging, they arrived in Boston about seven and a half days later. Hubert was given a thirty-day leave and then he traveled to Texas and on to Fort Lewis, Washington, for his discharge.

Hubert declared that he would be "an Army man forever!"

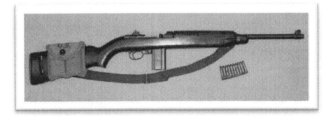

WWII – M1 Carbine

Photos Courtesy of Hubert Andrew

Ruel Hale Barrus
U.S. Army
WWII
1943–1945
POW

*"I think my overcoat saved
my life."*

When Ruel Barrus stepped out of the movie theater that afternoon on December 7, 1941, in rural Idaho, he did not know that the news he heard about the bombing of Pearl Harbor would greatly impact his life a few years later. He was just seventeen years old.

After graduating from high school in 1943, and knowing he would be drafted for military service, Ruel first tried to join the Air Force, but he couldn't pass the eye test. He did, however, pass the Army tests for enlistment. He was told he was eligible for a program called the Army Specialized Training Program, or ASTP, which meant an eligible recruit would be able to attend two years of college, compliments of the Army, after he finished basic training. However, the Army terminated the program just before Ruel could be enrolled in it. Instead, after basic training in Ft. Benning, Georgia, he was sent to the 94th Infantry Division, Third Battalion, 302 Regiment, Co. L, Third Platoon. This assignment was clearly not where he wanted to serve. After six or seven months of training at Camp McCain, Mississippi, Ruel's unit was put on a Cunard Line cruise ship sailing for England. This ocean liner had been refitted as a troop carrier and used for that purpose for the duration of the war.

Landing in England, the unit spent a few weeks camped outside of London. For a country boy from Idaho, seeing Europe was an exciting experience; but the idea of going into combat always loomed over his head. Ruel's unit landed on Utah Beach two months after D-Day. He said that the beach by the time he arrived was pristine, and no one would have known that such a bloody battle had taken place there. His first combat experience was in the hedgerows in France. The American Army had been unexpectedly slowed down by the overgrown hedgerows. Tanks couldn't get through them. Ruel's assignment was to go out on night patrol with his squad. On a particular night he and his men had a close call. They accidently tripped some kind of device that turned on lights and lit up the entire field. A hidden enemy machine gunner opened up on them from one of the hedgerows. They were lucky to escape with their lives.

Ruel's unit was then sent to the Normandy Peninsula. They manned a line across the peninsula to keep 60,000 German soldiers trapped there. It had become a ready-made prison camp. The American soldiers lived in foxholes that they dug 200 yards from the German line. There were two men in a foxhole and they ended up living there for three months. They took turns at guard duty and on night watch, trying to make the best of the situation. Finally it came time to move on.

In December 1944 Hitler's forces broke through the Allied lines, which resulted in the Battle of the Bulge. All the U.S. Infantry units gathered together and headed north. In the dark, Ruel's unit moved to the front line, then through a mine field to the Maginot Line. This line of defensive fortifications was erected by the French to protect themselves from the Germans. The soldiers were set up in a rotation that had them spending two hours in a foxhole and then two hours in a bunker. They were so close to the enemy that they could easily be seen by the Germans. Mortars continuously fell and exploded all around their unit. When the assignments were made for the rotations, Ruel was given a later one. The next morning while he was taking his allotted time inside the bunker, there was a commotion outside. Ruel grabbed his rifle and grenades and went out to investigate. German guns were going off everywhere, and he lobbed a grenade in the direction of the guns. Then a German machine gun began to fire at them. The sergeant ordered everyone to get back to the bunker, while he remained outside to keep watch. Once inside the bunker the men secured the door. The Germans demanded that they surrender. They initially tried to smoke the GIs out, but the soldiers stuffed their coats into the air vents to keep the smoke out. Sometime in the afternoon, they heard their sergeant yelling. The Germans had captured him and were threatening to shoot him if the rest of the unit didn't come out of the bunker. That was when the Americans decided to surrender; but only after they had destroyed their rifles so the Germans couldn't use them.

Ruel was the first man out. Burp guns were jabbed into his ribs and the Germans pointed to one of their dead soldiers. He thought they were going to shoot him right there, but all the men were herded as a group to where other prisoners were being held, and then led to an old truck. Since it was December, outside temperatures were freezing. They passed a wounded U.S. soldier from their platoon, who lay in the snow on the side of the road, crying out that he was cold. He had no coat, so Ruel took his coat off and gave it to him–then moved on to the truck. A short time later, another soldier came up to Ruel and gave him back his coat. He never knew what became of the other soldier, but he could guess. "I think my overcoat saved my life because later on we were so cold," he said.

The prisoners were taken by truck to a group of buildings that were behind enemy lines. Their jewelry was stripped from them. One by one they were taken away to be interrogated. Ruel was surprised when it came his turn to be questioned. His interrogator sat behind a table and looked like a typical German from the movies–a big swastika hanging on the wall behind him. He spoke excellent English. The guard prodded him with a rifle and asked for his overshoes. He said, "No," twice. The German behind the desk told him to give them up, and he did. At first there was pleasant conversation and Ruel was offered some refreshment, which he refused. Then he was asked about his outfit. He gave his name, rank and serial number. Over and over again this same questioning went on, until the German grew angry. He threatened to have Ruel shot if he did not respond correctly. Ruel refused to say anything more. He was then pushed out into the snow, stripped to his waist, and left there. Ruel commented, "I got awfully cold, but what saved me was that the guy watching over me got cold, too." He was soon taken back inside and questioned again. Since he refused to answer any questions, the German official grew frustrated and told the guard to get him out of there.

The next day the men were taken by truck to a prison camp near Limburg, Germany. There was one warehouse untouched by the bombings and they were housed in that building. They slept on lice-infested straw. They had to work, building a sign that read "POW Camp," as well as pile sandbags to protect German antiaircraft gun emplacements. At the camp Ruel's leg became swollen. When told he was going to have to march to another prison camp, he knew he had to comply or else he wouldn't survive. The POWs were given Red Cross supply boxes with food in them. They were forced to walk for five long days. Ruel recalled that a man named John Bockman, who walked beside him, died during the march.

Arriving at Bad Orb Prison Camp, the captives were told to strip and shower (Ruel's first and only shower during imprisonment). To kill the lice, all their clothes were run through an oven. They were then taken to the barracks that would become their home until they were liberated. The barracks had no beds or facilities; i.e., no toilets, kitchens, or showers. There was a hole in the floor for a toilet, and one water faucet that only worked part of the day. The prisoners slept on hard wooden floors. To keep warm the men slept six together–rotating who would be on the outside–and that kept everyone equally warm. There was a lot of sickness, with burial details conducted daily. Their food consisted mainly of a soup made from water, cabbage and possibly a little horsemeat. Each day, two guys would be sent to the kitchen to pick up the food for the rest of the men. One day it was discovered that two of them had been stealing some of the food before bringing the remainder back to the barracks. The rest of the prisoners formed a court with a jury, and they held a hearing. The jury was made up of six starving men. The offenders were convicted and sentenced to sit out in the street "using hammers to make little rocks out of big rocks."

Every day the men could hear the sound of American bombers–this kept them going. One day they heard artillery shells that kept getting closer. Soon afterward, tanks from the 776th Armored Division came in to liberate the POWs. The tanks knocked the pole gate down. Ruel met a soldier from Idaho who was from the town next to his. The soldier offered to help notify Ruel's family that he was alive and had been liberated. While he was being held captive, what Ruel worried about most was that his mother wouldn't know he was alive.

Three or four days later Ruel was taken to France to Camp Lucky Strike (the contribution of the tobacco company to the war effort). Here the freed POWs were given beds and all the food they wanted. Ruel was there for ten days and then trucked to a liberty ship. He was among the first group of POWs to arrive back in the United States, landing in New York City in December of 1945.

Inside one of the Barracks
of Bad Orb POW Camp

Bryan E. Brewer
U. S. Army
WWII
1942-1946

"I was in three major battles and never got a scratch, until I was in a vehicle accident near the end of the war."

Born in Comanche, Oklahoma, Bryan Brewer found himself working as a senior gardener or landscaper for the city of Glendale, California, when Pearl Harbor was attacked on December 7, 1941. That Sunday was his day off and he had gone out hunting in the woods. He had returned to town to get gas, and it was then that he heard on the radio about the Japanese attack on the U.S. Naval fleet. At age twenty-one and already married, he decided not to volunteer for the military. Two of his brothers, however, did join–one in the Seabees and one in the Infantry. In the end, his married status didn't make any difference, and he was drafted a year later in December 1942 and sent for a year to Camp Hollis, Texas. He recalled his stay there as being really hot in the summer and very cold in the winter. From there he was reassigned to Louisiana, an even hotter, more humid place. Here Bryan trained for ten weeks in the swamps. He was being trained for eventual battle in the South Pacific, along with training in the use of explosives. Instead of the South Pacific, however, he received orders to the European Theater and was sent to Camp Kilmer, New Jersey, for two weeks before boarding a troop ship and heading for England. Due to U-boat sightings, his ship was diverted to Scotland, and from there he traveled by train on to London. After two weeks stationed outside of London he was sent over the English Channel to France.

Bryan was with the 84th Infantry Division, 309th Combat Engineers. Landing in France his group crossed the Siegfried Line just after a battle that had lasted several weeks. The Allies were pinned down outside of Geilenkirchen, Germany, but they later took control of the town. From Geilenkirchen it was on to Belgium where Bryan fought in the Battle of the Bulge. The U.S. military suffered a great number of casualties in the battle. The worst weather on record took its toll on the suffering troops. It was freezing cold and the men had not received their arctic overshoes. Bryan's frostbitten feet from that experience continued to bother him the remainder of his life. It was so cold that the juice in their canned peaches froze before they could eat them. They remained there and fought in the area for several weeks.

Bryan was the radio operator for his unit. At one point he was stationed alone in sub-zero temperatures, manning a transfer station at the base of a mountain. He got so cold that he realized he needed to get into some shelter. He found a shack and after entering he discovered a dead German soldier who had a gunshot wound in his stomach. The soldier's body was frozen solid. Bryan tied a cord around the soldier's ankle and pulled him out into the snow and left him there.

After the Battle of the Bulge, Bryan's unit went back to Germany. Their job there was to construct bridges across the Rhine River. Once the bridges were completed they moved on with the task of building one across the Ruhr River. However, they were unable to build it because the Germans had bombed the dam and flooded the valley. Because of all the mud and water, the Army couldn't construct the bridge. After two weeks, when the water finally receded, they were successful in erecting the bridge so that the military could make the Ruhr crossing. The unit also built foot bridges wherever the troops needed them.

On the way to take Hannover, Germany, Bryan's unit came upon a "displaced persons" camp of 1,000 men. He and his first sergeant were the first soldiers into the camp, and they came upon a horrendous sight. Of the 1,000 men they found, only ninety-one were still alive, and they were barely surviving. The men who died had perished from malnutrition and disease. After freeing the prisoners, the GIs continued on to Hannover where they captured that city and then crossed the Ruhr River again and moved on to where they met the Russians at the Elbe River.

After being transferred to the 12th Armored Division, Bryan suffered his only injury of the war. It was a bad one! He and a group of other soldiers were on a two and a half ton truck going into the town to take showers, when their truck was hit by two drunks driving another vehicle. The spare wheel of the truck hit Bryan on his side. He was taken to the hospital in town, suffering from a ruptured spleen. He was hospitalized for about six months until he was finally sent to Bremen, Germany, and then put on a hospital ship back to the States. He landed in New York and was again sent down to Camp Kilmer, New Jersey. He stayed there for three weeks. The Army then transported him to Ft. Lewis, Washington, for six weeks, before he was finally able to travel down to California and return to his wife and job.

U.S. Tank from Battle of the Bulge

Helen Maag French
U.S. Army Nurse
WWII
1942-1945

"I went AWOL to fly in a bomber."

Helen Maag French was born in December of 1918 on a farm outside of Buhl, Idaho. Her parents had emigrated from Switzerland and the family spoke German-Swiss before they learned to speak English. There were six girls and three boys to help with the farm chores. Their mother died in 1928 when Helen was ten. Her dad was a carpenter by trade and after his wife's death he hired a man to manage the farm and he went to work in town as a carpenter. He never remarried.

Helen went to high school in the town of Buhl–a long way from the farm. During the school week she stayed with a "nice, old lady" who had three birds and three large birdcages. Helen kept the cages clean in exchange for her room and board. She went home Friday after school and helped the other kids cook and clean the farmhouse. She returned to Buhl on Sunday afternoon. While Helen was completing high school, her older sister Alice was already in nursing school at St. Alphonsus in Boise, Idaho. Once Helen completed high school she worked for three months and then began her nurse's training at St. Alphonsus. It was a three-year course and during that time she always had a sister (younger or older) in training with her. All six of the sisters graduated from the St. Al's Nursing School, as did their mother.

After graduating Helen worked for a doctor in Buhl. She told him that she wanted to enroll in a post-graduate course in Boston so she could "see the country." He told her that she wouldn't be

16

happy being a scrub nurse all her life, and he suggested that she consider training in physical therapy. Subsequently, he loaned her enough money to enroll in a physical therapy course at Northwestern University in Chicago.

Northwestern University had a history with the U.S. Army. In 1916, a surgeon with the university organized a general hospital unit to assist the Allied war effort in Europe. During WWI it was called the U.S. Army Base Hospital #12 (Chicago Unit). In February of 1942, the unit was revived as the U.S. Army 12th General Hospital.

Two weeks prior to course completion, Helen was allowed to leave Northwestern and join the U.S. Army. She was looking for adventure, and in December of 1942 Helen was a nurse aboard the U.S. Army 12th General Hospital ship as part of a convoy en route to Oran, Algeria. The convoy went through the Strait of Gibraltar and into the port at Oran. The hospital was set up and put into operation five miles away at Ain el Turk. The unit embarked from Oran in December of 1943 and arrived at Naples, Italy, four days later. In June of 1944, the unit took the ship to Anzio, Italy, and then set up operations near Rome. In November they shipped to Leghorn (Livorno), Italy, and set up the hospital just north of the port. By July of 1945 the hospital had discharged its last patient and the unit officially disbanded September 1, 1945.

For three years Helen worked with wounded soldiers and loved being able to help the injured men until they were able to return to duty or to be sent home.

Helen said the Army took "really good care" of their nurses. The physical therapy department was closed on weekends and sometimes the airmen would drop their bombs on enemy targets and then return to base to pick up nurses who wanted to go for a ride. Helen said she went "AWOL" one day to ride in a bomber.

She sat in the nose of the bomber and loved her "free ride," but acknowledged that they had wasted fuel.

Helen loved being in the Army and completed her service with the rank of captain. She stated that, "It was a good unit, good doctors and I made good friends."

She found her adventure!

Hospital Ship – *USS Haven*

Leo Hammond
U.S. Army & National Guard
WWII & Korea
1942–1966

*On V-E Day he rang the bell of
the Leaning Tower of Pisa.*

Leo Hammond was born in Ashton, Idaho, in April of 1914. He was drafted in July of 1942 and was assigned to officer candidate school in Fort Belvoir, Virginia. Leo was commissioned as a second lieutenant in March 1943 and assigned to the Engineering Aviation Battalion at Fort Bliss, Texas. In August of 1943 he joined a troop convoy to North Africa. After the Allied invasion into Italy, he was sent there to equip the Army Air Corps. Leo moved, in December of 1943, with the troops from Corsica by LST (landing ship-tank) to southern France. Then in late 1944 he went to Marseilles, France, where the soldiers lived in tents that they heated with gasoline-fueled stoves.

Leo's engineer group followed the U.S. troops to Livorno, Italy, and then to Florence and Naples. On V-E Day he rang the bell at the top of the Leaning Tower of Pisa. Leo went back to Pisa in 1978 and rang that same bell again.

After the war in Europe was over, Leo was sent to Boston and then to Salt Lake City for discharge. In late 1948 he joined the Idaho National Guard in a Combat Engineering Battalion with the rank of lieutenant colonel; and in 1950 he was assigned as operations officer in a training unit at Fort Belvoir, Virginia.

In April 1951 Lt. Colonel Leo Hammond was sent to Pusan, Korea, to establish supply routes in support of the U.S. troops. A year later he was transferred to Japan, then to California, and finally to Colorado. The National Guard formed a combat unit in

1961, to which he was assigned. Leo was promoted to brigadier general in 1966 and retired after twenty-four distinguished years in the National Guard.

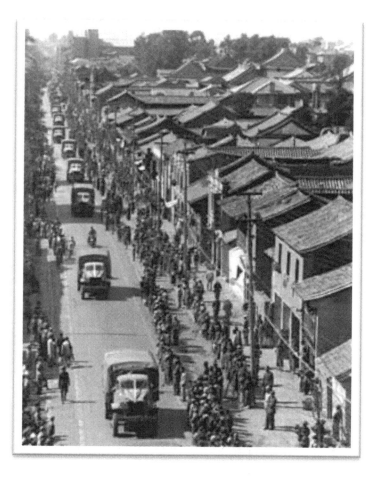

WWII Convoy of Allied Supply Trucks - China

Harold K. Herre
U.S. Army
WWII
1941-1945
Two Purple Hearts
Bronze Star

"He put a sulfa patch on the hole in my chest and said, 'We will be back for you.' "

Harold was born in Chicago, Illinois, and grew up during the Great Depression. He lived with his mother, father, two sisters and two brothers. Harold graduated from high school but couldn't find steady employment, so when he was offered a job with the CCC (Civilian Conservation Corps) he was able to help with the expenses at home.

I ran a rock crusher and built berms [small dikes or embankments]. I didn't know how to do anything, but we learned by doing. They ran it like the Army—we lived in barracks housing thirty men. I had read books about the Army and my uncle was in the Army in WWI. I was there [in the CCC] for six months but then wanted out in civilian life again. I worked for several years in office supplies and hung out at a pool hall (not a bar). I was a pool shark and made a few bucks there. I had a couple of nick names—one was Sparky, and well, that's enough. Across the street was a bookie and I worked watching the door for police. Wherever there was a job, I would do it. I bought a new car, a

Hudson, for $600. I gave people rides to work and charged them so I could make the payments.

That's where I met my wife. She came to work there and she was a doll! I was dating her when I went into the Army. When I made cook, I told her I was going to go into the paratroopers, which was 200 miles away from Camp Wheeler. She thought it was too dangerous. I told her I would come home on leave and we could get married. She was only nineteen and just out of school. I was twenty-three years old. Down to Georgia she came and I got an apartment. She got a job as a telegraph operator at the air base. But she was soon pregnant and I sent her home. I became a drill sergeant and that's when I got my orders. During that time we were quarantined for whooping cough, but I worked to get a seven-day leave and went home to Chicago. But they said I was AWOL. As punishment, they wouldn't let me leave the barracks.

I shipped overseas from there on a ship with thousands of other guys, and we had destroyer escorts. At midnight we landed in Liverpool, England, and it was still light because they had double daylight savings time. We stayed on the ship for a couple of days, and then we went to a camp. We marched in the rain with full field packs. We found out they were emptying the "honey buckets" into the potato fields. We could tell because we saw the toilet paper in the fields. I never liked mashed potatoes after that.

We went into London one weekend without permission. We had stuffed our beds with blankets to make it look like we were sleeping in them, but somebody snitched. While we were in London we were caught in an air raid and had to go underground. When we got back, they wanted to court martial us. I spoke first and said I had something to say. They asked me, "What is it, soldier?" I said, "We've already been punished for a week up in the kitchen. You can't court martial us." He said, "You are excused." So we got out of that, luckily.

We got on a boat and landed in France. We didn't hit when the other guys did (D-Day), but I felt for them, because I saw the mess. We went down the ladders into the water, hit the shore, and started walking until we got to Saint-Lô, fifteen-twenty miles down the road. We spread out into the hedgerows. There were still some Jerries in there and you just had to make sure you ducked. We kept going until we were just ten miles outside of Paris. I suggested we go to see Paris. (I was a bit of an agitator.) We had fun, but the MPs caught us and they just sent us back. We got in box cars on a train [traveling through] the countryside of France. We marched through the woods looking for the enemy and ended up in Belgium. All of a sudden we were all rounded up by a [U.S. Army] company. General Patton gave a speech to us. From there we went to the Hürtgen Forest. We were there for thirty days, holding the line. We were on a river and the Jerries were on the other side. Four of us made a raft out of brush and canvas to cross the river. It was running about twelve miles an hour. Two of us were lucky. We ran into a tree and held on. The guys on shore got a boat and a rope and got a boat out to us. I had a little Bible I always carried and it got soaking wet. We got out of there to a small town and had a chance to clean up a bit. In three days the Jerries attacked us with heavy artillery. I found a rifle and two bandoliers. I had thirteen men go through the forest looking for the Jerries. When I whistled, we started firing. We hid behind trees, but they must have had a sniper with a rifle because all of a sudden I got hit in the arm. I knew to fire and move, but I had such a good spot that I stayed there and, when I stepped out, I got hit in the right chest. To this day I don't know how I survived. I think about it, but not sure how I survived. A captain came along and wanted to roll me over, but I said, "No." I was face down. He put a sulfa patch on my hole and said, "We will be back for you." I was in the snow and couldn't feel my feet. All I knew was that I didn't want him to take my gun. I must have passed out. My partner Brownie didn't make it; he was also hit in the chest. Four guys with a stretcher came to get me, and put me on the stretcher face down, then on to a jeep to the first aid station. They took us in an ambulance and finally we got to a hospital behind the lines. They looked at my wound, and they told me they had to take care of it, but not to worry. That's the last I remembered until I woke up. They used butterfly stitches. All of a sudden they evacuated the hospital. They took us to Paris on a train. I think what saved my life was penicillin, which had just been developed. They were shooting me with it every hour.

Eventually they took us by truck to a ship and then back to England. I wound up in another hospital there. A doctor came by and he started snipping flesh off without any anesthetic. Eventually I went to rehab and I survived that. They gave me a whole pile of mail that I hadn't received.

While in England I checked with the Red Cross and found out my brother was also in England and had been shot in the leg. He was in a different hospital, but they let me go to visit him. I went to the recreation room in a wheelchair and there he was, playing the piano. We played piano together!

I was sent by ship back to the United States and several weeks later I was discharged and they gave me $200.00. I got some jobs in car manufacturing plants back in Illinois. Eventually, I became a parts salesman making $1.00 per hour. In a few years they told me I needed to move to a dry climate, so I packed up the car with my wife and seven kids and moved to Arizona. We bought several homes and did well there.

Bob Hibbs
U.S. Army
WWII
1942–1945

"War is hell, and cold, cold,
cold!"

Bob Hibbs was born in September of 1923. He attended the University of Florida, participated in ROTC, and enlisted in the Army Reserve. He was called to active duty in April of 1943. He completed his basic training at Fort Sill, Oklahoma, and then had specialized training in field communications for two quarters at the University of Mississippi. He was then assigned to the 94th Infantry Division in a communication platoon. Bob traveled on the very crowded Queen Elizabeth II cruise ship to Scotland. He offloaded via a shuttle boat and then took a train into England. In August of 1944, he went to Southampton, England, and boarded a "liberty ship" to Utah Beach, the site of the earlier June Allied invasion.

In France Bob saw action as a Jeep driver with a communication trailer and then fought in the Battle of the Bulge. The troops experienced the coldest weather that area had seen in forty years. They were constantly out following wire and splicing breaks. The only way to find the break in the line was to hold onto the line as the crew moved forward. German patrols would cut the lines and then stay to ambush the repair crews. The shelling was intense and, when not repairing communication lines, Bob pulled guard duty. The communication unit traded cigarettes for repair items they needed. While on the Siegfried Line, the Army's machine guns ran short of ammunition. Although they had no tank

26

support and no air cover, they did have good artillery. The 28th Division was overrun by the Germans, and Bob's 94th Infantry Division went in right behind them. Because of the freezing weather, many soldiers experienced frostbitten feet.

From battalion headquarters to company command, everything was in short supply, so Bob's crew reused everything they could. Bob was in the Bulge area for two to three weeks. In February and March his unit advanced across the Saar River. There they set up a switchboard in the basement of a six-story building that had been gutted by German 88 artillery guns. Initially, boats were used to cross the Saar and reach its banks on the opposite side. The soldiers carried ladders to scale those banks. Despite the very swift current, General Patton insisted on crossing prematurely. (According to Bob, Patton was not well thought of by some of his troops.) Upon crossing the Saar River, Bob fell in as he was trying to exit the boat. It was freezing!

It took from January to March to advance fifteen miles. One particular area was heavily mined. The soldier in front of Bob stepped on a mine and so did the medic going to help him. The soldiers were heading for the Rhine River and for weeks were in constant combat. Bob lost much of his hearing as the result of a close mortar shell explosion. In the Dusseldorf area they overran some horse-drawn artillery and released the horses. They marched into Czechoslovakia and with the Russians occupied that country.

In October 1945, Bob traveled through Germany and then to France, before boarding a ship to Boston. The Atlantic crossing took ten days, after which he took a train to Florida. There he was assigned to temporary duty and eventually discharged. Bob used his GI Bill benefits and earned a Ph.D. at Washington State University. He attended a 94th Division reunion in 1999 in Munich during Oktoberfest, and two years later attended another reunion in France.

Hiram A. Lorenzen, Jr.
U.S. Army
World War II
1941–1946

"Roosevelt est mort!"

Hiram was born in Emmett, Idaho, in January of 1919. He was an electrical engineering student at University of California, Berkeley, and he completed four years of ROTC. He was an accomplished musician and worked his way through college playing his trombone in dance bands. He turned twenty-two years old on January 15, 1941, and was in final exams and about to receive his Bachelor of Science degree in electrical engineering, when he was called into the office of the ROTC commander and was offered the rank of second lieutenant in the U.S. Army Signal Corps. He thanked the commander who shook his hand and handed Hiram his orders to report immediately for active duty. He did not graduate.

Hiram reported to Hunter Liggett Military Reservation in California on June 1, 1941. One of his first assignments at Hunter Liggett was to take a crew of men into King City (twenty-five miles NE) to set up a communications unit. Upon arriving they found that their future two-story communications center was occupied by a house full of prostitutes. The women moved across the street.

On July 11, 1941, Hiram was sent to Fort Monmouth, New Jersey, for further training. There was a long line of new recruits being questioned by a sergeant, and he asked Hiram if he was interested in high frequency techniques. He was interested and he was then diverted to a colonel's office. The colonel offered to double his lieutenant's pay of $125 per month and offered further education in high frequency techniques. The colonel informed him that he would have to forego signal school and had to be willing to go anywhere for his training. On September 12, 1941, Hiram and thirty-five other young men were heading north on a train. At the time, he was not aware of the other men being on the same train; he just knew that he was in the Electronic Training Group Number One, and that he couldn't tell anyone where he was or what he was doing. The last thing that his family and friends knew was that he was in the Signal Corps in New Jersey. As the train went through New York, a newspaper headline stated that the U.S. Navy had been attacked by German U-boats while on patrol duty in the North Atlantic.

Upon arriving at a Canadian port, the men were immediately boarded on the *Empress of Asia,* which was an old ship converted to a troop carrier. Hiram was assigned to a "one-person cabin" with five other men and three-tiered bunks on two sides of the cabin. The ship was escorted for two miles into the Atlantic by Canadian corvettes. The convoy of fifty ships that assembled in the North Atlantic was then escorted by the U.S. Navy. Along the way the Navy dropped explosive charges on any sub they could find, and that action was appreciated by the convoy. Twenty-four days later the convoy reached Liverpool, England.

On October 4, 1941, a small group of men were taken to the town of Bury and there Hiram was billeted with an English couple. He recalled that he was served oatmeal the first morning, and that he applied a teaspoonful of sugar taken from a small bowl in the middle of the table. He remembered that the sound of his hosts drawing deep breaths was obvious in the silence of the room. He later realized that the very small bowl represented one month of their sugar ration. The next day he went to the British Military College of Science where he was schooled in antiaircraft radar (radio detection and ranging). The short course was very intense and Hiram learned to maintain and calibrate the equipment. As secret as the course content was, the men in training were in U.S. military uniforms every day, and there was no attempt to hide that the U.S. military was their employer.

NEWS FLASH: On December 7, 1941, the Japanese Bombed Pearl Harbor!

Hiram completed his training in December of 1941 and then he was sent to Tynemouth on the NE coast of England. He was the only American officer they had seen and he was their radar officer. The equipment was in good condition but in need of calibration. British officers were each assigned a "batman" as a personal assistant. Hiram's batman was an elderly gentleman who drove his jeep and took excellent care of "the naïve young idiot," as Hiram called himself. The British treated him with great respect and he appreciated the sincere friendships he made.

Tynemouth was in the direct line for German bombers trying to get to the port at Liverpool, and there were bombing raids three or four nights every week. Young women manned the radar and very elderly men manned the 125th Rocket Battery. Hiram was very impressed with the dedication of the British people, and they were all aware that the German pilots were determined to eliminate that antiaircraft facility. One very foggy day the radar screens became severely distorted and Hiram could not find the cause. The interference was very strong and made early warnings or any operations useless. They later found out that the German battleships *Scharnhorst* and *Gneisenau* and the heavy cruiser *Prinz Eugen* had been stuck in a Spanish port. From there the ships had made their way up to Brest, France. The Germans wanted them back, so they blanked out all radar frequencies so the ships could make a run up the English Channel without being detected and attacked. The enemy operation was successful.

Hiram told of one "humorous" incident during the horrid bombings. The radar provided a predictor computer with data that allowed the gun position officer to give verbal directions to the gun crews. One night when German flares were dropped and the targets were illuminated, and the guns were being accurately directed to eliminate the flares, an off-duty gun position officer arrived. He was in his bathrobe and slippers and it was quite obvious that while off duty he had been enjoying his beer. He began to issue verbal orders to shoot down a bright flare appearing over a group of trees. It was the moon!

Hiram eventually got word that he was leaving the British and being sent back to the U.S. Army. In his words, "That was not fun!" He lost his British stipend and he lost his batman–no one to shine his shoes or drive him around. He had to participate in a twenty-five mile hike with full pack, gun and side arm. Hiram had to return to reality. He was reassigned in September of 1943 to the 62nd Coast Artillery Regiment which had recently arrived in the south of England. The regiment had arrived without anyone trained to man their SCR 268 radars (Signal Corps Radio Number 268–the U.S. Army's first radar system). The trained personnel had been removed for further training before the 62nd left for England. Hiram had to train those that remained, but he couldn't do that in England because the U.S. radar equipment was still on a ship. They soon boarded the ship and set out for Gibraltar. Hiram did not see the equipment until they arrived at Oran, Algeria, in North Africa.

Matters became more difficult for Hiram when he discovered that the manuals and all of the schematics (due to their secret classification) had been removed before shipment. Again, Hiram didn't know their destination until they docked there. The ship stayed in port until all was ready for their entrance into the Mediterranean. During the night they were suddenly called to report on deck with their life preservers. A Navy scuba dive team had caught an Italian crew in a small submersible, attempting to attach an explosive to the bottom of their ship. The Navy saved the 62nd from a cold swim and the loss of all of their equipment.

Once the ship docked at Oran, Algeria, they offloaded all of the equipment from the ship. They set up the radar quickly in anticipation of trouble from the Germans or Italians. Hiram said it became apparent that Rommel was having too much trouble in Egypt to worry about them in Oran. It allowed them the time they needed to train operators and find out how to maintain the radar.

Hiram had a very smart master staff sergeant who helped him set up a workbench in a stable. It was the first time Hiram had seen an American radar system, and he was thankful for his British training and some of his college work. He and his master staff sergeant were able to trace all of the circuits and write a maintenance manual, showing resistance and voltages on schematic drawings. The manual was copied and sent to other units in the area. After getting settled in Oran, information was relayed about a counter force coming in by sea. All units were on high alert. Looking over the Mediterranean late that night, their radars reported targets off shore, with close ones approaching Oran. The Navy denied any activity on their radars. Hiram said his Army unit asked for permission to illuminate the nearest targets with their searchlights. The lights revealed a naval vessel. If it was a "friendly" vessel it would be a sitting duck for enemy action, so they quickly turned off the searchlights. Then they started to plot the fixed targets. The plots showed that the radar beams intersected in Spain. That seemed impossible since their equipment had a range of only twenty-five miles. What they didn't know at the time was that an anomaly existed. Under certain atmospheric conditions, the radar signal could bend over the horizon and return a signal from the peaks of mountains in Spain. As it turned out, the vessel that they had illuminated was part of a secret convoy that the Navy did not want anyone to know about.

Finally they got the order to move eastward, and the convoy, limited by the slowest vehicles, began the slow journey to Bizerte, Tunisia, about 700 miles away on the NE coast of Africa. When the convoy started down a long hill into Algiers, Hiram's radar trailer got stuck on a switchback. He said it took a lot of time and a lot of sweat to free the trailer. They overnighted and then continued on, passing some of Rommel's burned-out tanks along the way. Eventually they reached Bizerte. No trees! No shade! Very hot! They wore the uniform of Patton's Army–boots, leggings, wool pants, shirt with black tie and helmet with chin strap fastened. While waiting for the landing craft to arrive so they could join the invasion of Sicily, Hiram stretched out under a truck and "pondered" a thick chocolate shake. The landing craft arrived and they all lined up to go aboard. They had to pass through two checkpoints and each man received injections in both arms. The trip to Palermo, Sicily, was uneventful for them. Earlier, it had not been so easy for the tank crews and foot soldiers in General Patton's 7th Army; but the Americans had successfully arrived at Messina before British Field Marshall Montgomery and completed the Allied conquest of Sicily.

Hiram's job changed radically when he received new orders to immediately return to Washington, D.C. He left Sicily on a small cargo plane headed to Algiers, and then got a slightly larger plane to Marrakech, Morocco. From there he flew to Dakar and then over the Atlantic to Natal in Brazil. The plane was not pressurized and the ride was very uncomfortable. The plane refueled and flew on to Georgetown, British Guiana, and then to Havana, Cuba, and finally Washington, D.C. Hiram reported to the office of the Chief

Signal Corps, General Code. He declined the opportunity for leave and was assigned to the Electronics Maintenance Test Branch, Maintenance Division at Bradley Beach, New Jersey. It was a great assignment, and he began to enjoy life. Then came another assignment.

Lt. Colonel Preston, Lt. Rudeen, Lt. Ireland and Hiram (a captain by then) were to go to Italy on March 12, 1944, to study how the troops were doing with the maintenance of their communications equipment. They started in Rome and went north, ending up in Florence. It was a miserable time of the year with a lot of snow. Hiram developed pneumonia and spent a little time in the hospital. The rest of the team returned home; but on April 3, 1945, Hiram flew to Paris, France, to finish his assignment.

His room in Paris was on the second floor of a building with a balcony that looked into an airshaft. A French family lived across the way, and one day while Hiram sat working on a report, the man went out on his balcony and called out to Hiram, "Roosevelt est mort!" That was the first Hiram knew of the death of the U.S. president. He was invited to join the family for dinner and discovered the gentleman was a member of the French Resistance. The man must have been well connected because the meal lasted four hours, and it was punctuated with wine and cognac. Hiram staggered downstairs, into the lift, and collapsed on his bed. One night before leaving Paris, Hiram returned their generous hospitality by taking the family out on the town.

Hiram was in London prior to returning to the United States, and it was there that he was able to celebrate V-J Day on September 2, 1945. That was the day a formal surrender ceremony was held at Tokyo Bay onboard the *USS Missouri*. Soon afterwards he returned to Bradley Beach, New Jersey. He was relieved from active service, having obtained the rank of major, and was discharged on November 17, 1945. He later resigned his Reserve commission on December 8, 1954.

After Hiram was discharged from active service, he worked for American Totalizer for a couple of years and then Lenkurt Electric for ten years. He also worked for Lockheed Corporation in Sunnyvale, California. Initially he worked on Polaris and Poseidon missile systems. In addition, he was part of a management group that monitored the accuracy of information as it went up the chain of command from lower to upper management. His last endeavor was classified, working with computers and satellites. He worked for Lockheed for twenty-six years and retired in 1984. Hiram and his wife of thirty-five years, Marilyn, then moved to Emmett, Idaho, to enjoy retirement.

Hiram was happiest when he was serving others, and he had an amazing list of accomplishments during his "retirement." He participated in the foster parent and the foster grandparent programs, was a computer instructor for the Boise Library, volunteered at the Emmett Police Department, was a court bailiff, and an EMT, worked with students at the Warhawk Air Museum, and he loved being a substitute teacher. He volunteered as a math tutor working mainly with disabled students. He usually tutored in algebra, but spoke about working with an advanced student that needed help with trigonometry, and he loved that because it helped keep his brain active. Hiram was the Gem County Man of the Year in 1990 and was named Idaho Statesman Distinguished Citizen in November of 1992.

Epilog:

At the time of his Veterans History Project interview in October of 2004, Hiram still did not have a copy of his DD 214. (The form declared his record of military service.) He said the history of the Electronics Training Group was shrouded in secrecy.

The Veterans Administration agreed to help him secure a copy and at that time he was hopeful he would then be able to verify dates and places in his military history.

The University of California, Berkeley, eventually granted Hiram his Bachelor of Science degree in electrical engineering.

Mobile Radar Unit

Robert W. Pitts
U.S. Army
WWII
1943–1945

*There was incredible fire
power on both sides.*

Robert "Bob" W. Pitts was born in
1918, in Oakwood, Missouri. His
family moved to Oakland, California, shortly after his birth. He
attended school there and graduated from high school in 1936. He
enrolled in an Emeryville, California, seminary to study for the
ministry. He was employed by Montgomery Ward at their
warehouse in Hayward when he met his wife and was married.
They soon added a son to the family.

When asked about December 7, 1941, the Japanese attack on
Pearl Harbor, Bob recalled alarms and sirens and a blackout. He
received his draft notice October 30, 1943, and went to Fort Ord,
California, for enlistment. From there he traveled by train to Camp
Wells, Texas, for thirteen weeks of basic training. After a week or
so of leave he was suppose to head for Fort Patrick Henry in
Virginia. By mistake he ended up in New Jersey, where he
boarded the ship *Argentine* and convoyed to Liverpool, England;
then across the English Channel to Omaha Beach, where he landed
in August of 1944. He and his unit boarded trucks to a bivouac
area and then were sent to the front. As the new recruits passed
through the area that is now the American Cemetery above Omaha
Beach, they marveled that there were still so many bodies of
unburied soldiers, killed in the D-Day invasion.

On the 5th of August Bob joined the 2nd Infantry, which was
part of the 3rd Platoon of Company G, 9th Infantry Regiment. This
made up the Indian Head Division that joined in combat on August

37

5, 1944, at Vire, France. Bob's infantry unit took the town of St. Lô. In Vire, as they walked into town, they encountered six or seven German scouts, and both sides began digging and scrambling into foxholes and trenches. He found himself behind German lines and at one point was facing a German tank, a radio man, and about fifteen German soldiers. Both sides exchanged fire for a while but, once the Germans brought in their artillery, his unit moved back out of range. Bob was made buck sergeant for one night during that encounter. He endured the heat of battle for 276 days. During that time his platoon lost their leader–his replacement was killed two days after taking over command. They then began fighting through the hedgerow country. There was incredible fire power on both sides, but visibility of the enemy was very difficult. His platoon leader was hit and his squad leader was killed. Bob carried hand grenades, so he decided to toss one over the hedgerow. He didn't throw it high enough and it bounced off his side of the hedge. Fortunately it rolled away from the men and went off without anyone getting hurt.

At one point Bob was supposed to carry a message to another unit, but as he was running and crouching down to reduce his target size, a bullet or shell from a big gun just missed him, passing close enough to burn his rear end. He was shot at many times, but sustained no injuries. The Americans took the city of Brest and captured many prisoners. They were then trucked to Belgium and fought to the Siegfried Line in the Battle of the Bulge. His unit was involved in building a bunker for his division, as they were constantly under fire–sometimes from the German 88s. In December the 106th Infantry finally relieved his unit. Bob remembered it was bitter cold and the soldiers slept in bags covered by double blankets. If they were lucky, they could occasionally get a shower.

As they advanced toward a forest, Bob's unit was pinned down by German machine gun fire. They hurriedly dug foxholes and hunkered down below the lip of the ground. It snowed and as it melted, the foxholes started filling with water. At that point the Germans began using mortars, setting shells to explode above ground, keeping the shivering troops even lower in their holes.

Bob witnessed the first German buzz bombs while on his way to the hospital to be treated for laryngitis and trench foot. While he was gone, his unit took several pill boxes and captured prisoners. Before rejoining his unit he stopped at division headquarters and found himself on KP (kitchen duty). It was there that he learned of the Army's need for MPs (military police) in the war zone, and he volunteered for that duty. He was in the combat MPs for the rest of the war, directing military traffic as the front kept moving toward Germany. They "policed" the many towns as they were overrun by the Allies. They found themselves all the way into Czechoslovakia, where they remained until the fighting finally stopped.

Bob and his unit drove trucks and jeeps to Le Havre, France, where on July 13, 1945, they boarded ships for the United States. He continued on by train to Texas, then to Ft. Bliss for discharge–still a private first class–then to Oakland, California. In the spring of 1947, using the GI Bill, Bob again entered school to study for the ministry.

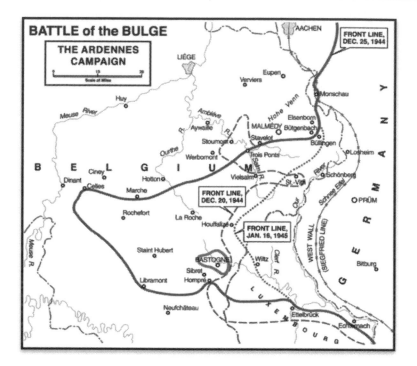

Battle of the Bulge Fox Hole

Sam Pollard, Sr.
U.S. Army
WWII
Bronze Star
Distinguished Service Cross

> *"Hey, Pollard, what happened?"*
> *"I don't know!"*

Sam looked out across what was once the town square of the small town of Cisterna di Littoria, Italy. Buildings on the far side had been reduced to a row of rubble. This had been a street of nice buildings not too long ago. At the far end of the street was an intersecting street of more bombed-out structures. Across the square from these buildings his nine-man squad was being pinned down by heavy automatic weapon fire. Sam knew that he was the only one with the possibility of moving into a better position and, as the senior man, it fell to him to try to do something. For a brief moment the thought flashed through his consciousness, "How did I get here?"

In 1943, Sam had landed in North Africa, near Casablanca, as part of a large invasion force that had fought all the way east through Algeria and French Morocco, until they were engaged with German Field Marshall Erwin Rommel's forces in Tunisia. After pushing the Germans out of North Africa, the Americans had fought in Sicily before moving to the Italian mainland.

As the Allies advanced up the spine of Italy they encountered increasingly stiff opposition. The Germans and Italians had built huge lines of fortifications and were very well dug in on high ground that controlled all roads through the valleys. Progress had ground to a halt near Monte Cassino, and the Allied forces were taking large losses from a well-entrenched enemy. A decision was

41

made by Allied commanders that a landing from the sea to the north would be made at Anzio on the west coast of Italy. They hoped that a flanking move would catch the enemy off guard, trap some of the Germans who would now have the Allies behind them, and clear the way for their forces to finally get to Rome.

The landing had been made with fairly light resistance, but once the Germans realized what was happening, they quickly brought up reserve forces and the Allies found themselves hemmed in a pocket of land against the sea. Many days passed with intense shelling and casualties on both sides. The Allied forces were still not able to move forward. It was not until mid-May that they made a major thrust, using heavy shelling from naval units on the sea and aerial bombardment. American units were able to breach the pocket they were in and move in to capture the road to Rome. The small town that lay immediately ahead of them was Cisterna.

* * *

Sam had been born in the tiny farming community of Roswell, Idaho, in 1921. He was the oldest of nine children. His parents had an eighty-acre farm. Everyone helped out on the farm, doing whatever each one was capable of doing to make sure that the family had enough to eat. This was dryland farming back then, and growing and cultivating crops was a lot tougher than later when irrigation and mechanization were available to do most of the heavy work. Hay, wheat, alfalfa, onions and potatoes were principle crops in this area. All farms had their own vegetable gardens to feed the family and put up enough food for the tough winters.

Sam attended a tiny Roswell school where he played American Legion baseball with kids from Roswell and nearby Parma. He liked to fish and hunt and, like many young men of his generation, was a pretty good shot.

By 1940 the winds of war were blowing across from the European continent and young men in Sam's community were starting to receive their draft notices. It was a very uncertain time for everyone. After his junior year of high school Sam decided to enlist in the Army before he received a draft notice. This decision, he thought, might improve his chances of getting a better assignment and training. He enlisted that September and was sent immediately to Ft. Lewis in Washington State for basic training. Two months later his draft notice came in the mail.

After Ft. Lewis it was on to Ft. Ord in California for advanced training. Sam was pulled out of the barracks early one morning and taken to the firing range, where he qualified for his sharpshooter medal by putting three out of five bullets into a target 500 yards away. All those years of hunting had paid off!

On December 7, 1941, Sam was at Ft. Lewis, his permanent base, when Pearl Harbor was bombed. His regiment was told to set up on the nearby beach, dig in and prepare to repel the Japanese if they were to come ashore on the American mainland. This invasion didn't happen, and in 1943 Sam's regiment was boarded on trains and transported to Ft. Pickett in Virginia. Upon arriving they were taken on a twelve-mile hike. The next day brought another twelve-mile hike, and the day after that a shorter one. The men were then boarded on ships at Norfolk, Virginia. In all there were 600 ships. It was a vast task force, but many escort ships were needed to make sure they arrived to their destination safely. It wasn't until three days at sea that the men learned they would be going to Casablanca in North Africa.

* * *

Sam's mind promptly returned from the flashback, realizing he was in a "tight spot" in Cisterna. He quickly decided the only way to dislodge the enemy across from him was to run through an open area to a better position, off to the side of the Germans. He leaped up, firing his Thompson sub-machine gun as he ran. From the German position, bullets were zipping past him, but he was able to get where he wanted to be and quickly jump into a hole without getting hit. He then worked his way into a position where, after lobbing a grenade in their direction, he was able to force two Germans to surrender. Sam then moved stealthily along the line of rubble to where several more Germans were positioned. They also gave themselves up. He continued along the line of buildings, clearing his way with grenades and machine gun fire. It was then he spotted several more Germans running into a basement further up ahead. Sam followed them and yelled for them to come out and surrender. What happened next made Sam's jaw drop. Slowly the Germans began to file out with their hands up. Sam was partially hidden from their view in case one tried to come out shooting, but he had plenty of grenades and was prepared to use them if need be. The Germans continued to come out of the basement and formed a line. What they hadn't realized was that Sam was the only GI that they were surrendering to! The Germans just kept coming until there was a long column of them. In all there were 134 German soldiers, one of high rank and several lieutenants. By this time, some of Sam's squad had caught up with him, and together they marched all the prisoners back to their headquarters. As they came into their camp area one of the men yelled out, "Hey Pollard, what happened?" All Sam did was shrug and say, "I don't know." Sam was then told to return to his unit. The Germans were searched, interrogated and ended up giving the soldiers information that was useful to the Americans, as they continued to press on toward Rome.

The breakout from Anzio and then the capturing of Cisterna broke the German's ability to mount a good defense, and so the Allies were able to march into Rome with little resistance. After entering Rome, Sam's unit was sent back to Naples, where they got on a ship that took them to St. Tropez and Nice in southern France. The Allied Forces had now opened another front and were pushing the Germans northward. When Sam got to Grenoble in France, he was told that he would be going home. By then he had been fighting non-stop since he had landed in North Africa–except for a few days rest before the Anzio invasion. Sam was put on a ship in southern France along with several hundred soldiers and German prisoners. Many of these prisoners ended up in Idaho working on farms. Sam remembered the ship sailing into New York harbor past the Statue of Liberty. To see the famous statue gave him the most wonderful feeling. It was there that what he had been fighting for really came home to him. He was very happy to be back in the USA.

Sam was then sent by train to Ft. Douglas in Utah where he trained with a mortar unit and tested new munitions. He was told that he was going to receive some military decorations for his service and in due course these were given to him. There was no ceremony for the awarding of the medals. He received the Bronze Star and the Distinguished Service Cross (DSC) for actions in Cisterna, Italy. (The DSC ranks immediately below the Medal of Honor.) Sam was discharged on July 1, 1945.

Back in Idaho Sam worked for the Parma rural electric company for twelve years, followed by thirty years for the post office in Roswell. He was a scoutmaster for nine years, and also volunteered for his local fire department, and was an EMT. He had a long, happy marriage that produced three children and eight grandchildren. He was awarded an honorary high school graduation diploma by his old school.

Willard J. Rowley
U. S. Army
WWII
1943–1945

*"All I have to say about war is
that it should be avoided, if possible;
but if it is not–go to it!"*

Willard was born in 1916 in Camas, Washington, a small paper-mill town. His father died when he was only eight years old. He graduated from high school there and then went to work in the paper mill.

When WWII broke out Willard was drafted into the Army and sent to Fort Hood in Texas for basic training. He was then sent by train to Maryland for more training, and from there he traveled to New York, where he was put on a ship to Liverpool, England. Willard remembered that the North Atlantic was miserable and they lost two ships on the journey over to Europe. It was a rocky road all the way, with a lot of sea sickness.

Willard's first camp in England was St. Melons. He was assigned to the 635th Tank Destroyers. "We went to the beach where we boarded an LST (landing ship-tank) boat and left for France. We were told we could order anything we wanted to eat. The fellows joked that they were being 'fattened up for the slaughter.' We knew where we were going, but we weren't allowed to say anything about it."

The Allies had landed in France the previous day, and at 5 a.m. the next morning (June 7) Willard's group boarded more ships for Omaha Beach. Willard recalled the first few days of June 1944– the invasion on the beaches of France.

The day before [June 6] on Omaha Beach was tough. We didn't have much time to look around when we landed. The infantry had done a lot of work the day before. There was a lot of carnage on the beach, a lot of tanks blown up, [and] bodies everywhere! Our ammunition truck hit a mine about seventy-five feet onto the beach and was blown up. So our supply was gone. We had mine detectors and looked for mines on the top of the hill. We drove up to the top of a hill and from there to the woods. Somebody started firing a machine gun in a field right down the row we were going. The bullets were coming. We broke off and went to a bivouac area that was prepared for us. A woman had tied herself up in a tree and was shooting at German soldiers and hit a couple of them. But the German infantry took care of her. That was the welcome we had to France.

Our assignment was the right flank of the invasion. Two miles behind us was to be a small artillery outfit. We didn't hit any opposition whatsoever until we got up on the Cobalt Line. We had our first main scrimmage there. Someone figured there were 1,500 bullets fired in that scrimmage. We were on the line for a month. We dug fox holes and covered ourselves to keep shrapnel from getting to us. I got some cardboard to cover me to keep the rain out. Then I got some heavier stuff to keep the bullets and shrapnel out. After thirty days we were relieved by an outfit from Iceland. The next day they lost a lot of guys.

The first of July we were pulled off the line and were then sent to Germany. Some of the guys were so badly shook up from the bombing they couldn't see us move our hands in front of their eyes. We went behind enemy lines to find out what was there, but not a shell was fired. One time we were behind the German line for about two weeks and we got on King Leopold's estate. About the second night the lookouts told us there were 400-500 German tanks coming up the road. We went out and took the bazookas and lay alongside the road—but they never came. We were very happy about that. We had no radios or connection with home base and didn't know where the line was anymore. When we left the estate, we came into a place where the [front] lines were. A fellow from Company C said he couldn't pull the lanyard [line which is pulled to fire the cannon]. If he had pulled it, I probably wouldn't be here today, because the enemy was lined up to fire on us.

From there we went into the Hürtgen Forest. That [battle] is something people here [in the U.S.] didn't know anything about. We had too many casualties there. There were 2,800 people killed outside of Aachen, Germany. The battle lasted about a month. We had one of the heaviest fires we were ever under. They fired so heavily that the newly forested trees that were four or five feet high were cleared. One night there were 2,500 rounds fired on us. We never should have fought that battle—we didn't need that land. In one of the battles I picked up some steel in my elbow and I had to go to the hospital there. They put some yellow powder on it, and it was back to the war. The guys picked me up and we went back out to a farmhouse and barn. The Germans knew we were there and we knew where they were. They were out there in a concrete pillbox. We were sent to keep them there along the Siegfried Line, where they had a lot of concrete monuments that the tanks couldn't get over. Somehow or other we broke through it. One of the pillboxes opened and a red jacket was waved. Our guns were very accurate and we put one right through the opening. We didn't hear from that pillbox again.

I had trench foot there. When your feet have been cold [and damp] for several days, the blood quits flowing and congeals. During WWI many of them [the affected soldiers] had their feet cut off. But they learned how to treat it during WWII. They came by every half hour and poured alcohol on my feet. It was a very painful time. We could hear the German rockets going into the town just beyond us a little ways. We couldn't build a fire for heat because it would be seen.

After that was the Battle of the Bulge. We were assigned a crossroad on Christmas day and told to hold it at any cost. The Germans were down the road, maybe three or four miles. We could hear the battle going on. They only put one unit from every outfit on the road. On Christmas day the sun came out and that ended the battle, as the [Allied] planes were able to take over. We were happy about that. They served us a hot Christmas dinner cooked by a [field] kitchen. I didn't know we had one up until then.

We saw very little fighting after that. When the war ended, the Russians were on one side of the river, and we were on the other. Even though we heard the war was over there was still firing going on. One of our tanks shot down an airplane with German officers in it.

Fifty years later, Willard had the opportunity to return to Omaha Beach. "A fellow that I had gone to grade school with was killed there and his grave was there. I couldn't hold back my tears. I also saw children playing on the beach. It is hard to describe. We never would have thought of that back then."

"All I have to say about war is that it should be avoided, if possible; but if it is not–go to it!"

Omaha Beach: D-Day + 1

View from the Eyes of a D-Day Paratrooper

Robert Vernon
U.S. Army & OSS
WWII
1942–1946
Korea
1950–1951

*He had the feeling this was going to be
a very difficult assignment.*

Boise, Idaho, was an integral part
of Bob's early life. He was born and raised there, attended Boise
High School, and was a member of the first class to graduate from
what was then Boise Junior College. He was continuing his
education at Oregon University when WWII broke out. He was in
the enlisted reserve at the college until being called into service in
1943. Over two hundred of the university enlisted reserves were
called up at the same time. After being sworn into the service, a
big party was held for their unit on campus; and the next day, as
their train pulled out for Fort Lewis, Washington, numerous
students gathered to say goodbye. Bob remembered it as a very
emotional moment for him. His first assignment was with the
Army Air Corps and he was stationed at what was considered a
good place for training–Atlantic City, New Jersey. After a day of
training they would often go down to the Boardwalk and take a
swim in the ocean. When Bob was finished with basic training, he
was assigned to radio operator school, where he learned Morse
Code. Once he was able to transmit over twenty words a minute
he qualified as a high speed operator.

Bob became bored because his next assignment was put on
hold. All day long the men practiced operating the radio. One day
an officer came in looking for volunteers to join a special unit.
The officer explained that it would be a dangerous assignment and

the soldiers selected would have to learn to fight with a knife. There was a possibility these men would be sent behind enemy lines. Bob applied for the position and went through an interview process. One of the questions dealt with parachuting from an airplane. He had the feeling this was going to be a very difficult assignment. He was selected for a position and was assigned to the Office of Strategic Services (OSS). The OSS was a wartime intelligence agency and was formed to coordinate espionage activities behind enemy lines for the branches of the U.S. Armed Forces and was a predecessor to the CIA.

Bob's first training was at a country club in Washington, D.C. The men trained on the golf course and slept in tents on the tennis court. He received training in handling explosives at Camp David, which later became a retreat for U.S. presidents. He was trained in the use of all kinds of weapons, including German and Japanese firearms. Later he was placed in a thirty-man unit that had four teams, each supervised by an officer. Various specialists were assigned to them, including medics and radio operators (his job). Bob's unit was trained for work in France, and several of the men in his unit spoke both English and French.

After training, he sailed on a victory ship which was part of a 400-vessel fleet headed for the upcoming invasion of Sicily. His ship, however, was diverted to Casablanca, North Africa. From there his unit went by train traveling for several days to Algiers. The train was so slow that one day, when one of the men lost a gun part through a crack in the floor, he was able to jump out, find the part and still was able to get back on the moving train. In Algiers Bob received more radio training, as well as parachute training where he made four jumps.

Next, the men boarded a ship to Scotland. On the way there, one of the officers went to the toilet and found there was no available toilet paper. They had just changed their money to

English pounds and, not knowing the value of the money, he used one of the bills for toilet paper. Later he realized it was a five-pound note worth twenty American dollars–more than a week's pay at the time.

After more training in Britain, Bob was assigned to his first mission–to parachute into France and secure a power dam. The unit consisted of twenty men who were divided into groups and assigned to four airplanes. The French underground was supposed to light bonfires at their drop zone and assist them in their mission. However, upon arriving over the drop zone, no fires were located, and after several hours searching the area, they returned to England. They were disappointed to later find out that the other planes had dropped their troops and were able to complete the mission.

His next mission was with fifty other OSS members who were dropped close to Paris. He parachuted in the dark at 2 a.m., landing 150 miles behind enemy lines. This time they were met by members of the French Resistance. Their specific job was to cause disruptions and havoc behind the German lines.

By now the American Army was quickly advancing toward Paris, and thousands of German soldiers were surrendering. One day he and several men were given the duty to find twenty Germans who were somewhere in the area, and had made it known that they wanted to surrender. Bob's men scoured the countryside but could not locate the soldiers, so they returned to base. Later they found out that over 700 Germans were actually on the hill close to their scouting party and, when the regular Army arrived, they fired a few shells onto the hill, and all of the Germans surrendered. Had Bob's group found the Germans first, they would have been facing 700 instead of twenty of the enemy. The Free French Forces came upon their unit and, since their mission was over, they decided to join the French as they surrounded a

German fort.   Fortunately, the garrison of about 3,000 Germans again surrendered without resistance.   Bob's group was then sent to Paris, where they were given leave to enjoy free time and take in the sights of the city.

After returning to England, Bob received orders back to America.   He was told if he agreed to go to China he could stay in the OSS; otherwise he would be reassigned.   He decided he would go to China; so he was sent first to California, then by ship to Australia, and then on to India.   While in Calcutta, he was shocked to see dead bodies lying everywhere.   Smallpox was plaguing the country at the time, and when victims died they were often just left on the streets until they could be picked up.   He rode trains and drove a truck and finally arrived at a Chinese army camp, the trip taking about two weeks.   His duty there was to train Chinese soldiers to become commandos.   His group helped to rebuild an airfield that had been abandoned by the Japanese after they had destroyed the flight line.   Two thousand Chinese "coolies," using only hand tools, were brought in to rebuild the field.   The nearest city to them had a cholera epidemic, and daily there were funeral processions passing by Bob's barracks.   About the time the base was operational, the Japanese surrendered and his unit prepared to return to the United States.

Bob had enjoyed his time in the OSS, so he joined the Reserve when he returned home to Idaho.   In 1950, when the Korean War started, his unit was called up and he was sent to Korea.   He was stationed in Seoul, and he remembered it being severely cold there. Since he had seniority and was married he was rotated home in 1951.

Bob fondly remembered his time in the military, especially the OSS.   It was quite an adventure for a young man, because he had the opportunity to see parts of the world he had never expected to experience.

Bob Vernon's OSS Group

Russell Biaggne
U.S. Army Air Corps
WWII
1942–1945
POW

Daily provisions consisted of a cup of tea & a piece of bread for breakfast; one bowl of soup for dinner, & three cigarettes.

Russell Biaggne was born in New Orleans, Louisiana, in June of 1923. On December 7, 1941, he was attending Tulane University and was shocked at the news of the bombing of Pearl Harbor. He tested for entry into the Navy and scored high, but after two weeks they hadn't called him. He finished his term at college and enlisted in the Army Air Corps for flight training. Russell went to Santa Ana, California, in June 1942 and joined a cadet class in the 50th Squadron. He finished preflight and primary flight school, but washed out in the acceptance ride.

In 1943 Russell went to armament school in Fort Myers, Florida, and then to Salt Lake City, Utah, where he was assigned to a B-24 crew. He then was assigned to Boise, Idaho, for training, followed by a move to Topeka, Kansas, for a new airplane. Russell's next stops included Brazil, Africa, and Marrakech (Morocco) to join the 450th Bomb Group. Their group was later re-designated as the 449th and he was in Squadron 717. There were eighteen planes per squadron and four squadrons per group.

Russell's crew flew eight-hour missions out of Italy with 8,000 pounds of bombs. They did daily flights and then alternate days. They typically flew at altitudes from 22,000 to 24,000 feet. In all, Russell flew forty-seven missions. On April 4, 1944, the 449th group lost most of their planes to enemy engagement.

On their last mission to the Ploesti oilfields in Romania, they lost an engine over Bulgaria as they headed toward their target. Their plane could not maintain either the designated altitude or formation, forcing them to drop their bombs unarmed (without them exploding). An enemy ME-109 Bandit attacked them several times. After ten minutes under attack, Russell's plane lost all its on-board radios. The waist area of the aircraft was on fire. Donning their parachutes, he and one other crewman bailed out through the camera hatch and, although they were fired on by enemy ground forces, they landed safely away from the Germans. Unfortunately, they were eventually captured by German artillery troops. Two Germans in black Gestapo uniforms came up in a field car and demanded the prisoners be turned over to them. The German artillery officer refused, saying that he could also benefit from the two captured Americans. Russell and his comrade were taken to a small town in Bulgaria and then to the capital, Sofia. The B-24 crew members all survived and were brought together, but Russell and his buddy Bob were the only two who were unhurt.

The POW camp they were taken to had over 300 prisoners, and they were detained there eighty-five days. Their daily provisions consisted of a spoon, a cup of tea, and a piece of bread for breakfast; one bowl of soup for dinner, and three cigarettes. Soup was made daily in a held-over WWI field kitchen. Prisoners also endured periodic interrogations by their captors.

In late 1944, the Russians were pushing to take Bulgaria. A captured lieutenant colonel, a U.S. major, and a British major were sent to Sofia to negotiate getting the POWs out of Bulgaria before the Russians took over the country. Russell believed this was part of a prisoner exchange between the Allies and Bulgaria. They went by train to Istanbul, Turkey, and, dressed as Turks, the men were loaded onto a Turkish cruise ship. They were onboard for two weeks before arriving in Cairo. They then flew with the 15th

U.S. Air Force to Naples, Italy, before boarding an American ship to the United States. Altogether there were 330 former POWs on the ship. They landed in Norfolk, Virginia, and had a week's leave before heading to a hospital in Santa Monica, California. Finally they arrived in Galveston, Texas, for discharge.

Russell used his GI Bill benefits to attend school and purchase a house. After the war, the 449th Bomb Group held a reunion every other year for many years. At their last reunion there were only three of Russell's crew mates in attendance.

Russell Biaggne's B-24 Crew

John Edward Blake
US Army Air Corps
US Air Force
WWII
Korea & Vietnam
1942–1974
Silver Star

"At my level I was a little cog in a big wheel."

John was born in June of 1923 at Pocatello, Idaho, and because his mother was a deputy U.S. Marshal, they also lived part time in Boise. He had one brother and two sisters and they spent a lot of time together "chasing frogs and scorpions" in the hills. They loved exploring in the brush and fishing. It was a good life. He loved making airplane models and hung out at the airport whenever he could. He completed high school in Pocatello. John's grandmother was a school superintendent and a principal. He shared her love of books and learning and completed two years of college. He was nineteen and working at the Elks Club as a bartender when World War II broke out. He wanted to fly, but even though his mother was the draft clerk for Bannock County, she was not happy with his desire to join the military. Eventually she gave him her blessing and John enlisted in Pocatello on July 9, 1942. He was appointed aviation cadet on September 2, 1942, and trained through June of 1943. He loved his training and enjoyed the learning and the associations with the people who trained him.

John was in the European Theater of Operations from September of 1943 through October of 1945. He was a ferry pilot throughout the war and was mostly based in England. As a result of being in a ferrying squadron, he got to fly just about everything: B-24, B-17, P-38, F8F, P-51, P-61, P-47, etc.; whatever aircraft needed to be delivered to a location for servicing or to a combat unit for use. He also flew aircraft that were pulled from use and flown to locations for storage. The smaller aircraft were cocooned in fiberglass and shipped to England on freighters. There were three depots in England where aircraft were readied for use. The larger multi-engine aircraft were flown to England, and John discovered that opportunities for ferry pilots were numerous.

John had heard about a Navy pilot who once got into trouble for flying under the San Francisco Bay Bridge. Before John and his wingman were to depart England and ferry aircraft to a base in France, he considered the possibility of flying under the Eiffel Tower. En route he told his wingman to take the lead and go directly to the destination base, and then John peeled off–flying over the two wings of the Trocadero and along the Champs-Elysees. But his wingman had decided to follow him, as did another flight leader and his wingman, who had joined with them for a flight of four. They flew under the arches of the Eiffel Tower one after another (1-2-3-4), then went back through a second time and, after a third pass, they left. They flew about fifty feet above ground level, but John commented it wasn't hazardous and any trained pilot of that time could have done it.

Ferrying missions and equipment moved with the battles– Scotland to Liverpool to East England to France; and also Belgium, Spain, Algiers, and Italy. When the war ended it was a big problem determining what to do with all of the equipment that was spread all over the war zones. Some was kept. Some was not. Some equipment was disabled or destroyed. John was made commander of his ferry squadron and spent five months organizing the remaining aircraft, relocating or salvaging them. He closed out the unit and then spent a few months in France as a storage officer for light aircraft that the Army used. He got them flyable, so the Army could take the ones they wanted.

In the winter of 1945 he was shipped down to Southern France. He was then transported in a "forty and eight," which was a World War I vintage boxcar, intended originally to carry forty men or eight horses. He rode the train all the way down to the Mediterranean in preparation to be shipped back to the U.S. The trip home was tough, as storms raged and damaged the bottom of his ship. John said that all but ten of the 2,500 soldiers on board were seasick. They rode out the storms and ended up down by Bermuda, and then finally arrived in the United States.

John was assigned to the Portland Reserve Training Center from June of 1946 to July of 1950. It was during that time, in 1947, that he had a blind date and met a beautiful young lady named Alice. They were married on New Year's Day in 1948. John was a maintenance officer in charge of the testing and certifying of reservists. He was responsible for prepping aircraft for ferry pilots to fly to assignments or storage. He was still sorting out aircraft when the Korean War started at the end of June in 1950. Two days later he was put on alert. Since he was current in flying the P-51, C-46 and A-26, the Air Force decided that the A-26 would be his aircraft. He was sent to B-26 (A-26 redesigned) training for four weeks at Langley Field, Virginia, in August of 1950; and then he ferried a B-26 to Japan, where he joined his squadron flying out of Iwakuni. His unit of B-26s was known as the "Grim Reapers," 13th Bomb Squadron of the 3rd Bomb Group. He was a pilot when flying in the aircraft and maintenance officer when he was on the ground.

During that time John was sent to Indo-China on a mission which included experimenting with "night intruders." Night missions were effective in slowing down the enemy's ability to move their troops and equipment. At that time, half of the U.S. aircraft flew day missions and half flew night missions. He was assigned to a classified mission with an operations officer from the

13th and five mechanics of John's choosing. They were not to discuss the mission with anyone. They were transported in a C-46 to Seoul and then to Clark AFB in Manila. The French picked them up in a C-47 and flew them to Indo-China. The B-26s arrived on a boat, and John and the operations officer each had two pilots to train during a six-week period. John had two French flight commanders, and the operations officer had two French generals. Upon completion, John, the operations officer and the mechanics returned to Iwakuni and did not discuss the mission with anyone. In August of 1951, the squadron moved to Kunsan Air Base, South Korea, taking their combat missions closer to the targets. John was in the 3rd Bomb Group for one and one-half years. When he had flown seventy-five plus missions, six of them in Indo-China, he was moved from the squadron to the wing as the materiel officer. The military extended his time overseas by six months and promoted him to lieutenant colonel.

His next assignment took him to El Centro, California, in April of 1952, where he was with the Air Force 6511th Parachute Development Test Group. He was there until May of 1955. He did extensive flying and made thirty-one jumps. He was at a command and staff school from June 1955 to May 1956. From June of 1956 through March of 1960 John was deputy base commander of Olmstead AFB in Pennsylvania during the building of a new runway. The base housed a helicopter unit which was responsible for presidential support in the event of nuclear war.

In May of 1960 John went back to Korea in the "advisory business." Initially he was at the Seoul Air Base for four months, then stationed at Taegu Air Base, where he was commander of the southern district in an advisory capacity. His family (wife, kids, dog, and cat) was able to join him for that assignment. They had a good time and got along well with the Koreans. John was involved with building a depot and got the Koreans started overhauling their own F-86s, T-33s and C-46s. He flew with them and helped with maintenance.

In July of 1962 he was reassigned to the Air War College for a year. During that time his fourth and last child was born. Next stop was the Pentagon in operational requirements from June of 1963 to February of 1967. John said it was a good experience and involved assignment of units and the strength and equipment of units worldwide. He was a chief under the Secretary of the Air Force and got to meet with him three or four times a month.

After his assignment at the Pentagon, John was in C-130 Advanced Pilot Training and promoted to full colonel. Subsequently, the military found that they didn't need another full colonel in that capacity, so from August 1967 to October 1969 he was stationed at the Yokota Air Base in Japan with the 441st Combat Support Group. He was deputy base commander for six months and then base commander.

During the Vietnam War John was in Udorn, Thailand, where he headed the 7th Airborne Command and Control Center for a year. A C-130 would fly at 25,000-30,000 feet in a back and forth pattern. Because radio frequencies could not reach north to south, the C-130 would relay communications and information about moving fighters around. The C-130 had a twenty-eight man crew, including a pilot, copilot and navigator. The back of the aircraft had rows of seats for the battle staff and display boards for monitoring aircraft movement.

In October of 1970 John went to Travis Air Force Base in California. There he was deputy base commander and was involved with base modernization. His last assignment was in an advisory role. He was deputy commander of the Civil Air Patrol headquartered at Maxwell AFB in Alabama.

John Blake always loved flying. He flew six days before his retirement in July of 1974. He had 8,400 flight hours, thirty-two years in the military, and no complaints. Reflecting on his years of service, John said that, "At my level I was a little cog in a big wheel. I just watched it go by and did my job as best I could. I think I did it pretty well, but I don't know what everybody else thought."

- Epilog -

Silver Star–awarded for actions during the Korean War.

The President of the United States of America, authorized by Act of Congress, July 9, 1918, takes pleasure in presenting the Silver Star to Major John E. Blake, United States Air Force, for gallantry in action against an enemy on 21 April 1951. On that date, Major Blake was pilot of a B-26 attack bomber from the 13th Bombardment Squadron, (L-NI), 5th Air Force, on a single plane low-level combat mission over Korea. Major Blake successfully reached the target area despite the hazardous weather conditions. In the vicinity of the target he encountered intense and accurate fire from many dug-in gun emplacements. Although his plane did not have turret guns to give additional protection during the low level attacks, he proceeded to bomb and strafe repeatedly, destroying a multiple mount 50 caliber gun emplacement, and silencing all antiaircraft fire in the area. Major Blake then located five railroad engines in a marshaling yard south of Songchon. Again under heavy antiaircraft fire which shot two radio antennae off his aircraft and inflicted other damage, he made repeated attacks, destroying one locomotive, damaging four others, and damaging fifteen boxcars. After expending all bombs and ammunition, Major Blake remained in the target area until after daylight to observe any movement of rolling stock. At daylight he called for fighter aircraft and led them to the railroad yards. Disregarding the fact that he had no armament, Major Blake made a simulated attack on the targets and positively identified them to the fighter aircraft, insuring complete destruction. He then turned homeward after five hours in the target area. Through his outstanding skill, heroism and devotion to duty, Major Blake reflected great credit upon himself, the Far East Air Forces, and the United States Air Force.

General Orders: Headquarters, Far East Air Forces, General Orders No. 540 (November 20, 1951).

Martin B-26 Marauder

Charles (Chick) W. Blakley
U.S. Army Air Corps
WWII
1942–1945
Purple Heart
Winged-Boot Award

*"On that one mission I got almost
all the medals I earned."*

Chick was born in rural Idaho, outside of Parma, one of seven children. After attending college for a year, he ran out of money and decided to go to work for an auto parts company. On December 7, 1941, he was working on a car at a station, with the radio playing in the background, when the announcer related the news of the bombing of Pearl Harbor. Chick knew that it was only a matter of time before he would be drafted. He continued to work for the auto parts company until August 1942, when his draft number came up. He was informed that the Army Air Corps would be his duty assignment. Boarding a train, he went to Ft. Douglas, Utah, where he was given all of the required immunizations and his uniforms. The next stop was Keesler Field in Biloxi, Mississippi, for basic training.

Chick spent about five months training in Biloxi while he attended aircraft mechanics school. It was then on to Ypsilanti, Michigan, to the Ford Motor Company plant which was building B-24 airplanes. That training lasted six weeks. Next up for Chick was Laredo, Texas, where he completed gunnery school as a machine gun operator. He recalled that when they arrived it was sweltering, and all they had were their issued wool uniforms!

Chick's travels continued to the air base in Salt Lake City, Utah, and then to Clovis, New Mexico, for the first phase of bomber-crew training. He then went on to phase-two training at

Pueblo, Colorado, where he became part of an actual bomber crew as engineer gunner. The engineer gunner was responsible for the preflight checking of the plane. In Lincoln, Nebraska, in mid September 1943 the crew picked up their airplane. They flew it east to Presque Isle, Maine. From there they "hopscotched" across the Atlantic: Labrador, Canada; Iceland; Belfast, Ireland; and finally England. The crew spent a week there and then was sent to combat training school where they learned to identify enemy aircraft. The crew was finally part of the 68th Bomber Squadron, 44th Bomb Group, 8th Air Force.

On November 3, 1943, Chick's crew flew their first mission to Germany. They arrived back at their base with twelve or thirteen flak holes in their bomber. Four more missions were flown in November–two to Germany and two to Oslo, Norway. On one of the flights to Norway, the crew had to proceed to an alternate target because the original target was no longer viable. On December 11 they headed over to Bremen, Germany. The crew took enemy fire on this mission. One crew member was badly injured and, when Chick deplaned, he noticed his boot was full of blood and discovered he had been hit by shrapnel in the back of his knee. For this injury he was awarded the Purple Heart. His entire crew was awarded two air medals for that one mission. Chick recalled that he earned almost all his medals on that one flight. Of the next three missions he flew, two were aborted and the third was to southern France.

Chick's life was about to take a drastic turn. In early January 1944 the crew was sent to Kiel, Germany, with the target a shipping facility. For the first time, P-51 fighters escorted them. It was bitter cold and they encountered many problems due to adverse weather conditions. On January 21 their mission took them to western France. It was supposed to be a four-hour mission. But, because of the low clouds, the colonel in charge of the twelve-member squadron could not locate the target. They circled three times over Abbeville, France. On the third pass the squadron took antiaircraft fire. Four of the twelve planes were lost, including Chick's. Three command pilots lost their lives on that mission, and all four of Chick's officers were killed. Chick's plane caught fire and the entire crew bailed out. Chick was the last man out of the burning plane. He had to exit through the camera hatch. He parachuted down and after landing hid his parachute in the bushes. Eventually, two more of his crew members were killed and two were taken as prisoners of war.

Chick and three others, including a camera man on that flight, survived and were picked up by the French Resistance. While hiding in the bushes, Chick saw one of his crew members following a French woman, so he decided to join them. She left the two of them, explaining that she would be back after dark. They again hid in the bushes and could hear German soldiers searching for them. That night the woman and two other Frenchmen came back to get them and led them to a house. There they met up with the other two survivors. They stayed at the house from Friday until Monday, when each man was outfitted in French clothing. Chick, who had much larger feet than most Frenchmen, had to make do with a pair of patent leather dress shoes. One of the Frenchmen had "underground" connections. They gathered the fugitives into a group and headed southwest to freedom. When they started out on their trek there were thirteen airmen. The survivors boarded a train to Paris; and after they arrived there they were moved four different times, even staying for a few days in a room over a bakery. After two weeks, they were led by a railroad worker to another hideout. One day they even took the metro to a studio to have photos taken for their fake IDs.

On the first of March the airmen headed south by train and arrived in Toulouse, France, where they spent the day roaming around the city. That night they were put on another train, and their French connections instructed them that before they came to the next small town, when the train slowed down, they were to jump off before it arrived at the station. Skirting around the town they hiked south to the Pyrenees Mountains. They eventually arrived at a farm and were put up in the barn loft. Because of a snowstorm they had to remain there for three long days. The men were nearly starving, so they caught and slaughtered a sheep and devoured the whole thing! At sundown on the third day, they left and continued south over the mountains. One man became ill and was left behind in a shed that they passed on the way. They even took shelter one night in an abandoned castle. In the dark, on the night of March 13, they had to work their way through a low tunnel, keeping bent over and walking side to side to stay upright. Finally they emerged into daylight, sat down to rest and, looking down the valley, saw the Spanish frontier.

Crossing the border into Spain, they stayed close by one night and then moved on to Andorra where they settled in for three days. The next day, half of the men moved on and the following night Chick's group resumed their journey. A car was found and they drove overnight to Barcelona, where they met up with the British consul. Better clothing was issued to them. Chick was sad to give up his patent leather shoes in exchange for sandals. He later wished he had kept his nicer shoes. The men stayed several days in Barcelona, then took a train going to Madrid. From Madrid they went to Gibraltar and there they were presented with new uniforms. The consul arranged to put them on a C-47, flying to Casablanca, and, after three more exhausting days, they were transferred to a C-87 for the trip back to England. Their harrowing ordeal had finally come to an end! Because Chick was able to evade capture and "walk out" of enemy territory, he was presented with the winged-boot award.

Once in England the men reported to 63 Brooks Street, which was a debriefing site for all servicemen who had escaped capture and made it back to safety. Chick had developed a sinus infection while in Casablanca, so he made daily visits to a clinic to get treatments. On April 14, 1944, Chick was on a train to Scotland and there he picked up his ride on a C-54 transport plane back to the United States. He was just twenty-two years old.

Winged-Boot Award

Downed Airmen Take Refuge in a Barn Loft

Ceil Dennis
U.S. Army Air Corps
WWII
1942–1945

"They're not even letting them get out of high school now."

Ceil was born in 1923 at Blackfoot, Idaho. His father was a traveling salesman for Henninger Creamery. Work took him to Missoula, Montana, so the family moved there soon after Ceil was born. One of his earliest memories was of seeing an airplane fly over his house. When he ran outside to see it, he was told that it was Charles Lindberg. From that time on Ceil was fascinated with aviation.

The family relocated to Buhl, Idaho, when Ceil's father started a produce business selling chickens, separated cream and other foodstuffs. He attended school in Buhl from the second grade through high school.

Ceil had a particularly good history teacher at this time who challenged him to think critically and question the status quo. This often caused him to butt heads in conversations with his father, but it helped Ceil think about possibilities in his life. He had always loved airplanes and made many models. This hobby helped him understand flight dynamics and characteristics. He wanted to join the Army Air Corps, but learned that he would need two years of college to be considered for flight training. Ceil decided to correspond with the Canadian Air Force about being accepted there for flight training. The Canadians, who were already fighting in WWII, did not require two years of college, but were training men to be sent to England for the RAF (Royal Air Force). Ceil was accepted, but he was very reluctant to go to Canada. He felt

72

like a small-town boy and worried that he would be really out of his depth. He tried to get friends to go with him, but when that failed, he backed out of going.

On December 7, 1941, Ceil was out with friends shooting ducks below the Bell Rapids on the Snake River. They were not having a particularly good day so decided to head back to the car. It was then that they heard on the car radio about the attack on Pearl Harbor in the Pacific. He was only eighteen years old at the time, but the attack on Pearl Harbor changed everything. The Canadians stopped accepting Americans into their program; however, the U.S. Army Air Corps changed their requirements, allowing a candidate to test into flight training if they showed enough aptitude.

Ceil enlisted in the Army Air Corps and was called into training five months later. He did well on his testing, particularly since all his years of making models helped him understand the principles of flight. He also had a second hobby of photography, which helped him with many of the questions on the test. In addition, he also had a reasonable grasp of mathematics and of proportionality, which further helped him get through the test. He was asked what his preferences were–did he want to be a pilot, navigator, bombardier, on a single- or multi-engine airplane, etc.? Ceil chose to be a pilot and was sent right away to Ryan Field in Hemet, California. Here he was trained in the basic flying class to fly the Ryan PT-22. Ceil was in class 43-K, but when he broke his wrist during training, he was put back into class 44-C. This class graduated in March of 1944 at Luke Field in Phoenix, Arizona. Ceil had flown T-6 advanced trainers as well as P-40 fighters. There he earned his wings and gold bars of a second lieutenant. He was expecting orders that would send him overseas to join the fight; but, instead, found out he was being sent to Camp Stoneman at Pittsburg, California, to be put in a "pool" of men awaiting orders. In the meantime he was given some semi-menial tasks and told to take soldiers on hikes and marches.

This didn't last long though, and soon Ceil was on his way to Ft. Lewis in Washington in a crowded "cattle car train." This train consisted of long carriages with a potbelly stove in the center of each car. Bunks dropped down from above and the lower bunks converted into uncomfortable seating during the day. It was a very tough, crowded way to get to Ft. Lewis. Once there the men were sent on to Oahu, Hawaii.

Ceil arrived in Hawaii in April of 1944. He was stationed at an airfield on the northwest corner of Oahu. There was a surplus of pilots and not enough airplanes, so once again Ceil had to do some busy work, which included censoring mail and policing an assigned area. As they became available, he was able to fly T-6s and a couple of converted Navy planes. The men were then sent to Bellows Field on the other side of the island. Here the men realized they would have to completely refurbish the barracks themselves before they could inhabit them. The barracks were full of bedbugs, and Ceil took charge of eradicating them. From April through December they were able to fly P-47 fighters which had become available for their squadron's use.

In January 1945 Ceil was able to fly P-51 Mustangs that had also just become available. The men were told that they would be taking these Mustangs on an aircraft carrier, the *Sitkoh Bay,* to the island of Saipan. The planes would then be catapulted off the deck of the carrier and land on Saipan. After much testing it was finally deemed too risky for the Mustangs to take off from an aircraft carrier, because they were built too fragile and could not get up enough speed for lift-off. So the aircraft were put on a crane and moved to shore. For the move, each aircraft was covered with cosmoline protectant. This covering all had to be scrubbed off prior to again flying the airplane.

On the 8th of March the Mustangs were flown to Iwo Jima. Ceil felt lucky to draw the last plane available because, again, there were more pilots than planes. The other pilots were taken by sea and had to come ashore at Iwo Jima in a landing craft. Fighting with the Japanese was still going on at Iwo Jima, and the American forces only held about one third of the island. The Mustangs were the first land-based airplanes to actually land there. When Ceil landed and taxied to a stop, Marines swarmed around his plane. These were the first Mustangs they had seen up close, and it meant they would be getting some help to drive the Japanese off the island. Fearing that the horizontal flight surfaces might be damaged if the Marines got too close, Ceil hurriedly stood up in the cockpit and took off his helmet to yell out to them. He was fairly short of stature and looked very young for his age. One of the Marines yelled back, "They're not even letting them get out of high school now!" Ceil spent quite a bit of time talking to the men and explaining things about the plane and even let some of them sit in the cockpit. The Marines were laughing and smiling and having a good time, but their eyes told a different story. They had been through "hell" on Iwo Jima and still had plenty of fighting to do. They fought for several days at a time and then were replaced by other Marines while they had a brief rest. Then it was back into the fight. Ceil felt lucky to be doing what he was doing.

There were no barracks or living quarters for anyone on Iwo Jima. The pilots all had to dig out a makeshift burrow that would then have some wire netting and sandbags put on top. There were still mortar shells falling from the Japanese soldiers who were able to get close enough to the American lines. Ceil named his burrow, which he shared with two other men, the "Iwo Hilton."

Ceil and his fellow pilots did some dive bombing and strafing of the Japanese on Iwo Jima, as well as targeting some neighboring islands. There were still many more pilots than available planes.

The flights made to Japan from Iwo Jima would only be flown by a pilot every fourth day. The missions were so long, a minimum of six and one-half hours, and so stressful that the flight surgeon recommended this interval. It meant that airplanes would be shared among pilots. Those pilots not on a mission and without a plane assigned to them were known as "yardbirds." They were treated somewhat contemptibly by the more senior pilots. Some of them went out of their way to belittle the junior pilots. This mistreatment did not sit well with Ceil. He felt that they were all putting their lives on the line to fly these very long and dangerous missions, and Ceil felt that the junior pilots deserved more respect.

The P-51s were assigned to join up with B-29s coming from Guam and Tinian and fly from Iwo Jima to the mainland of Japan. The P-51s would provide top cover for the B-29s while they made their bombing runs. The Japanese sent up fighters to intercept the bombers, but found out the hard way that tangling with the P-51s was very dangerous. The American tactic of flying four-man formations, split into two aircraft a short distance from each other, was very effective. The idea was that each two-man flight would look across at the other flight and make sure no enemy aircraft was entering into their airspace. If that did happen, the two flights would perform a crossing maneuver which would draw the enemy into the path of the second two-man flight. This worked particularly well with Ceil's four-man group. An enemy plane was shot down and blew up right over Ceil's airplane.

The P-51s didn't have much in the way of navigation equipment, so they depended on B-29 bombers that had been designated to guide them both to Japan and then back to Iwo Jima. The P-51s were free to strafe ground targets when the bombers had made their runs and were out of harm's way. On one strafing run Ceil's flight of four lost two planes, because very accurate enemy radar-controlled flak scored a direct hit on one P-51 and severely damaged the second. Both pilots were killed and Ceil felt very lucky to have escaped unscathed. He and his wingman were both very late getting back to the point where they were to rendezvous with the B-29. Fortunately the B-29 turned around and waited for them. Both planes were extremely low on fuel, and by the time he landed back on Iwo Jima, Ceil found out that his name was in the process of being removed from the pilot list.

When the atomic bomb was dropped on Hiroshima and the second bomb on Nagasaki, Ceil was told that they would not be doing any more missions to Japan. He was discharged from the Army Air Corps in October of 1945 and returned to Idaho. Ceil considered becoming a lawyer, but thought that banking suited his personality and belief system better. He met his wife-to-be at the Idaho National Bank and together they had two children. Ceil lived a long and successful life. He was a boy scout leader for more than twenty-five years, where he mentored many young men. He also did a lot of volunteer work and often shared his wartime experiences, holding students spellbound as he described his experiences on Iwo Jima.

Boeing B-29 Superfortress

North American Aviation P-51 Mustang
Cadillac of the Sky

Ken Gurr
U.S. Army Air Corps
U.S. Air Force
WWII
Korea & Vietnam
1942–1969

*"We got our news from Tokyo Rose.
She knew where we were going before
we did."*

Ken was born in Southern Utah in the small town of Richfield, where he completed his education up through high school. In May of 1941 he moved to California with the idea of becoming rich; however, his plans were interrupted by WWII. He was living in Oakland and working for Standard Stations Incorporated when, on the morning of December 7, 1941, his first customer of the day came in and exclaimed, "Did you hear what happened in Hawaii? The Japanese bombed Pearl Harbor!" At first it didn't mean much to Ken, but after five or six more customers mentioned it, he realized the enormity of what had actually occurred.

Ken knew that as an eighteen-year old he would be drafted into the military, so he spoke with a recruiter about entering the Army Air Corps. He was in luck, because the Air Corps had just dropped the college-degree requirement, and he was able to join the cadets. He signed up February 2, 1942. He left Oakland on a steam-powered train for Buckley Field, Colorado, arriving there two days and two nights later. After some basic drilling and receiving their uniforms, the recruits left again on another steam-driven train and four days later they arrived in Minneapolis, Minnesota. They marched two and one-half miles to a stadium, which became their living quarters. Ken completed a one-year college course in five

79

months and received ten hours of dual-flight instruction. The officers in charge encouraged the formation of a drum and bugle corps. Because Ken had participated in a high school marching band, he was given a blank check to go buy the instruments. A number of volunteers with band experience were recruited. For five months they marched and played. Ken discovered several others had previously been in big-name swing bands, so they also formed a dance band. It was a good five-month tour.

Ken then went to Santa Ana, California, for training in military discipline. Members of his group were not formal cadets yet, so it was necessary for them to learn the Corps' very strict military regulations. One of the challenges he ran into there was Morse Code. The requirement was thirty words per minute. Ken struggled, but with help from a kind tech sergeant, he was able to pass the test. Morse Code was important because the range (navigation) stations were identified by it. If a pilot was flying into the station, "A" (*dit da*) was on his right and the "N" (*da dit*) was on his left. If he was on course, the signals would overlap and make a solid tone. The names of the stations were also identified in Morse Code.

Ken was then off to Thunderbird, Arizona, and there he trained in the PT-17 Stearman, which was a bi-wing, open dual-cockpit plane, with the flight student in the rear seat. Before his first flight, the instructor told him, "Make sure your safety belt is tightened." During the flight, the plane suddenly rolled upside down. He was then told to put his hands over his head for several rolls–and that was his introduction to aerobatics!

At Lancaster, California, Ken flew BT-13s, which were mono-winged airplanes with more horsepower. Then he was sent on to Luke Field in Phoenix, Arizona, to fly AT-6s, with training in air-to-air gunnery practice. He graduated as a cadet on April 15, 1944. His mother was one of the few parents that came down for the graduation. After fifteen days leave, he went to advanced training at Mather Field in Sacramento, California. There he volunteered for night-fighter training. A flight demonstrator came from the Northrup Company to demonstrate the capabilities of the P-61 to the group of fifty volunteers. The P-61 was a dual-engine, dual-fuselage night fighter named the "Black Widow." It was one of the first fighters to use onboard radar. At Mather they then flew twin-engine bombers, the B-25, which required two pilots. At Lemoore, California, they flew A-20s, again a twin-engine airplane that required only one pilot. At Salinas, California, they did more twin-engine flying.

At Fresno, California, they finally completed the night-time P-61 training. Ken remembered it was a "piece of cake." They were scheduled to go to England, so they assembled all of their cold weather gear. In a few days the orders changed. They found out they were actually being sent to the Pacific, so they returned their cold weather gear. They were loaded into a B-24 with canvas seats in the belly, and flew to Hawaii, where they stayed at the Royal Hawaiian Hotel for two weeks. From there they flew to New Guinea and then on to the Philippines, where Ken was assigned to the 550th Night Fighter Squadron. They practiced what he referred to as "aerodrome protection and launch"–if unknown aircraft entered the area they would immediately launch their aircraft and run an intercept. Ken said, "This was when I found out there are no lights and no horizons in the Pacific; so at night we always flew 100 percent on instruments." Toward the end of the war, Ken was scheduled to go down to Sanga-Sanga, the most southern island in the Philippines, and from there flew to Borneo and back. It was a six or seven hour flight.

Ken recalled the following nighttime experience.

One night my radar man Don said, "Hard port and bust her," which meant turn left thirty degrees and firewall the engine. I just got established and he said, "Hard starboard," which is a little difficult [to do] at night. When I got into the turn the airplane bounced a little bit and finally I rolled out and asked him if we were chasing rain clouds. He said, "They look like airplanes to me." [I responded], "On the next run I am going to go through [the clouds]." At that time my left engine started to backfire severely. So I throttled it back and feathered the engine as we were taught to do. I asked for a heading home and Don said, "I don't know where we are." I said, "We flew down on a heading of 180 degrees, so we will fly north to home." But we didn't know what the wind was or anything. I was watching the fuel, but I knew we wouldn't make it home on one engine. Luckily for me, [I remembered reading]…a paper from Charles Lindbergh [which] said that to extend one's cruising range by twenty to twenty-five percent, reduce the RPMs as much as possible. So, I set it up that way. I decided to start the other engine to see if it would work, and it worked [fairly well] at low cruise speed. Don couldn't see any land on his radar scope. Finally Don said that we were about fifteen miles from a convoy, but no land. I knew we had to decide to either ditch or bail out pretty soon–a no-win situation. I decided to go twenty minutes past the convoy, and if we still didn't see land, we would come back to the convoy. After thirty minutes, I started to turn and he said, "I've got land!" We flew toward it, and he thought it was Sanga-Sanga.... I had been "squawking" emergency but nobody had been talking to me. We landed, and it WAS Sanga-Sanga. As we turned off the runway, the engine quit, as it was out of fuel. The flight was eight hours and fifteen minutes–the longest combat mission I know of!

Ken also reminisced about the following.

During fourteen night-fighter missions, I was able to correspond with my family. I would use code names to tell her [my wife] where I had been and where I was going. She got one letter and all it said was, "Dear Mary Lou.... Love, Ken." All the rest had been blacked out by the censors.

We got our news from Tokyo Rose. She knew where we were going before we did. We would listen to her to hear the big bands. We didn't take her seriously.

Our living conditions during the war were not what I would call ideal. We lived in eight-man tents. The shower was a burlap-screened area. The mess hall was in a building. [Earlier] a guy had told me, "When you ship your foot locker, ship all the booze you can get in it." I told him that I didn't drink, and that it made me sick. He said it didn't matter, take it! So I did. While we were in the Philippines at Leyte, there was a lumber yard on the beach. I found out who the boss was, and I told him I wanted wood to build a hut. He said, "Sure. You have any booze?" The next day I brought a truck and they filled it with lumber and corrugated steel. I gave him a quart of booze, and I think we built five huts from the materials. We had opportunities to do lots of swimming, and softball, when we weren't flying.

Ken came back home as one of 5,000 soldiers on a liberty ship. He stayed in the Air Force serving in Korea and Vietnam until 1969, when he retired as a lieutenant colonel. Ken had met his wife in Sacramento, California, and on October 14, 1944, they were married. He had been told by his friends not to get married, because war-time marriages never lasted. However, after a daughter and two sons, and fifty-nine years, Ken felt his marriage had been successful. He and his wife eventually moved to Fish Lake, Utah.

Northrop P-69 Black Widow
(Night-Fighter/Interceptor)

David Haggard
U.S. Army Air Corps
WWII
1940–1945

*"I went in as a snot-nosed kid and
came out a man."*

Dave was born and raised in Boise, Idaho. After graduating from Boise High he had trouble finding a job and, since his draft number was close to being called, he decided to enlist. He thought about joining the Navy, but when he talked to a recruiter he discovered the Navy had a six-year commitment; so, instead, he joined the Army Air Corps.

Dave was sent to Fort Lewis, Washington, for basic training. However they had additional draftees coming in, so they gave his group the option of going straight to the Philippines for training or to Stockton, California. He originally thought going to the Philippines would be a good idea, but for some reason changed his mind. Looking back at that decision, he was very happy about it because otherwise he would have been in the Philippines when the Japanese invaded soon after the war started. His training in Stockton wasn't actually a boot camp, just general training. One time the recruits were asked if anyone could drive a truck, and since he had previous experience, he volunteered. He was then assigned to a work detail–pushing a wheelbarrow. That taught him to be careful about volunteering! He had initially signed up to train in aerial photography, but his unit had only one person with any knowledge of photography, and their equipment was very antiquated, so his training was limited.

On December 7, 1941, Dave and his group were outside playing volleyball. A radio was playing in the window of their barracks when they heard about the Japanese bombing Pearl

Harbor. He felt that the Army was ill-prepared for war at that time because his unit had received little training, owned poor equipment and, in fact, most of the men hadn't even been issued a rifle. He began having second thoughts about being an aerial photographer. One day he noticed on the bulletin board an announcement recruiting for glider pilots. He decided that sounded interesting, so he volunteered for glider-pilot training.

Dave underwent a variety of tests in order to qualify for the glider program, and he successfully passed them. He was then sent to Plano, Texas, for ground school. The glider program was still in its infancy and did not have a lot of equipment with which to train; even the place he stayed had been a Boy Scout camp prior to it being turned into a military base. His next assignment was at Big Springs, Texas, where he learned how to fly small aircraft– primarily Piper Cubs. The men were trained to do "dead stick" landings. After turning off the engine they had to glide the aircraft to a landing strip. Next he was sent to California to a glider-training base in the desert. The pilots practiced on several different types of gliders, and they also used Piper Cubs that had their engines removed. A bigger plane would pull the glider up in the air and release it, and then the pilots flew them as they glided down. Flying in the glider was very similar to an airplane with an engine, except the pilots could not regain altitude unless there was a strong wind undercurrent.

Again, Dave's unit was sent back to Texas where they trained on the Waco glider. As this training progressed, the program itself seemed to be in jeopardy. Some of the Army generals wanted to continue the program, while others wanted to drop it. Many of the trainees transferred to other duties due to the uncertainty of the situation. Dave stuck with it and continued to train in the glider program. A 375-foot tow rope attached the Waco glider to a cargo plane (usually a C-47), which would then pull them up into the air.

A flashing red light on the cargo plane alerted the glider pilots to be ready for detachment. Once that light turned from red to green, the glider pilots had three seconds to disengage the rope. Dave remembered that one time there was a mistake and the C-47 released the attached rope. It immediately came rushing back toward the glider, making a noise that sounded like hundreds of cackling geese. Each glider had two pilots, and they would take turns flying the aircraft. Eventually the decision was made to deploy Dave's glider group and send them to the Orient. However, at the last minute there was a change in plans and instead they were assigned to report to England.

On the trip to England, Dave celebrated his twenty-fifth birthday. His unit was assigned to an airbase in England where they continued their training. In order to get flight pay they had to have a set number of hours flying each month, and that became a challenge, since there were not enough planes and gliders for the number of pilots stationed there. England was a beautiful place, but it rained constantly. Dave thought the girls were very nice, and they liked Americans. (A fact, Dave said, that was not appreciated by the British soldiers.) Everywhere he went he saw soldiers from different countries and different units.

The servicemen knew that the Allies would eventually invade France, but no one knew when and where. As the D-Day drew closer and it became very apparent that something was about to happen, more pilots were sent to Dave's base. The base was secured, so no one was allowed out or in without special permission. To maintain security, armed guards watched them even when they marched. When D-Day finally arrived, Dave was on a standby status. He later recalled being very relieved that he wasn't part of the first wave, because, as the cargo planes returned, almost all of them were shooting off red distress flares. Many of the planes crash landed coming back to the airfield–almost all of them had wounded on board.

After D-Day, half of Dave's unit was reassigned to Italy. They were stationed at a base north of Rome, staging for the invasion of southern France. On the day of the invasion, his glider was forty-fifth in line. At four o'clock in the morning, he got up to start the flight to the invasion area. In his glider they carried a Jeep and four British paratroopers. As they were getting ready to fly, one of the paratroopers pulled out a bottle of whiskey, and they all had "one for the road." They were delayed getting into the invasion area since it was fogged in, but eventually they continued their flight. They were released from the cargo plane and glided down, landing in a vineyard. They then helped the British get their Jeep out of the glider. About that time another paratrooper came up with a German soldier, who was carrying a white flag. A group of Germans wanted to surrender, but they insisted on surrendering to an officer. There was no officer around, so Dave told the interpreter to tell the German if they didn't surrender the Allied soldiers were going to blow up the house where the Germans were hiding; they would use a howitzer that was in their glider. The Germans decided to surrender! Dave was very grateful, because there was no ammunition for the howitzer.

Dave's next assignment included being part of Operation Market Garden in Holland. Since the Army Air Corps was short of glider pilots, most gliders took only one pilot on this mission. However, Dave's glider had two pilots because they were transporting a highly-secret intelligence team. Landing in Holland was fairly easy because the country was very flat, with few obstacles preventing a safe landing. As they were landing, the glider in front of him hit and injured a cow that then lay suffering on the ground. Being a farm boy, Dave walked over and shot the cow to put her out of her misery. (Years later, while Dave was working for a telephone company, he was talking to one of his coworkers about his war experiences. They discovered they were both glider pilots in Operation Market Garden. His coworker recalled that when he landed his glider he accidentally hit a cow and broke her back, and some other pilot came over and shot her. Surprised, Dave told him that he was the one that had shot the cow. They were amazed that years later both of them ended up working with the same company.) After landing the glider, the pilots were expected to be part of the infantry and, in Dave's case, he was assigned to guard duty watching German prisoners. While he was assigned there, the prison camp was bombed and shot at by German artillery.

Dave's final mission was the invasion of Germany. The plan was that the gliders would have an airborne drop across the Rhine into Germany. Prior to their landing, American artillery shot numerous smoke bombs to hide the gliders. Unfortunately, this also made it difficult for the glider pilots to see their position and, as they were coming in, Dave's glider barely missed hitting the top of a house. The glider then went through a power line before it came to a stop. Once they landed, the men were under heavy mortar fire, so everyone had to get out fast and find a safer place. As Dave was escaping from the glider, the person in front of him fell. At the same time a mortar hit between the two of them. Luckily, just prior to the invasion, the farmer who owned this particular field had plowed his ground, so the mortar charge went off into the soft earth. That plowed field softened the explosion and saved Dave's life!

After the war in Europe ended, Dave was sent back to the United States for reassignment. He was in California awaiting orders when the war ended. He had thought about remaining in the military and going to helicopter flight school, but decided against it. He was married in California and worked at the Ford Motor

Company for a short time before deciding to return to Idaho. Back in Boise, he worked for a telephone company for thirty-five years. In talking about his military experience, he stated that he went in "as a snot-nosed kid and came out a man."

Waco Glider Hitting the Dirt

Pressciliano Herrera
U.S. Army Air Corps
WWII
1942–1945
POW

"When I awoke they had a rope around my neck and strung over a tree branch."

Pressciliano Herrera was born and raised in New Mexico. Like many young men during the Great Depression, he quit high school in order to find work. He was living in Boise, Idaho, when Pearl Harbor was attacked, and he was called up for military service in May 1942.

Leaving Boise was especially hard for him, since by then he had a wife and a small child. He was first sent to Wichita Falls, Texas, for basic training. He then volunteered to be an airplane mechanic, and since that school was at the same base as his initial training, he only had to walk from one end of the base to the other to continue his training.

Pressciliano's next assignment landed him in Seattle, Washington, where he received training on the B-17 Bomber. After going to gunnery school, he got a pleasant surprise. He was transferred to Boise's Gowen Field for more B-17 training, which allowed him to spend three months with his family before being sent to England. There he joined the 388th Bomber Group as a flight engineer. He used one word to describe England, "Wet!"

His duties on the B-17 included manning the top-turret machine guns. He was credited with shooting down two German planes during his tour. On his twelfth mission his plane's heating system malfunctioned, and he ended up with frost bite in his toes and fingers that required him to be hospitalized. At that time, the doctors didn't know much about treating frostbite, and his hospital stay extended to a month. While he was there, the crew that he had been assigned to since being in Boise was shot down over Germany.

At this time during the war, bomber crews were transferred after doing twenty-five missions. But in Pressciliano's words, "I was to do twenty-four and one half," since he was shot down in the summer of 1943 during his 25th mission. The aircraft was on a bombing run to Berlin when, shortly before reaching the target, it was hit by antiaircraft fire that killed the bombardier and navigator. He and the rest of the crew bailed out of the plane.

Pressciliano remembered being told during training that the recruits were not to open their parachutes right away after jumping from the plane, so he waited as instructed; however, he almost waited too long, because his chute barely opened before he hit the ground. The force of the landing injured his knee. Now on the ground, he realized German civilians from a nearby village were waiting for him. He struggled to stand up, but one of them hit him in the head with a rifle, knocking him unconscious and leaving him with a scar which was visible the rest of his life.

When he awoke, the villagers had a rope around his neck and had strung it up over a tree limb. They were attempting to hang him. Just about that time, two German soldiers rode up on bicycles and rescued him from the crowd. He was taken to a building in town where he was left in a cellar for a week. Then he was put in a cattle car with a hundred other POWs and sent to a prison camp in Austria. Back in the States his wife and family were notified he was missing in action. It was over a year before they were sent word that he was alive and being held as a prisoner of war.

There were over 4,000 prisoners in Pressciliano's POW camp. They were separated by nationality: American, Russian or French. To keep track of the prisoners the Germans had frequent roll calls, forcing the men to stand in lines on the parade grounds, often for extended periods. His frost-bitten toes from his previous hospitalization started to blister, and for a while he couldn't walk and had to be carried to and from the roll calls by other POWs.

In attempts to escape, the prisoners dug several tunnels under the fences. Pressciliano, himself, escaped one time, but he was caught and placed in solitary confinement with a bread and water diet. During his thirteen months in the POW camp, he lost sixty pounds. He remembered that the Germans shot two prisoners who had tried to escape; however several prisoners were able to successfully make it back to the Allied lines.

In 1945, as the Russian Army advanced closer to the camp, the Germans evacuated the prisoners, forcing them to walk back into Germany. It was very difficult, since many of the prisoners were sick and unable to walk, and others had to carry them. They finally came to a forest, where the Germans abandoned them. Shortly thereafter they were found by the American Third Army. Pressciliano remembered many of the men crying as the American soldiers came into sight. The rescued prisoners were sent to France to recuperate and then transported back to the States. When he arrived in New York he went to the mess hall and ordered a steak and a quart of milk. Even though it tasted wonderful he was not able to eat all of it.

After returning to Boise and being reunited with his family, Pressciliano decided to stay in the military and joined the Air National Guard. His unit was called up for the Korean War and was sent to an airbase in Iceland. Later, he spent his Guard time working on the various planes that were assigned to Gowen Field. He retired from the Guard in 1979 and spent much of his retirement time volunteering and enjoying his grandchildren and great grandchildren.

Casper (Cap) D. Kramis
Royal Air Force
U.S. Army Air Corps
WWII
1941–1945
Soldiers Medal

*He knew he wanted to fly
anywhere, anyway he could.*

Casper or "Cap" Kramis was born to Swiss parents in November of 1914 in Hamilton, Montana. His dad homesteaded in the late 1800s in the Bitterroot Valley of Montana, and Cap's mom immigrated in the early 1900s. At that time there was a boom in the valley and thousands of acres of apple orchards were planted. Cap's dad sold his first farm and purchased acreage with apple trees. It was there that Cap grew up with two brothers and two sisters. In 1921 Cap was outside chopping wood and an airplane flew high overhead. That was it! He became enthralled with flying. He stayed in Hamilton, graduated from high school and was employed until 1941, when he enlisted in the Royal Canadian Air Force.

Cap joined the Canadian Air Force because he had started flying in a program in the U.S. called the CPT (Civilian Pilot Training), and by October 1941 he had his private pilot's license. He knew he wanted to fly anywhere, anyway he could. He tried to join the U.S. Army Air Corps or U.S. Navy, but at twenty-seven years old he was considered to be too old; plus he lacked sufficient education, and his eyesight wasn't very good. He had a friend who had gone to Canada and was very happy with his experience there. That friend was instrumental in getting Cap interested in the Canadian Air Force.

In December of 1941, Cap and a friend arrived in Vancouver, British Columbia, to enlist and were told that because of Pearl Harbor they couldn't be accepted immediately, as they had expected. There were numerous conversations between Canada and Washington, D.C., before the U.S. decided that Americans joining the Royal Canadian Air Force didn't jeopardize the United States' citizenry. So Cap and his friend joined the Canadian Air Force and began their training.

In January of 1942, they were shipped to #3 Manning Pool in Edmonton, Alberta, and were housed in facilities that had once been fairgrounds–complete with cold showers and unheated barracks. They learned to bathe, shave, shine shoes, polish buttons, maintain their uniforms and otherwise behave in the required manner. They participated in physical education, marching, rifle drill, foot drill, saluting and other routines. After four or five weeks a selection committee decided which recruits would be trained for air crews and which for ground crews.

In April 1942 they went to #7 Initial Training School in Saskatoon, Saskatchewan. This training was basic ground work and, more than anything, Cap thought it was a test of their learning ability. By August 1942, they were off to #6 Elementary Flight Training School at Prince Albert, Saskatchewan. This was primary training in Tiger Moths, until October 1942. From October 1942 to February 1943 the boys were back in Saskatoon in the #4 Service Flight Training School, and received their training in the twin-engine Cessna Crane (Bobcat). They were then finally commissioned as officers.

In March 1943, they went to #3 General Reconnaissance School at Summerside, Prince Edward Island, for ocean patrol and navigational training. That course lasted until May 1943. The commanders wanted to make Cap an instructor and make his friend Duane a fighter pilot, but Cap didn't want to be an instructor and

Duane didn't want to be a fighter pilot. They both wanted to go to Europe and fly "big airplanes." So, they were shipped to Europe for additional training. The Canadians kept Cap and Duane together when they went to Bournemouth at the Personnel Reception Center from June until July 1943. From there they were sent to South Cerney, Wales, for #3 P-AFU training (Pilot Advanced Flying Unit).

Cap and his friend were flying the Halifax, a four-engine heavy bomber, and then they started with the Royal Air Force 502 Squadron Coastal Command. They had completed a number of missions when they received a message from the U.S. Army Air Corps (8th Air Force) telling them to report to London. Once there they were told they had several choices: the 8th would send them back to the U.S. to fly B-17s; they could choose not to make any changes; or they could take a commission at their current rank and stay with the Royal Air Force, completing their own RAF missions. Cap decided, along with about ten other Americans, that since the British trained them they would continue what they were doing. However, they wore American uniforms and were paid in American dollars.

Cap and Duane flew numerous missions out of Wales with the intent of bombing German shipping, submarines and shore installations. Later they were moved to the Outer Hebrides Islands. During one bombing mission, Duane was shot down and spent a day and a night in the ocean before he was rescued. Upon returning from survivor's leave, his very first flight was as a volunteer to replace a copilot on a night-crew training mission. Duane's plane crashed and he and the entire crew were killed. Subsequent to that, Cap lost another dear friend from California, who joined the 8th Air Force and was also killed.

Most missions were between eight to twelve hours and all were at night. Some of the missions out of the Outer Hebrides were almost to Iceland, but most were off the coast of Norway, where they attacked German shipping. (Cap didn't relish the idea that some day he might end up in that cold water.)

Cap recalled one mission when he and the crew were flying through clouds at night and encountered what was at that time called St. Elmo's Fire. The electrical field built up on the tips of the propellers and on the wings, making them look like they were sparking or on fire. It became very intense, and after a minute or two there was an explosion, and the bright light temporarily blinded Cap, who was trying to hold the aircraft in level flight. The copilot found a flashlight and illuminated the instrument panel so Cap could see. He credited the copilot with "saving the day." When the electrical charge exploded from the trailing antenna on the bottom of the aircraft, it blew the wire and the antenna off and left a hole that was about four inches in diameter.

According to Cap, it wasn't bad flying at night. He remembered having tea first before each departure. All missions over the ocean were flown at about 5,000 feet above sea level and the usual attack position was at 1,500-2,000 feet and then on down to as close as 50 feet above the target. Once up to cruising altitude, Cap would set the course and go back and get another cup of tea, and then rest until they arrived at the target area–at which time he would return to flying the aircraft. Once out of the bombing area, his copilot would fly until landfall, and then Cap would complete the flight and land the plane. Upon returning to base, the routine was to have a tot of rum (a tot was a daily ration of rum given to sailors on Royal Navy ships and was about one eighth of a pint), debrief, have a Q&A session, and then sleep during the rest of the day. The next day would be a practice mission and then another operational mission on the third or fourth night. The way the British managed their missions, it took at least four to five times longer to accomplish their required number of missions as it did, for example, a U.S. Air Corps B-17 pilot. Cap said that the missions accomplished in a year and a half flying for the British would be comparable to the number of missions a B-17 pilot would have flown in three to four months. He thought the British were really nice, and he enjoyed his experience working with them because they didn't see the need to rush anything. He made many really good friends. His crew was an interesting group of men with varying nationalities: one each from Spain, Russia, Holland, Australia, New Zealand, and two from Canada.

On January 21, 1944, when he was still flying the Halifax bomber with the 502 Squadron Coastal Command and guarding the crucial western approaches to Britain, Cap's plane was returning from a rough flight on a stormy night. It had flown almost to Iceland and back. Cap was flying copilot that night and, as they made their final approach to St. David's Airfield, there was a loud explosion. They lost total control of the airplane, but couldn't determine the cause. They landed on one wing and on the nose of the plane, and it caught on fire. It was later determined that the propeller on one of the inboard engines had sheared off and had flown into the fuselage just back of the pilot's cabin. The errant propeller severed the control cable to the ailerons and elevator. There were depth charges on board the plane and an explosion was likely. After the hazardous landing, Cap quickly lifted the unconscious navigator out of the aircraft by way of the pilot escape hatch. He reentered the burning plane to help the captain and flight engineer extricate the other crewmen. On April 1, 1944, the Office of the Commanding General of the Headquarters of the U.S. Strategic Air Forces in Europe awarded Cap the Soldier's Medal for his heroism.

The 8th Air Force had a headquarters location at Chalgrove Airfield, Oxfordshire, about forty-two miles NNW of London. The base had a flight section with aircraft of all types that were utilized for courier work and transport of VIPs. In March of 1945 Cap joined them and had a grand opportunity to fly numerous aircraft. In all, he flew forty different types of planes during his military career. At Chalgrove they had small aircraft such as the Piper Cub and all the way up to B-17s, with fighters in between. They had a P-51 engineered with a passenger seat and, when the Colonel from the 8th needed to go to Brussels, it only took about twenty-five minutes to get him there. Many times Cap had the honor to fly with General Doolittle. He would fly from his airfield over to General Doolittle's small airfield near London. Upon arriving, he would shift to copilot and Doolittle took over. Cap stayed with the Chalgrove group until October of 1945.

In October of 1945 Cap went to the 653rd Bomb Squadron Light at Wattisham Airfield and flew the British de Havilland Mosquito on meteorological missions. These planes flew completely unarmed and depended on their speed and altitude to keep out of trouble. The missions were not flown in groups, but as a lone aircraft with a pilot and a navigator trained in meteorology.

In November 1945 Cap went to Snetterton Heath and spent two weeks with the 339th Bomb Squadron, 96th Bomb Group. Later that month, Cap was aboard the *RMS Queen Mary* which departed Southampton, England, with 11,682 troops plus 843 ship crew members. They disembarked at New York City. From New York the soldiers went to Camp Kilmer, New Jersey, which was the main center for the reception and processing of soldiers returning from Europe and the Pacific.

About forty years later, Cap found the phone number for his wartime copilot and called him in England. When a man answered, Cap asked him if he was John. He answered, "Yes," and then asked the caller, "Is that you Cap?" John said that after all of the war missions they had flown together, he would always be able to recognize Cap's voice. As a result of that conversation,

John became interested in the war history they shared together, and he researched information about a German submarine that they had bombed in the English Channel about the time of D-Day. He found out that one of the survivors of the sub had managed to get to shore and eventually moved to London. John decided to visit the German sailor, and Cap teasingly warned him to be careful, because he might still be mad at them. (There was a twinkle in Cap's eyes when he related this story during his Veterans History Project interview.) John later reported that he had enjoyed a wonderful visit with the man.

Cap enthusiastically said that his military experience guided and motivated him from the very beginning to do the very best he could. He learned to give it all he had, and felt that even if he had failed he would have the knowledge that he had done the best that he possibly could. He spoke to his children about the importance of having drive and determination, sharing that, "It isn't whether you are a ditch digger, a carpenter or a college professor–I am proud of you if you do the best you can and lead an honest and honorable life."

On November 5, 2004, Cap celebrated his 90th birthday flying members of his family over Boise in a Cessna. He celebrated his 100th birthday on November 5, 2014.

Donald Lloyd
U.S. Army Air Corps
WWII
1942–1946

*The wind was so fierce they had
to crawl on their bellies to get
the food.*

Donald was raised in the Portland, Oregon, area where he graduated from high school in 1939. Because of the Great Depression, Don found it very difficult to get a job in the Portland area, thus he joined the Civilian Conservation Corps. The CCC was a program started by the federal government during the depression years to help young people learn skills needed to get employment. Don spent some time working for the CCC in the Idaho and Oregon area before being transferred to Alaska. While there he was able to secure employment in a lumber mill where he worked for a short time. He was then able to get a job with the Army Corps of Engineers working on a survey crew.

Returning from Alaska, Don was visiting his parents when the news of the Japanese attack on Pearl Harbor was announced. He remembered listening to President Roosevelt on the radio talking about the bombing of the U.S. Naval Fleet at Pearl Harbor. He continued working for the Army Corps of Engineers until he received his draft notice.

Don's military training was very extensive. He was first sent to Fort Lewis, Washington, to do some testing. After the testing he was assigned to aircraft armorer school. He was sent on to Denver, Colorado, for six weeks basic training and then additional armorer training. When the training was completed, he stayed on there as an instructor. After a short time, he was sent on to an additional basic engineering class. This training at a Catholic college in Denver consisted of basic college courses in engineering and lasted for eight months. One day the supervisor came in and told the men that classes were over and Don would now be headed to Oklahoma to commence basic infantry training.

While there he was assigned to the 42nd Infantry Division. One day on the parade grounds the generals advised the men that they were being deployed to Europe. They were immediately sent back to their barracks to get packed. While gathering his belongings, Don was summoned back to his captain's office. There he was told that since he was originally in the Army Air Corps, he would not be going to Europe after all, but would be sent to Boise, Idaho, where he would be starting aircraft armorer training again.

Finally, Don was sent overseas to the Dutch New Guinea Islands. From there he went on to the Philippines. He was assigned to the 38th Bomb Group, where his duties included working on B-25 airplanes after they returned from bombing missions, reloading and checking the mechanisms to make sure they were in working condition. They also were responsible for loading bombs onto the aircraft.

The men lived on the beach in small huts that had been constructed by local labor. They also had a Filipino boy who cooked for them. Don was in the Philippines for approximately six months before his outfit was transferred to the newly-liberated island of Okinawa. One time on Okinawa they were warned that Japanese paratroopers might invade that night. He had to stand guard duty to make sure that his unit was safe, but no enemy paratroopers ever appeared. While on Okinawa the island was hit hard by a hurricane. Don's sergeant took their squad up a hill where everyone was ordered to lie down in a pit. He sent Don and another soldier back to camp to get food supplies. The wind was so fierce they could not stand up, but had to crawl on their bellies to get the food, and then crawl back, pushing the boxes ahead of them to the pit.

They rigged up a makeshift theater in the pit, and the soldiers sat around the perimeter to watch movies. One night they were watching a cowboy movie when suddenly all of the antiaircraft guns started firing. Word came down that the Japanese had surrendered and the war was over. The entire island erupted in a great celebration.

Soon Don was sent to Japan, and he was assigned duties to assist in the occupation of that country. While there he was very surprised to discover that the Japanese people were quite friendly with the Americans. One evening he and a buddy were invited to a Japanese home to share a meal. Two young boys were in the family and, when Don discovered they were going to engineering school, he challenged them with an engineering formula that he knew was impossible to solve. The boys worked on it for some time before they finally realized he had given them a bogus equation. He spent several months in Japan before being sent back to the United States. On the way to the ship his train traveled through the two cities of Hiroshima and Nagasaki that had been destroyed by atomic bombs. He was able to witness firsthand the devastation that the bombs had caused.

Don returned to the United States where he was reunited with his wife, whom he had married while he was stationed at Denver. They moved back to Oregon, where he used the GI Bill to go to Oregon State University and complete the civil engineering degree he had started while in the Army. He spent the rest of his career as an engineer working for different companies, including the city of Idaho Falls. He joined the American Legion and was active in it for many years. Just prior to his interview with the Veterans History Project, Don turned ninety years old. His neighbors held a huge block party, where everyone came and celebrated his birthday. He enjoyed a great life and felt that he owed a lot to his experiences in the military during WWII.

Consolidated B-24 Liberator

Martin Luther
U.S. Army Air Corps
WWII & Korea
1942–1952

*Thus began the biggest humanitarian
airlift ever attempted.*

Martin was born in September of 1921 in Mt. Vernon, Tennessee. This was a fairly remote area in eastern Tennessee and, when he was still very young, his family moved to Madisonville. He had two older brothers and two older sisters. His father was in the state house of representatives and also operated a cotton gin, as well as had other business interests.

When Martin turned eighteen in 1938, he decided to seek his fortune by moving to California. A relative helped him obtain a job working in the research department at the American Potash and Chemical Company at the Trona Mine. Martin took two years of chemical engineering via correspondence courses while he was working at Trona. He also learned to fly by taking lessons at nearby Dry Lake. After a skiing trip in the Sierra Mountains near the town of Bishop, he stopped on the way home and heard about the Japanese attack on Pearl Harbor–December 7, 1941. This event changed everything for him, along with millions of others.

On the 9th of November 1942, Martin enlisted in the Army at San Pedro, California, and passed the test for the flying cadet program. He flew the Stearman biplane and the Fairchild monoplane as part of his progression through the training. His desire was to fly bombers and he was given the chance to fly the four-engine B-24. He was assigned to pilot training at Liberal, Kansas, where he graduated as "first pilot." This then took him to Topeka, Kansas, where he and his crew picked up a brand new B-24. Martin's crew was made up of nineteen- and twenty-year olds.

They flew their B-24 first to Cuba, then Belem in Brazil, and on to Dakar and Casablanca, and finally to Stornara, Italy. This was to be their base, and from there they began flying bombing missions to northern Italy, targeting railway marshaling yards, refineries and airfields. They then expanded the bombing to take in areas of France, Germany, Austria, Hungary and Romania. This was extremely dangerous work, and many planes were shot down or badly damaged by flak or enemy fighters. In all, Martin flew fifty-three missions.

One of the worst missions Martin remembered was when he flew to the Shell Oil refinery in Budapest, Hungary. Seven out of nine planes in Martin's squadron were shot down during that bombing run. His ball gunner was killed and his tail gunner was critically injured. Seven of the other crew members were also injured to a lesser degree. The crew did their best to apply tourniquets wherever they could to stop the gunner from bleeding to death. For the next four and one-half hours, the B-24 limped home and eventually landed in Foggia, Italy. The aircraft was shot up so badly, that it was missing its vertical stabilizer, and the flaps and hydraulics no longer worked. The only way Martin and the crew were able to get the plane stopped was by deploying their parachute chest packs out the side windows. The B-24 was damaged so badly that it was scrapped.

After WWII Martin flew C-54 and C-47 transport planes. Because of his familiarity with these aircraft, in June of 1948 he received orders to report to Germany to become part of the Berlin Airlift. The Soviet Union, who controlled East Germany, had blocked off all surface routes into and out of Berlin, and the people of West Berlin (the part of the city held by the Western Allies) were running out of food and other essential supplies. Their prospects looked grim until the U.S., British and French Allies decided to send by air the essentials that the Berliners needed.

Thus began the biggest humanitarian airlift ever attempted. Martin was working for General Tunner as staff operations officer and was stationed at Weisbaden, assigned to the Combined Airlift Task Force. In this capacity he helped organize operations, as well as flew a lot of the supplies into Berlin. By the 26th of June the Berlin Airlift officially began providing food, fuel and medicine to two and a half million West Berliners that had been cut off from the rest of the world by the Soviet Union blockade. Aircraft flew continually to West Berlin for 462 days, despite foggy and rainy conditions and less than perfect navigation and landing aids. At the height of activity, aircraft were landing every ninety seconds. This meant that they had to be unloaded very quickly and made ready to leave Berlin to make space for more incoming aircraft.

Sometimes, when aircraft were being unloaded, pilots and crew would take a quick opportunity to stretch their legs by taking a walk around the airfield perimeter fence. One day Gail Halvorsen, one of the pilots, encountered a small group of German children just outside the airbase fence. He wanted to give them something, but all he had in his pocket was a couple of sticks of gum. He passed the gum to the kids anyway and was impressed by the way that they shared the gum amongst themselves, each receiving a small piece. He told them that the next time he flew into West Berlin, just before the airplane landed, he would drop them some candy. He would "waggle" his plane's wings to let them know it was him. Thus began the "Candy Bombers" crusade. Soon, most of the incoming planes were dropping candy received from donations from all over the United States. By the end of the "Big Lift" (September 30, 1949), 277,569[1] flights had taken place, delivering in excess of 2.3 million tons of cargo.

---

[1] Miller, Roger G. 1998. To Save a City: The Berlin Airlift, 1948-1949. Air Force History Support Office, Bolling AFB, DC 20032-5000.

A total of eighty-three[2] military and civilian personnel, associated with the airlift, died due to accidents in the effort to keep the people of West Berlin alive. Berliners were so appreciative of what the Allies had done to save them after WWII that they organized a huge celebration in May 2009 on the 60th anniversary of the Airlift. Martin and his family, along with fifty or sixty "airlifters," were invited to Templehof Airport for the celebration. An estimated 160,000 Berliners turned out to say, "Danka!" One of these, now a grown adult, was one of the children who had received dropped candy from Martin and his fellow pilots. She became a good friend of his family.

In 1950, Martin was next assigned to Combat Cargo Command in Ashia, Japan, to support U.S. operations during the Korean War. He delivered critical medical supplies and ammo, and he helped with air evacuations of the wounded. He also flew behind-the-line drops of OSS personnel. He participated in psychological warfare by flying low in a C-47 that was outfitted with huge speakers and dropped propaganda leaflets into the country side. He also flew into the Chosin Reservoir airstrip in support of the First Marine Division.

After the Korean War, Martin returned to civilian life and fulfilled a number of assignments for Douglas Aircraft, as well as working for the Martin Company, where he wrote flight handbooks and procedures for missile-systems launch crews. For the next forty years, he owned and operated a Chrysler, Plymouth, Dodge, Jeep dealership in Bishop, California. He also owned and operated an air charter service. In 2003 Martin and his wife moved to Ontario, Oregon, to be near their children, grandchildren, and great grandchildren.

---

[2] Ibid.

Joseph Meyers
U.S. Army Air Corps
WWII
1942–1945

"I did all fifty missions in a ball
turret on a B-17 bomber."

Joe was born in Pennsylvania and was raised there until he graduated from high school. His father was a butcher and his mother a homemaker. On December 7, 1941, he and a friend were out deer hunting, and they came home excited to tell about their hunt. When they arrived everyone started yelling at them to listen to the radio, because the Japanese had bombed Pearl Harbor.

Joe thought about joining the Marines, but he had just gotten out of the hospital and didn't think he could take the training. So, in the spring of 1942 he decided to join the Army Air Corps where he underwent six weeks of basic training at Atlantic City, New Jersey. Joe commented that the training was very strenuous in Atlantic City because he had to do a lot of marching and running in the sand on the beach there.

His next assignment was gunnery training at Fort Meyers, Florida. He recalled that the men would be put in the back of a pickup truck, each given a shotgun and would be driven into the Everglades, where clay pigeons would be thrown up for them to shoot. From there they trained in a two-seater airplane where the gunners sat in the back seat and shot a machine gun at towed targets. Joe was the smallest one in his crew, so he got the assignment of ball turret gunner. The space where a ball turret gunner operated was very compact, which meant that the person operating that gun could not wear his parachute. If the plane was in trouble before he could jump from it, he would have to first extract himself from the ball and then put on the parachute.

The next assignment for Joe's crew was Boise, Idaho. While there they learned to fly together as a team and did extensive gunnery practice. They then transferred to Walla Walla, Washington, where they did additional training, including flying night missions out over the Pacific Ocean. Finally, Joe's crew received their orders to go overseas. They flew their plane first to Brazil, then to some islands in the Atlantic, before landing in North Africa. He stated that North Africa was extremely hot during the day, but in the evening it cooled off so much that the men had to have a blanket to sleep. Their missions were mainly to bomb German airfields. When approaching the target, they were often shot at by the enemy. He felt very nervous about the antiaircraft fire, because there was nothing he could do to protect himself except sit in the turret, watch it all, and hope for the best. Because he was in the bottom of the plane, one of his jobs was to make sure when the bombs dropped that they all cleared the bomb bay doors. On one of his first missions, Joe's airplane was attacked by an Italian fighter plane. As the fighter followed underneath his aircraft Joe was able to shoot it down. During the war, he flew bombing missions to France, Italy and Greece.

It was on his 16th mission when Joe's plane was badly damaged by antiaircraft fire. The pilot got on the radio and announced that the plane was going down and asked if everyone wanted to parachute out. All of the crew decided to remain with the plane. As their plane left the formation, they found themselves alone, and they were still being attacked by German fighters. In a normal firefight, many different gunners from different planes would shoot at the same target, so it was hard to tell which gunner actually shot the plane down. But in this case, they were the only ones shooting at the Germans. Both the tail gunner and waist gunner in his plane shot fighters down and, as one flew underneath the plane, Joe shot at it and blew it up. They downed three fighters in a very short time. As they descended closer to the water, the crew members squeezed into the radio room and sat down. Joe grabbed a radio, so when they exited the plane they would have some communication. As the plane hit the water it tore the bottom off the fuselage and twisted around and around like a washing machine. The airplane was equipped with two rubber life rafts. Unbelievably, neither of them was damaged, so they both inflated. Joe couldn't believe that the rafts had not been damaged since the airplane had numerous bullet holes in it. Miraculously, none of the crew was hurt, and all of them escaped the plane safely.

The entire crew struggled into the life rafts and started rowing hard toward an island they could see in the distance. Joe's job was to crank the small radio that sent out an SOS signal. When the plane went down, some people living on the island spotted the airplane crash and, knowing there was a Navy boat on the other side of the island, they ran over and alerted the Navy that a plane had been shot down. The ship was a submarine chaser and it immediately took off to rescue them. The crew members were glad to see a ship coming to their rescue, but they also worried about whose ship it was–theirs or the enemy's. Everyone was relieved to see that it was American, and they were rescued shortly after crash landing.

On another of Joe's missions, just as they got over their target, the plane took a hit from antiaircraft fire. The pilot made radio contact with everyone, but two crew members did not respond. Joe climbed out of the ball turret and checked on the two waist gunners. Both had been hit by enemy fire, and one was in shock. Joe helped him put on his oxygen mask. The other gunner had been hit in the chest with shrapnel and was dead. After that mission, his crew didn't fly together very often. He flew with other crews because there was always a need for a ball turret gunner. He was the first of his original crew to finish the fifty-mission limit.

After returning to the United States, Joe was reunited with his parents, who were very relieved and happy to see him safely home. While stationed in Boise, Idaho, he had met a girl and corresponded with her while he was overseas. She came out to Pennsylvania, where they were married. Because he had some health problems, he was given quite a bit of time off, which enabled him to spend it with his new bride. His last assignment was as a gunnery instructor, and he was sent to Mountain Home, Idaho, where he was stationed until the end of the war.

After being discharged, Joe and his wife decided to stay in Idaho, and there he found work as a machinist. Many years after the war, a B-17 Bomber came to Boise. Joe paid for his three kids to take a ride in it, and he proudly labeled the photo taken of them, "Mission #51!"

Joe Meyers' Crew - Boeing B-17 Flying Fortress

Luther D. Moore
U. S. Army Air Corps
WWII
1936–1945
POW

"All of a sudden it quieted down and someone said, 'Here come the P-38s, God bless 'em!' "

Luther was born in 1916 to parents that homesteaded in Montana just outside of Lewistown. During the Great Depression he went to a little country school. His uncle sent him to a prep school and a junior college named Boiling Springs College in North Carolina, which was run by Baptists. It later became Gardner Webb University.

After graduating, Luther couldn't find a job, so he decided he would go into the Army or the Navy. He went to the Navy recruiting office and was measured and weighed. He was small of stature, so they said they couldn't use him. He then went to the Army recruiting office. Because many applicants couldn't read or write, he was given a literacy test, which proved to be fairly simple for him. After grading the paper, the officer asked Luther where he would like to go. He responded, "The Army Air Corps." He was told, however, that he needed to enlist in the Army first, then apply to the Air Corps. It was suggested he would fit in with the Corps of Engineers and, if he went overseas, he would only have to serve two years. Luther was sent to Panama and after two years he re-enlisted in the regular Army Reserve. As he was leaving the recruiting office, the commanding officer came in and said to him, "Hitler just walked into Austria. The War Department says we will be involved in a major war within a few years, and we won't be prepared, so we will keep you in the Army Reserve."

113

Luther's new assignment was with the Military Police. One day a truck showed up with the lettering "Air Corps" written on it. Luther ran up to the vehicle and said he wanted to join them. He was told he needed an engineering degree and some political pull if he wanted a chance to become a flying cadet. Because of his two years of college, the Air Corps eventually let him take an exam to see if he was qualified. Luther was then sent to Pine Bluff, Arkansas, to attend a civilian flight school, class of 42H. If the cadets could solo a PT-19 in seven hours, they could take their choice of becoming a bombardier or a navigator. Luther chose to become a bombardier.

He was sent to Spokane, Washington, to attend B-17 training, and while there he was commissioned in the ORC (Organized Reserve Corps) and eventually became a bombardier instructor at Davis-Monthan Air Base in Tucson, Arizona. Finally attached to a squadron, he was given a Sperry bombsight (which he did not like as well), instead of the Norden bombsight on which he had been previously trained.

Luther's group was sent to Casablanca and then into Italy in November of 1944 to join the 515th Squadron of the 15th Air Force. They arrived just months after the Benghazi-Ploiesti attack, where the squadron had lost fifty-three airplanes. (In military circles, this disaster became known as "Black Sunday.") They were forced to wait for more planes to arrive, some coming from the Ford Motor Company. They were stationed in southern Italy near the Foggia complex of B-24s. The men did not have much chance to interact with the Italians; but when they did, Luther found out the Americans were well received. One time he stayed in a flat (apartment) in Capri. The Italians there told him they would fight the British, but not the Americans.

Luther made thirty-five missions into France, northern Italy and Germany, before his plane was shot down. All his missions were day missions; only the British flew at night. Luther's plane bombed the rail yards in Budapest, Hungary (they were supplying arms to the Russian front), the industrial complexes and aircraft factories in Austria. The rest of the story is told in Luther's own words.

One of the roughest missions was when they sent us to Steyr, [Austria]. When we went into the briefing they told us not to expect any fighters [for protection], and when we got there and started the bombing run, the sky became black with [German] ME-109s. There were B-24s [American bombers] ablaze and blowing apart–engines, propellers, parts of men, blowing up and burning. Some of the guys jumped to get out of the burning planes. I think we lost nine planes. After they finished with the B-24s, they started on us. The nose gunner said, "Here they come at 9 o'clock." The tail gunner would pray awhile, then swear awhile. After awhile he said, "I'm out of ammunition and they are still coming." He got credit for shooting down two of them. A bullet came through one side of the skin [of the plane] and out the other, right behind me. And then all of a sudden it quieted down and someone said, "Here come the P-38s, God bless 'em!" They got them off of us. They were short on fuel, and some had to crash land on the beach, but some made it back.

[During] the 36th mission we were shot down. We were hitting a Messerschmitt assembly factory. The main thing was to crush the Luftwaffe [German Air Force]. To win the war you had to invade and, to invade, you had to get across that [English] Channel. We were trying to cut off their fuel supplies. By May we had whittled down the Luftwaffe.

For the bombs to be accurate, we had to fly straight and level at one air speed. They threw up a wall of flak at our altitude. This time we had a direct hit in the left bomb bay. In a B-24, that is where all the control cables are, and it severed the control cables. The pilot had no control over the yoke or rudders. So we started a flat spin from 20,000 feet. We didn't hear a bailout call, but the tail gunner came up saying, "get out!" [The gunners] in the nose couldn't wear parachutes because it was too close. We had chest packs and we put them on the navigator's table behind us. Our way of escape was through the nose wheel door. I realized it was pretty bad. I put my chute on with clip-on straps. I opened the doors and went feet first. I was whipped around with no control. Finally I got straightened out and the chute was up above me. I pulled the rip cord and it worked. Coming down I could hear rifle shots coming off of my chute. I don't know if they were shooting at me or something else below. I landed in a little park area. They [the civilians] were all in air raid shelters. I realized my left shoe was full of blood and my left leg was pretty bad. I guess a piece of flak hit me.

I followed instructions. First thing you do is get rid of the chute so they won't see where you are. I got under some trees and vines and tucked the chute under there. All of a sudden here came some German troops looking around. I got down low and they walked right by me, looking up in the trees, thinking I had landed up there. They didn't find me. One of them might have seen me, but he didn't let on. They were Austrians. I was right near some German barracks and I could see troops coming and going. I thought this was a good place to stay until after dark. They won't think to look for me next to the barracks. So after dark, I started off. We were supposed to go south towards Yugoslavia. If we got in the hands of Tito's group, he would see that you got to the border, and they had submarines that would pick us up and take us back to Italy. If you got in the wrong hands, they would sell you to the Germans or work you over themselves. One of the guys that finally got back said the Yugoslavs castrated him and sewed his testicles up in his mouth and sent him walking into the other lines. Those are the kind of things they had to put up with.

I headed south, but didn't realize what I was getting into. I started walking and it was dark. Here came a couple of German soldiers on bicycles. They asked, "Are you Ruski?" I said, "No, I'm not a Russian." They told me to wait there. They weren't armed, so I put my hand in my flight jacket where U.S. airmen wore their handguns, and the bluff worked. I walked away and they didn't follow. I got into a rye field and hid there. I had to cross a stream and almost drowned–I was soaking wet. I got into a small town with rock houses and they all had dogs. The dogs started "raising cain!" I finally got on top of the hill and tried to dry my clothes. I was in my long johns hopping around on one foot, getting my stuff to dry and I guess it was quite a sight. The local people would pack a lunch and when the air raid sirens went off they would take it and go to the woods. So here they came. When the women saw me they started giggling. One of them saw my jacket, and she screamed out in perfect English, "Look, a parachutist!" The men had orders to bring the men [downed flyers] to a gym there. They took charge and kept the women away. I got dressed and they hauled me down to the town, and women were screaming and dogs yapping at my heels. When I got to the gym, I found a lot of people there. The copilot from our plane was there. He told me that he knocked the navigator out [of the plane] before he got out. I asked about the pilot and he said he resisted getting out. One waist gunner got out. Six were killed, including the pilot.

They took all government property, including my jacket. They took a straight razor and shaved around my leg, [and treated it] with iodine and put brown paper bandages on the wounds. That afternoon they took us to a mess hall with a full life-size picture of Hitler. We ate a stew with vegetables and meat. They told us to eat well, because we were taking a long trip on a train. My leg was getting infected–all red and swollen. I was getting a fever. They put us on a train to Frankfurt where the interrogation center was. We spent the night there and they gave us some clothes. We were lucky we were with the Luftwaffe. Goring, the second in command under Hitler, was a paradox. He was a Nazi, but he had the idea that all flyers should take care of each other. So, he said he was going to take care of us the best he could, under the Geneva Convention. It was a POW camp, but they allowed the Swedish and Red Cross to send food parcels in. They had a small hospital with [both] a captured American and British doctor. They had medical supplies from the Red Cross that the Germans didn't have. The doctor cleaned my leg. They didn't have penicillin then, but they had a lot of sulfa, so he packed it with sulfa and nice bandages. I stayed in the hospital, and the first night was bad; but eventually it got a little better, so I could walk a little bit. They sent me back into the camp with the group. There were a lot of people there. It was the West Lager camp. The original Lager camp was for the RAF before we came in. They started getting so many Americans they had to build a whole new camp. I heard there were 20,000 [POW] soldiers. They had a loud speaker and once a day we could hear some of the German news. But we also got BBC news on a crystal set. So that the Germans wouldn't find it, several people each kept a part of it, and when it broadcast they would get together to assemble it and listen, then spread the news throughout the camp.

We had a lot of privileges there that other prisoners didn't get. We arrived just after the "Great Escape" [had occurred] and some of those guys were coming back in. The Germans knew they [the POWs] were tunneling and brought in seismographs. The [prisoners] had little stoves in each room and it was under [one of these] that they started the tunnel. They all had to carry a little dirt in their pockets and every day would walk all around spreading the dirt out. They used wood off of the beds to build the tunnels. They escaped in March of 1944 but were caught and rounded up. [The Germans] shot fifty of them.

The worst part of the whole thing was our "famous march." The Russians were close, so the Germans decided to move us. It was thirty degrees below zero and a blizzard when they started walking us out of there. The guards were in their sixties or so. (The Germans were scraping the bottom of the barrel.) We walked for two nights and three days until we got near the Czech border. Some of the elderly guards died of hypothermia and exposure–same with the guard dogs and the horses. The camp commander came with us. They considered us as exchange for negotiations. They put us in French boxcars, fifty prisoners and one guard in each car. There had been horses in there and they hadn't cleaned it out, so we had a smelly ride back to Nuremberg. We were there a short while. The barracks were loaded with lice. The Germans had us dig zigzag trenches outside, because the air raids were coming over. The Germans decided their final holdout would be down in Bavaria, near Hitler's home. I had come down with pneumonia and was in the German army hospital for a few days.

We started out to Moosburg and Patton's 3rd Army came in. He looked like a Greek god in his shiny helmet, riding in a special car. He looked around the barracks, then got up on his car to make a speech. They had been cutting Nazi flags down around the camp. He saw one that hadn't been cut down and said, "I want that son of a bitch cut down, and I want the guy who cuts it down to wipe his ass on it!" Then he looked around and he said, "I guess you sons of bitches are glad to see me!" A cheer went up.

We were sent back to Camp Lucky Strike [in France] for delousing–and we had them! They [the lice] would get in the seams of our belt linings, and we had a time with them. We got on a British ship in Southampton, England. We had a bunch of British war brides on the ship with us. We came into New York Harbor and got to see the Statue of Liberty. Then a long trip back to California. They released us pretty quick and gave us some [new] clothes. I had married a California girl and we decided to stay in California. We took a train back to see my family in North Carolina and some of my family lived near Arlington, Virginia. I still had a bad case of pneumonia, so I would take a bus to the Pentagon, and they took care of me.

So that's how it was. We got back to the States. I was a young lieutenant with most of my time in the service. I was married and had a family, so I had to go to work and couldn't use the GI Bill for an education. I stayed in the Reserve, though, and retired as a lieutenant colonel.

Lockheed P-38 Lightning

Stalag Luft III - Germany

Warren Harding Roberts
U.S. Army Air Corps Reserve
WWII
1942–1945
Korea & Vietnam
U.S. Army Service Award

"They seemed so young, not even shaving yet."

Not everyone involved in a conflict, such as WWII, was an active duty soldier, sailor, airman or marine. There were some people who served in civilian positions that were just as vital to assist in the war effort. One such person was Warren Roberts, a pilot who flew our troops and supplies during three conflicts: World War II, Korea and Vietnam.

Born and raised on a farm outside of Caldwell, Idaho, Warren was in his third year of college when World War II broke out. He was home from school and out on the ranch the day Pearl Harbor was attacked. He knew he and his brother would now be inducted into the military service. Warren joined a Reserve unit in Caldwell and took flying lessons there. He was sent to Texas for a while and then up to Seattle, Washington. He was drafted from the Reserve by Pan American Airlines. They had huge military contracts to provide aircraft to transport troops and equipment. Warren flew training planes (C-54s) for the company. He was in the training unit for some time. He then flew C-54s all over the world: Brazil, England, India and Africa; moving troops, deceased military personnel and cargo back and forth. He flew out of Miami and New York dozens of times. His job lasted until a year after the war was over.

After WWII, Warren retired his commission from the Reserve (never really serving any time as a commissioned officer) and moved to San Francisco to work for the Pan American Corporation as a pilot flying DC-4s. He was still carrying some troops, but also tourists. During the Korean War he flew roundtrip from San Francisco to Seoul, South Korea, and back again. This job lasted one and a half to two years. Then it was back to flying commercially until the early years of the Vietnam War. He first flew DC-4s to Saigon. With the new 707s coming off the assembly line, Pan American created a training facility for the jet pilots on their campus at LaGuardia Airport, New York. That is where Warren learned to fly the 707s. It was a one-month course. The jets then came into full service and he flew 707s to Saigon for two years. Because of the dangers surrounding the airport, the pilots could not overnight in Vietnam. They had to fly in, unload the plane (sometimes carrying ammunition, which worried him), reload with outgoing personnel and cargo, then leave before nightfall. His airplane was fired on several times. When asked about the troops he was carrying in and out of the war zone, he said, "They seemed so young, not even shaving yet." But he said they were all fit and in good shape.

Warren spent the next twenty years flying around the world for Pan American. He then retired to his farm in Caldwell, Idaho. For his service to his country during the Vietnam War, the U.S. Army awarded him a Service Award.

Glenn (Dick) Rosenberry
U.S. Army Air Corps
WWII
1939–1945
POW
Two Purple Hearts
Good Conduct Medal

*"The Japanese got my left leg and
the Germans the right."*

Dick was born in 1921 and grew up in Uhrichsville, Ohio. He was always fascinated with flying, so in 1939, soon after he graduated from high school, he enlisted in the Army Air Corps. After completing basic training he was stationed in Hawaii.

He was there at Hickam Field on December 7, 1941, when the Japanese attacked Pearl Harbor. At first, everyone thought it was a training exercise but, when the bombs started falling, it soon became apparent that it wasn't. One of the Japanese planes flew so low that Dick saw the rear gunner wave to him. Dick immediately ran to the armory where he was issued an Enfield rifle. This was a bolt-action rifle made for a right-handed person, but Dick was left-handed. As the enemy planes flew overhead, it was difficult for him to get off many shots. He took cover and was lying flat when a plane dropped a bomb right behind him. The shock wave from the bomb propelled Dick up into the air; he remembered actually looking down on palm trees. When he landed, he realized he was still in one piece, although his leg and foot pained him. He then set about helping other soldiers who had been seriously wounded, driving them by truck to the base hospital. During the bombing, the truck he was driving was damaged, and Dick was barely able to drive it back to the motor pool. There they issued him a staff car, and Dick hurried back to pick up more wounded soldiers and drove them to Tripler Army Hospital. After he helped deliver all the wounded, he realized the floor of his vehicle was covered in blood–his blood. He limped inside, where his foot was temporarily treated. It was a full two weeks before his foot was operated on and a piece of shrapnel removed from his heel. He was given two more weeks to recuperate.

Because he was still determined to become a pilot, Dick applied several times to Officer Candidate School and was finally accepted. (The regulations were changed to allow high school graduates to test into the Aviation Cadet Program.) He was sent to Santa Ana, California, in December 1942 and graduated as a second lieutenant in August of 1943. He was selected as a bombardier and sent to Victorville, California, for further training. He was then sent to Mountain Home, Idaho, for night-bombing training; and then to Casper, Wyoming, for additional training, before being placed in group training with a crew in Alamogordo, New Mexico. His group became the 492nd Bomb Group of the 8th Air Force and assigned to North Pickenham Airbase in England.

After an uneventful trip across the South Atlantic by way of Florida, Trinidad, Brazil, and Morocco, they finally arrived in Wales. Dick's crew did a lot of practice flying before embarking on their first real mission to Germany on May 11, 1944. On their third mission to Brunswick, Germany, they were attacked and shot down by German fighters. Nine of the thirty-six B-24 bombers in his group were lost on this mission. Dick managed to bail out and was one of the four survivors from his ten-man crew. As he bailed out he was hit by debris, which broke his right leg.

After landing, Dick was picked up by German civilians and transported to a hospital, where his leg was put in a brace. Later he was transferred to a POW hospital, and his leg was put in a plaster cast. He stayed there recuperating for over two months. Then he was taken to the notorious Stalag Luft III (POW camp) in Sagan,

Germany; the location of the "Great Escape" (later depicted in a war movie of the same name). Dick was initially put in with a group of British airmen who were less than kind to him. Because he looked extremely young for his age, they continually harassed him by saying that he couldn't possibly be an officer; he hadn't gone to a military academy like them! Dick was finally transferred to the American prisoner compound.

In January 1945, as the Russians were approaching from the east, the Germans closed the POW camp and marched all the prisoners westward. Thus began a very arduous and dangerous journey. At times temperatures reached twenty-degrees below zero, and the men had only some threadbare blankets for protection against the cold. Before leaving the camp, they were permitted to raid the area where the Red Cross parcels were kept. Dick picked up as many coffee and tea rations and cigarettes as he could carry. Having these supplies later paid off, because he was able to trade these items with German citizens for bread and, at one time, even a chicken. Since there were over 12,000 POWs on the march, they were quite loosely guarded. On the way out of camp, some of the prisoners broke into the administrative offices, where they absconded with their personal files. Dick also managed to recover his own file, which is now on display at the Warhawk Air Museum in Nampa, Idaho.

During the long cold march the men spent quite a bit of time foraging for themselves. They found barns and other places to bed down. The Germans guards by now didn't have the capacity to feed and care for them, or even guard them properly. The majority of the guards were older men who were also trying their best to survive. One lighter moment on the march came when a German staff car, a baby pram attached to its top, pulled up to the line of men. The pram was removed from the roof and, after a prisoner got out of the car, it was given back to him. He was then told to get back in line with the other prisoners. It seemed that while foraging, he had gotten too far away from the rest of the prisoners.

The march continued until the 20th of April, when the men were finally liberated by General Patton's Army. Dick was standing just a few feet away from him when General Patton stood up and addressed the freed prisoners. Scolding them, Patton said, "He…had never seen a cruddier group of officers." According to Dick, Patton's words didn't sit well with the men, given that they were extremely desperate at that point. At least a third of them turned their backs and walked away. Dick remembered that the last bath he had taken was several months previous, and the only clothes he and the other men had were what they were wearing. At this point the men were agonizingly hungry, since they hadn't eaten for three days. They finally received some food from their liberators and, within a few days, they were picked up and flown to Camp Lucky Strike in France. There they were fed very well before being put on a ship back to the USA.

After being discharged from the military, Dick headed home, married his high school sweetheart and decided to go to law school in Laramie, Wyoming. He graduated in 1950 and began a legal career which lasted for over fifty years. He served as prosecuting attorney for Washington County, Idaho; was an assistant attorney general in Guam; and eventually moved to Caldwell, Idaho, where in 1956 he started a private practice.

For his dedication to his country, Dick received two Purple Hearts, a POW Medal, Good Conduct Medal, Asiatic Pacific Campaign Medal, European Campaign Medal and a WWII Victory Medal.

Lee Smith
U.S. Army Air Corps
WWII
1942–1945

He was standing at the back of the vessel when a Japanese kamikaze headed right toward him.

Lee was born in Missouri and moved to Oregon when he was a teenager. He was working at the Umatilla Army Ordinance Depot when the Japanese bombed Pearl Harbor, and he knew at that time he would soon be drafted. In March 1942 he was inducted into the Army Air Corps and sent to Wichita Falls, Texas, to start his basic training. He arrived in August–the hottest month of the year in Texas. It was so miserable there that in his words, "It wasn't hell, but you could see it from there!"

Lee's next assignment was in Colorado, where he was trained to use and maintain machine guns and various other kinds of ordinance. From there he traveled to Pennsylvania where he was trained to shoot machine guns on P-40 fighter planes. In addition, his assignments included different types of training in Florida, Virginia and Connecticut. While in Connecticut he worked on P-47 fighter planes. He found them much easier to work on than P-40s. He traveled extensively throughout the eastern United States, training in New York, Massachusetts and New Hampshire before being sent to California.

From California, Lee was shipped out on a troopship to Australia. He spent nineteen days on board–seasick most of the time. Upon arriving in Australia, he boarded a train for Brisbane, where his unit's airplanes had been sent. These were new planes and they required considerable work to unpack, clean and put in flying condition. Once they were ready, the pilots flew the planes to New Guinea, while Lee and the rest of the outfit got on a liberty ship and sailed toward the same destination. As the ship approached the Great Barrier Reef off the NE coast of Australia, there was some type of misdirection, and his ship went aground on the Reef. All the troops had to be evacuated off the ship and onto another vessel. Then other ships pulled the liberty ship off from the reef and the troops were reloaded. They sailed back into port to check for damage. After making repairs and loading up more supplies, they continued on to the island of New Guinea.

Lee remembered New Guinea as being very hot and muggy. Continual rain necessitated putting their tents on platforms. His duties on the airfield were helping repair the planes and maintaining the ordinance. One day there were several major crashes on the airfield, because a fighter plane ran into a parked B-25 bomber. As they were trying to clean up this accident, an A-20 aircraft came in about the same time as a P-38 fighter, and they almost collided. The P-38 was able to get away, but the A-20 pilot hit his brakes, which blew out his tires, and he crashed into an embankment. These crashes caused significant damage to the airfield. All the time Lee was on the island, they never had hangars, and the men had to do all the needed repair work outside in the heat and in all kinds of weather.

Lee recalled a very interesting event that happened to one of the pilots in his squadron. While flying, his plane was damaged, and he had to bail out onto the island of New Guinea. Other airmen in his unit could see that the pilot was safe, so the next day they flew in supplies for him. Because the ground there had grass about eight feet tall, a machete was included in the dropped supplies. The downed pilot had to cut down the grass in order for an airplane to land and rescue him. He labored for some time cutting enough grass to carve out a landing strip. A small plane was able to land, but they still didn't have enough runway length to take off. Both of the pilots spent two more days cutting grass before they finally had the needed length on the runway to build up enough speed to get airborne.

After the Philippines were liberated, Lee's unit was sent there for a short time to stage for their next assignment. He remembered the Philippines as a much nicer place to stay than New Guinea. The servicemen then boarded troopships and headed to another island. On the way, their convoy was attacked by Japanese kamikaze planes. Several of the enemy got through the antiaircraft barrage and damaged three of the U.S. ships. Lee was standing at the back of his vessel, behind a machine gun, when a Japanese kamikaze headed right toward the rear of the ship. He watched anxiously as the Navy gunner shot at it until he blew the plane up.

Lee's next station was on the island of Okinawa, after it had been secured by the Americans. They maintained an airfield there while they worked on the brand-new P-47s in preparation for the invasion of Japan. It was there that they heard the announcement that the atomic bombs had been dropped on Japan, and several days later the Japanese surrendered. He remembered there was a wild celebration all over the island, and people were firing weapons into the air. Lee knew "what went up must come down," so he put on his helmet and sat in a foxhole until the party settled down. From there he was shipped to a small Japanese island, where he waited for transport back to the States. While on that island a typhoon hit, creating winds of up to 150 miles an hour. During the storm he and a friend found shelter in an old burial tomb. They stayed there for three days until the typhoon subsided.

When he returned to San Francisco, it was a great feeling to see the United States again. He was mustered out of the service in Washington State and returned home. As a lifelong member of the VFW (Veterans of Foreign Wars) Lee attended several reunions, but each year fewer people remained to attend them. He took great pride in serving his country.

Nemeses of Allied Bomber Squadrons:
The German ME-109 & Antiaircraft Guns

Thoville George Smith
U.S. Army Air Corps
U.S. Air Force
WWII
1943 –1964

*"We almost got shot down by
our own chaff!"*

The following is Thoville Smith's account of his military experiences during World War II.

  I was born in August 1925 on a plantation near the town of Nirva, Louisiana. My father was a sea captain. When I was six months old my mother took me to New York, because my father was sailing for six months. After another six months, my father took us aboard the ship and we spent the next three years sailing between New York, Columbia, and Venezuela. In 1930 we ended up living in New Orleans and, as early as I can remember, I became fascinated with aviation. I remember seeing a dirigible fly overhead, and I was fascinated. When I was about nine years old we went out to the New Orleans airport and I saw my first military airplane, an Army bomber. I remember walking up to it, reaching out and touching the shiny propeller. We moved to a town called Houma, where I went to sixth and seventh grade. It was there on my eleventh birthday that I got my first ride in a Ford Tri-motor airplane. I had to sit on a fellow's lap, but I finally got in the air. We moved out in the country to Centerville, where I went to high school. After graduating, I went to Texas A&M, which had a military component. I wanted to get into the Army Air Corps, and I figured that was one way to do it…. In 1943 I went to Houston [to enlist] and the recruiter said it would take eighteen months. I figured the war would be over by then, so I went to the Army and they said nine months. When my eighteenth birthday came around I hadn't heard from them, so I went to Houston and walked in and said, "Here I am." They told me to go home and they would send for me in a couple of weeks. We were inducted there and sent to Amarillo, Texas, for basic training. It was cold and windy. From there we went to a college, training for three to five months, learning math, physics and Morse Code. Then we went to classification and took lots of tests to see what we were qualified to do: pilot, navigator, or bombardier. I qualified for all three so they gave me my choice. I chose pilot, but when I went to sign, "navigator" was typed on the papers. I explained there must be some mistake, and they told me, "No. Sign here." I went to see the Lieutenant and he said I had a choice of navigator or gunner. I then decided, "I always wanted to be a navigator." From there we went to gunnery training in Texas.

We finally got to go up in a B-24 bomber, and shoot at targets being towed by B-36s, flown by WASPS–lady pilots. They also had P-39s and we would shoot at them with plastic bullets that had electrical contacts on the leading edge of the wings that would flash a light if you were hitting it. They had a little trouble getting pilots to fly the P-39s! We finally went to San Marcos, Texas, where we learned navigation, dead reckoning, celestial, and some of the first LORAN [long-range navigation] training. When I graduated in November 1944, I received orders to go to Lincoln, Nebraska. They formed crews there and then we were sent to Gowen Field in Boise, Idaho, for B-24 crew training.

When we took off (because of weight and balance considerations) the navigator would first sit in the waist of the plane, and then after we were airborne, he walked forward to his station. One morning we took off with the bomb bay doors partially open, because fumes often collected in the bomb bays. I had fallen asleep and was called to come forward. I had my chest harness on but no parachute pack. I missed the narrow walkway with my foot and started to fall out the bomb bay door, but caught a rope and held on–I nearly went out of the airplane, but I was able to crawl back in.

We got on a troop train and went to Salinas, California, and picked up a brand new airplane. We got the plane all checked out and set up, then went to Mather Field in Sacramento, California. The Army Air Corps gave us a briefing to go overseas– first to Hawaii. We received sealed orders instructing us where we would go from there, but we couldn't open them until we got past the halfway point. We took off at night and I remember we passed the Farallon Islands off the coast of San Francisco. Halfway to our destination we opened the orders and they directed us to fly to Biak. Nobody had ever heard of the place. After we got to Hickham Field in Hawaii, we got out maps and found that Biak was off the west coast of New Guinea. On the way there we stopped at Canton Island, where I saw my first case of Atabrine color. (Atabrine was a medicine given to the servicemen to ward off malaria.) One of the side effects was that it turned skin yellow. Most people tanned easily while in the Pacific, so the yellow condition wasn't that apparent. But this particular fellow had not been in the sun, and his skin was very yellow.

We island hopped and finally landed in Biak, where we lived in tents for a couple of days. One night they came and woke us up and told us to bring all of our gear and to get on a bus. They put us on a transport and flew us down to the Markham Valley of New Guinea (without our airplane). The main Japanese forces were gone, but there were pockets of Japanese soldiers in areas that we were assigned to bomb. The first mission was to a place called Monokwari (which meant on the ear of the dragon). We were briefed that the Japanese were using English code, signaling [our] planes that Biak was closed and they needed to proceed to Monokwari. So we had to bomb them. As soon as we dropped our bombs, we broke to the right and the Japanese almost hit us with antiaircraft fire. The pilot wanted to go directly back to the base, but I didn't have a course to do that. I only had maps that had big blank areas in them. The pilot was lost, but I managed to get us back to base.

From Biak we went up and joined the main squadron in the Philippines. On the way up we landed at Halmahera where there were some clearings in the jungle here and there. They issued us some gear to sleep overnight, and told us there was an open-air movie playing in the next clearing. After the movie, we were walking back to our tents when we heard a loud commotion–a group of people crowded around a huge python that was about a foot in diameter and eight or ten feet long. It had already been killed, but someone remarked that pythons often ran in pairs. About 2 a.m. in the morning our antiaircraft started shooting and the air raid siren sounded. We had no shelter, so we started for the ditch, when some of us remembered the snake. A moment of truth was at hand. We had been issued machetes, so I grabbed one and headed for the ditch. One of the other guys said he would rather take the bomb! It turned out we got neither!

We headed up to the island of Samar in the Philippines. We flew some missions against Japanese holdouts on the islands there. Then we flew a mission to Formosa, where the Japanese had installed some antiaircraft radar. We carried chaff (bundles of aluminum strips that had a strap around them). When this strap was broken open and released, the aluminum strips would disperse in the air and the enemy radar would lock onto the strips, so that their flak would be aimed behind us. Sure enough, the first time we tried it, the last plane in the formation dropped their chaff and the Japanese flak was directed below and behind us. However, [the flight] leaders thought the flak came a little too close to our planes, so they ordered it dropped from the lead airplane. We were in a box formation, and my plane was down in the slot. The bombardier in the lead plane became very nervous and threw the entire bundle out. I heard a big bang and a thump, and thought we were getting hit by flak. Pretty soon the nose gunner in our plane screamed. But it turned out to be the bundles of chaff; which broke the Plexiglas in the nose, dented the engines, and tangled up all of our antennas, leaving us without any radio contact. [Thoville declared,] "We almost got shot down by our own chaff!"

Rumor was that some of the men were betting the war would be over in six weeks. And sure enough, about six weeks later, we heard they had dropped "the bomb" on Tokyo. After that we did some armed reconnaissance missions–no bombs, only guns. On one mission we went around Formosa looking for activity. When we got to the northern end of the island, we headed back, but I didn't know the speed and direction of the winds. I got one LORAN fix, then another, but it was so dark (there were no stars). There were some lights on in the town on Samar. The pilot thought it was our base, but I told him, "No, keep going!" When we got to the base we saw fireworks going off and search lights. And as predicted, the war was over. After we landed, everyone was out getting drunk.

We went to Clark Field in the Philippines in late October 1945. They let us fly an airplane back to the United States. We island hopped and on the last leg, from Hickam Field to Travis Air Force Base in California, we ran into something very unusual–easterly headwinds. We were in them for fourteen hours and when we crossed the Golden Gate Bridge, we were running out of oil and the oil pressure was beginning to fluctuate; but we made it back and landed.

From there we were on a troop train to Houston. I decided to stay in the U.S. Air Force because I still wanted to become a pilot. On my sixty-day leave at home I finally soloed in a Cub. In late 1946 when I was about to get married, the military had a reduction in force, and they wanted to discharge me. But I found out I could re-enlist as a master sergeant; so I did that, and ended up being a navigation instructor. I remained in that position until 1948, when I was recalled to active duty and sent to Guam on a troop transport. Previously, black troops were transported separately; but by Presidential order they had just ended [segregation], and we had some of the first mixed transports.

In Guam, I wrote my wife a letter telling her I was happy not to be staying there. But after mailing it, I found out I "was" assigned to stay on in Guam, flying on C-54s. I wound up flying troops between Guam, the Philippines, and Japan. I was still a navigator. After one and one-half years, our outfit was assigned to the Berlin Airlift, but instead we picked up a run to Guadalcanal. We flew support down there–moving troops around to Hickam Field, Hawaii.

Finally in 1949, I came back to the United States and was sent to Merced, California, in a B-29 and then transitioned to B-50s, where I had some interesting times with SAC (Strategic Air Command). I then was shipped back to Texas to fly the B-36. The general there thought we should be involved in the maintenance of our aircraft. One day we had to change the spark plugs. We discovered there were seventy-two spark plugs on each of the engines. We had to wear cotton gloves so they wouldn't create an [errant] spark.

In 1950, at age twenty-five, I finally went to pilot training in an AT-6 trainer. I was given the opportunity to decide if I wanted to fly fighters or transports. I wanted fighters, but I thought I was too tall, as I was six-foot-two. The officer in charge changed my paperwork and said, "You are now five-foot-eleven." Well, it turned out all right. I fit in the seat of the fighter planes and had headroom, because most of my height was in my legs. We flew the T-28. After that, we flew the T-33 and then the F-80. Just before we graduated in 1951, they sent Chuck Yeager [first pilot recorded to have traveled faster than sound] down to give us a talk. We thought he would arrive in an exotic airplane, but he came in an old yellow AT-6. He said that it was all they would give him.

Some in our squadron were assigned to Korea, but I was sent to help with gunnery instruction at Luke Air Force Base, and then up to Maine, flying the F-86D. At that time I was married and had children. I spent a few years flying in the ADIZ (Air Defense Identification Zones) along the coast and would rat race (dog fight).

I retired from the Air Force, but stayed flying in the Reserve. After doing various jobs, I thought maybe I should re-enlist in the Air Force, so I reapplied. Days later, I received two letters, one from United Airlines and the other from the Air Force. [Since] I was a captain, I decided to stay in the Air Force. I was assigned to Okinawa flying an F-86D, and my family was able to come along. The F-86 was designed as a bomber/interceptor and was an advanced airplane. It was good duty. I was later promoted to major and flew nine months in Canada and three months in Greenland. From there I went to Klamath Falls, Oregon, and flew some newer model airplanes. In 1964, I had twenty years in the military, so I resigned from the Air Force and began flying with the civilians.

I had already lined up a job. I began a second career in charter flying and flight instruction. In 1969 I read an ad for an FAA (Federal Aviation Administration) inspector in Oakland, California. I had been doing accident investigation and check rides for people in general aviation. I then went to work for the FAA until 1988, when I retired and started work in the flight-training department of Sky West Airlines. Then I had a heart attack and bypass surgery. Eventually I obtained a third-class medical, and in 1994 we moved to Boise where I continued as a pilot examiner.

Thoville Smith's Bomber Crew

Robert Sobba
U.S. Army Air Corps
WWII
1942–1945

During the two years Bob spent on the islands, he saw the sun four times.

Bob was born and raised in the small farming community of Fowler, Kansas. His father, grandfather and great-grandfather had all been Kansas farmers, and he was looking forward to the day when he could farm his own land. He excelled in sports during high school and upon graduation started to work for a local farmer, living in a small house on the tract of land. His grandmother, who was widowed, stayed with him to cook and keep house.

He was out in the field working on December 7, 1941, and when he came in for the evening meal he was told that the Japanese had bombed Pearl Harbor. The news was hard for him to believe. Bob knew that he would probably be drafted into the military, but at that time the draft age was twenty-one, and he was only twenty. Thinking he had a year before he would be drafted, he decided to marry his high school sweetheart. However, no sooner had they married when the law was changed to twenty and, within five weeks, Bob was drafted into the Army Air Corps. Leaving home was a big shock, since Bob had only been out of his home county one time during his life. He reported to Fort Riley, Kansas, where he underwent his physical. He then reported to Shepherds Field, Texas, for basic training.

Being a farm boy, Bob was in excellent physical shape and he never had any problem with the strict physical training in boot camp. He remembered a lot of the others, particularly kids from

143

cities, had a terrible time with the marching and other physical training. Being used to fresh food all of his life, he did have a hard time adjusting to the military food. While training there, he played on the Army baseball team and was also on the boxing team.

After boot camp Bob was sent to Illinois for additional training. He was trained in the proper care of parachutes and how to handle oxygen and CO_2. There were several thousand soldiers at this camp and at times he had to take his turn on KP (kitchen duty). He was amazed at how much food was wasted in preparing meals for that many people. He remembered one time, when he had to work in the kitchen that he spent the whole day just slicing bread for the evening meal. While in Illinois, he was on an Army football team when he dislocated his shoulder in a game. He had to have an operation on the shoulder. Because he was incapacitated, he was allowed to return home for a few weeks. While at home he and his wife made a decision to buy some land north of the town of Fowler, Kansas. They put a down payment on the land, and his father-in-law farmed the land while Bob was in the military. After recovering from his injury, he was sent to Salt Lake City, Utah, for further training. He spent six months in Utah, mainly training on weapons and keeping in good physical shape.

His unit was then given overseas orders, and they were told they were going to the Aleutian Islands in southwest Alaska. No one in his unit had any idea where the islands were, nor of what value they could be to the military. While they were waiting for transportation, a B-24 bomber landed and the engine caught fire. The men in his unit discussed who would be crazy enough to fly on one of those airplanes. Once the engine was repaired, they were ordered to get on that plane to fly to the islands. Bob then spent time on several islands in the Aleutians; including Kodiak, Adak and Attu, before settling in on Shemya. In building the airbase on Shemya, there was a plateau that was designed for the airfield, but it butted up to a small mountain. The mountain made it difficult for the pilots to maneuver and land; so the Army used tons of dynamite to blow up the mountain, and eventually it was all leveled so that the airfield was safe for take-offs and landings.

Building the airfield on the tundra was not a simple task. It required putting rocks on the surface of the frozen ground and then pouring ten feet of concrete over the rocks in order to make a safe, sturdy runway for the bombers to land. The island was roughly two miles wide and two and a half miles long, and at various times there were close to 10,000 troops crowded on it. Because of the damp weather and the corrosiveness of the salt air, it was impossible for planes with electrical systems to operate. Thus, most of the planes used there were hydraulic: B-24 bombers and the P-40 fighters. They had one B-17 that had a boat attached to its bottom, so if one of the planes went down they would try to drop the boat to rescue the downed aviators. However this B-17 had to be rotated out every six months or else the corrosion would eat up its electrical system.

The weather was brutal on the islands—cold and windy most of the time. There would be small storms they called "williwaws" that often had over 100-mile-an-hour winds. Ropes were attached to all the buildings, so the men could hold on to the ropes going between them; otherwise they would not have been able to stand up. On one occasion the island was put on alert, and for three days Bob hunkered down in a small bunker at his battle station while temperatures hovered at sixty below zero. The servicemen wore wool-lined boots and coats and slept in double-lined sleeping bags. They were in tents that were dug down into the tundra and heated with small gas stoves. If bad weather kept supplies from being delivered, which often happened, they would eat pancakes for three meals a day until the needed supplies arrived.

During WWII, the 11th Army Air Force in Alaska had a plane loss rate equal to the U.S. bomb groups in Europe. But many of the Alaskan plane losses were due to the extreme weather conditions. During the two years Bob spent on the islands, he said he saw the sun four times. Despite the weather, no one ever got a cold or pneumonia; however, if someone broke a bone, it would not heal, and they would have to be taken off of the island.

The primary mission of this airbase was to facilitate bombing missions over the islands that were held by the Japanese north of Japan. Because of the long flight to those enemy-held islands, the B-24 could only take half of a bomb load. Extra gas tanks would be placed in the other half of the bomb bays. One of Bob's jobs was to install CO_2 in these fuel tanks. The CO_2 prevented the tanks from exploding and blowing up the entire plane if a bullet hit them.

Bob was soon promoted to supervise the parachute shop. In the salt air of the Aleutian Islands, a silk parachute would soon mildew and then become unusable. So, every fifteen days the chutes had to be unpacked, dried out, and then repacked. He was also part of the rescue team awaiting the return of planes from their bombing missions. Bob's crew would stand by with rescue and fire equipment. He also got a lot of flying time, usually as a gunner in a PBY (flying boat or amphibious aircraft), doing patrol and supply delivery duty.

The men had very little entertainment on the islands, as they were too remote for celebrities to visit there. They often weren't paid for four or five months. But that didn't make much difference, because there was nowhere, not even a PX, to spend their pay. Being a boxing fan, Bob was happy when Joe Louis, the heavyweight boxing champ, landed on the island for a visit. He was there for three days, during which time Bob was able to talk with him about boxing. The servicemen had a basketball league that played in the hangars, and Bob coached a team that won forty games and lost only two.

In 1944 President Roosevelt promised that all military personnel would get a turkey for Thanksgiving. Bob was helping in the kitchen when the anticipated turkeys arrived, and he helped unpack them. What a surprise to discover that the entrails were still inside the frozen turkeys, and 1937 was stamped on each box. Despite it being seven years old, everyone on the island was extremely grateful to get a few bites of frostbitten turkey–a fitting Thanksgiving dinner for the "often frozen" men of the Aleutian Islands.

After the Japanese surrendered, Bob was in the service for approximately one more month before he was sent home to the States. He returned to Kansas and continued his farming. He kept in close contact with several of the men he served with during his duties in the Aleutian Islands. Bob joined the American Legion and the VFW and used the GI Bill to attend a farm program that the government had set up to teach ex-servicemen about farming techniques. When asked what he learned most from his military service, he mentioned two things–learning how to keep warm and being patient.

Howard D. Thompson
U.S. Army Air Corps
WWII
1942–1945

"I was hit many times, but not bad–always able to get home."

Howard "Tommy" Thompson was raised on a farm in Mitchell, South Dakota, one of seven children. After completing his elementary education he moved to Nampa, Idaho, where he attended college. It was there that he took flying lessons at the Floating Feather Airfield in Boise and received his pilot's license in 1941. There was much talk around the college campus regarding the world situation. Pearl Harbor was attacked while Tommy was on a train ride back to South Dakota to spend a semester break. He was in his third year of college, but he didn't return to finish the next semester. Instead he and three other men went up to Ft. Snelling, Minnesota, and joined the Army Air Corps. Two of his brothers also enlisted and, within two weeks of each other, all three were sent out to the Pacific Theater. He said it was extremely hard on his mother to watch three of her children leave for war.

The Air Corps sent Tommy to many bases to train him for war. He went from San Antonio, Texas; to Independence, Kansas; back to Texas, and then finally to Colorado to do his flight training. On his first solo flight in a B-25, an engine went out. He managed to land it safely, but on his second solo flight he blew a tire–not a great start to his flying career! After flight training he was sent to South Carolina with the 345th Bomb Group. He received a new plane and a crew and was ordered to the South Pacific Theater. The trip was a long one, including four stops along the way. He

148

flew to Hawaii and then out to New Guinea, where he was based. The mission was to free the Philippines so that Japan would feel compelled to surrender.

In all, Tommy flew thirty-nine missions. He recalled one flight to Borneo. It was a long flight in bad weather. He was supposed to hit a particular target, but he was off a little, so he saw an oil dump and bombed that instead. Unfortunately, his plane was struck by shrapnel from his own bomb, and it hit and damaged his engine. He was losing a lot of gas and the engine wasn't running properly. Approaching the airstrip were many other planes, and due to the engine damage, he had to go around and come in the wrong way. He barely missed a P-51 coming in for a landing from the correct approach.

Tommy's plane was hit again off the China coast. This time he was looking for a convoy and was strafing a Japanese ship when one of his bullets ricocheted off the ship and flew through his windshield, embedding in the area between him and the copilot. No one noticed it until they landed, and the ground crew wanted to know if he was trying to kill himself with his own ammunition. They also kidded him about trying to lose his plane, since he had already lost one on a run to Borneo. He said, "I was hit many times, but not bad–always able to get home." The P-38s, P-40s and P-51s (fighter planes) always provided cover for his sorties, and he really admired the work those fighters and pilots did.

Tommy's flight group kept advancing toward the Philippines. His most important mission was a run to bomb Manila in February 1945. The Allies badly needed to take Manila. There were too many planes in the formation and the weather was terrible. They could see waterspouts from a typhoon and the Navy ships couldn't see them because of the weather. Not only did they have to worry about the Japanese but, because of the heavy cloud cover, they were concerned that their own Navy may shoot at them since they couldn't be identified as U.S. planes. The group began the run, but there were so many planes it was hard to get into formation. Tommy's wingman crashed into a church, so he had no one to cover him. He came in over a line of sheds and, as he did, the walls came down and enemy machine guns started strafing the planes. His plane sustained 200 holes, the hydraulics started leaking, one engine stopped, and the engine control was gone! His radioman was hit twice in the leg. After the battle, his plane met up with an A-20 (a light attack bomber) which had been badly shot up and had two dead crewmen on board. Together the two planes limped to an island with a makeshift runway and proceeded to land. The A-20 landed first, due to the severity of the injuries on that aircraft. Tommy circled for forty-five minutes with his bad engine before he could land; and then he had to land without flaps, since the hydraulics were gone. They managed to land safely and deplane without further injury. After this mission, Tommy and his crew were grounded for a while and sent for R&R (rest and relaxation) to Australia. Two weeks later they headed back to the Philippines for a few more missions and then were grounded again. They waited until their points came up on the list that would send them back to the States.

A few weeks rest at home in South Dakota, and Tommy then proceeded to California to receive his next assignment. The war was finally over and the need for pilots was not as great, so when he was offered the chance to be released from the service, he accepted it. With only another year left to finish his degree, Tommy returned to Nampa, resumed his studies and received his degree. He married and settled in Nampa, Idaho.

Some of the medals Tommy was awarded were the Asiatic Pacific Theater Medal, the Air Medal, and the Philippine Liberation Medal. He also received numerous oak leaf clusters to go with these awards.

Donald Tolmie
U.S. Army Air Corps
WWII
1942–1945
POW

A German ME-109 suddenly appeared out of nowhere and shot off the tail of his airplane.

Donald was born in Blackfoot, Idaho, in 1921 and spent most his life in Idaho. His dad was in the produce business and they moved frequently, finally settling in Parma, where Don completed high school in 1939. He decided to go to the College of Idaho in Caldwell and spent about a year and a half there before taking a year off to work. He then enrolled at the University of Idaho in Moscow. Don was in his fraternity house on Sunday, December 7, 1941, when friends started yelling at him to come into another room and listen to the radio. There they heard what was happening at Pearl Harbor. Even as a young man he realized everything was going to change in his life–at some point he would be involved in war. After graduating in June 1942 he went to Gowen Field in Boise and enlisted in the aviation cadet program. At that time the program had more cadets than there were places to send them for training, so he waited until February 1943 before he actually got an assignment to Santa Ana, California, for boot camp and preflight training.

Don remembered that at Santa Ana, they had a basketball player from Stanford University who was their physical training instructor. He made sure their physical training was very intensive, often making them work out three hours a day. In addition to physical training, they did regular flight training where they learned the basics of flying. There were about 200 cadets in his particular squadron; many of whom were washed out and unable to keep up with the physical training. Some of the remaining cadets decided to become navigators and bombardiers rather than pilots. Don and the rest were sent to King City, California, for primary flight training.

After completing the preliminary flight school training, Don was given a choice of what type of airplane he wanted to fly: heavy bomber, medium bomber or a fighter. While at Santa Ana he had seen P-38 fighter planes and was impressed with them, so he chose to be a P-38 pilot. Because the P-38 had two engines, he was then sent to Phoenix, Arizona, to receive multiple-engine training. While in Arizona he also did gunnery training. This instruction consisted of shooting at a target that was towed by another airplane. Each of the people in the various units fired different colored bullets. After each gunner landed, they could go to the target to see if their color had hit it. They were excited if their color was on the target somewhere. After P-38 training Don was given a week off. He returned to Idaho and talked his girlfriend into getting married.

Don's next training was in Santa Rosa, California, where he flew the P-39. This unique aircraft had its engine in the back and the cannon in the front. The barrel went through the canopy so it had to be straddled. It was a difficult plane to fly and had a terrible vibration. At that time they used the P-39 to train "on-ground support." They would have four heavy sacks on their airplane to simulate bombs and tried to hit tanks below them on the ground. The men in the tanks were also training to avoid being hit, so it was a fun competition between the two branches.

The next assignment Don had was at Concord Airfield in California, where he again flew the P-38. After he graduated, fifty-three P-38 pilots went to Virginia with him, where they boarded a liberty ship. The liberty ship was very slow, and it took a long time to get to Algiers, North Africa, their first stop. From there the men were flown in a cargo plane to their base in Italy, arriving in late April 1944. The new base was quite crude and had a rough airfield.

On almost every mission, the planes took belly tanks with extra gas. The belly tanks held 165 gallons of extra fuel in addition to the 300 that were in the main tanks of the airplane. Some of the early missions were dive bombing enemy railroad lines. Don remembered one particular target was a railroad tunnel which had already been bombed many times. But, since it was still operational, their unit was assigned to destroy it. Each plane had a 1000-pound bomb on one wing, and an extra gas tank on the other. They dropped two bombs into the tunnel, "closing down" that German railroad line.

Often when they returned from missions, they flew low and were told to seek targets of opportunity. So they often shot at trains, trucks or anything that was a military target. Each machine gun carried over two thousand rounds of ammunition. On one particular mission, they shot at so many targets that when they landed, they only had one shell left among the whole squadron. This got the crew into hot water because they were supposed to retain some ammunition in case they were attacked before returning to base.

During his time in combat zones, Don had three different occasions when he aborted missions because of engine trouble. While flying two of them, he was able to return to base; but one time the engine trouble was so bad that he couldn't make it all the way back. Thankfully, the plane was able to land on an American airbase on the island of Corsica. Don went on numerous flights escorting bombers, including trips to Vienna, Berlin, and Czechoslovakia.

One time, while on what was considered an easy mission, a German 109 suddenly appeared out of nowhere and shot off the tail of his airplane. He had to bail out at 22,000 feet. As a recruit he was supposed to have had parachute training, but that never happened. He indicated that it wasn't too bad jumping out of the plane, nor was the flight down, but he hit the ground pretty hard. Even worse though, was the fact that he landed fifty yards from a German command post; and consequently he was immediately taken into custody. One ironic thing about his capture was the town he landed in was Parma, Italy–the same name as his home town of Parma, Idaho. He spent three days in a prison cell, and then was interrogated before being transferred to a prisoner of war camp in Germany.

This camp was for American prisoners of war and was next to a British camp. Later, this was the scene of *The Great Escape,* a successful 1960s movie. One hundred prisoners from the camp escaped through an underground tunnel that they had labored on for months. He stated that most of the people in his camp were navigators, bombardiers and pilots from B-17 or B-24 crews. During his almost one year in prison, he was never physically mistreated, but the food was extremely scant and, being under-nourished, he lost considerable weight while he was there. Don also recalled how boring life was at the prisoner of war camp. Every morning they had to get up at 6 a.m. so that the Germans could count the prisoners. This was repeated again at 5 p.m. A trail was worn around the camp where the men would walk for exercise. He remembered there were several times that some prisoners just couldn't take the stress any longer, and when the guards would open a gate, these men would make a rush for it and be shot by the Germans. The prisoners were supposed to get Red Cross packages every week, which contained food and other supplies, and all of the men looked forward to receiving them. But as the war progressed they received fewer packages, and the men suspected the Germans were keeping the packages for themselves.

Back in Parma, Idaho, Don's family had been notified that he was a prisoner of war. His wife sent daily letters to him, but he received very few of them. As the Russians got closer to Berlin, the prisoners could see and hear the artillery fire to the east of the POW camp. The Germans then evacuated them at gunpoint from the camp, and moved them away so that they couldn't be liberated by the Russians. They were forced on long marches, continually moving ahead of the advancing troops. Eventually, they ended up near Munich, Germany, where in April 1945 they were finally liberated by General Patton's Tank Corps. The starving and weary men were ecstatic to see American troops. They were given C-rations, but soon kitchens were set up to serve nourishing meals.

Don was sent to the U.S. relief camp Lucky Strike near Paris, where he waited to be shipped back to the United States. He had been confined for so long in prison, he and a friend decided they would go for a walk around to see the countryside. While they were out of camp someone called a headcount and obviously, since Don wasn't there, he was counted as being AWOL. As punishment, the Army delayed his trip back to the United States. But he soon boarded a troop ship back to America and then took a train and bus back home to Idaho. He was finally reunited with his wife and a daughter, whom he had never seen. He decided to re-enlist in the Army Reserve, but his wife found out about his plans, took the application papers, and destroyed them.

Don belonged to several military organizations over the years including the Ex-POW Association, P-38 Association, American Legion and the VFW. After the war he worked on a farm with his father, eventually taking it over. In his opinion, he had a great life of farming and raising three wonderful kids, before retiring.

Thomas R. Young
U.S. Army Air Corps
U.S. Air Force
WWII & Korea
1943–1953
POW

"The safest spot in the group."

Tom was born in September 1922 in Memphis, Tennessee, where he also grew up. On December 7, 1941, Tom was at home when he heard the news of Pearl Harbor. He and his college fraternity brothers at Memphis State University were anxious to join the fight. Tom applied for a position with the Army Air Corps. He worked for ten months, got married, and within two months of marriage received orders to report to the Air Corps. He finished his pilot training in February 1944. He was promoted to second lieutenant with silver wings and was happy to be called a pilot in the U.S. Army Air Corps.

The B-17 was his choice of plane to fly, and he undertook extensive training in that plane. The crew he trained with was dedicated to combat. They left their families behind. Their first duty station was at Foggia, Italy, where they joined up with the 774th Bomb Squadron, 463rd Bomb Group. Tom was checked out by the squadron commander and flew his first two missions with him. Tom flew his third mission with his own crew. The squadron commander called him into his office and told him that, when it was time for the 774th Squadron to lead the group, it would be Tom's plane in the lead position. The commander assured Tom that the "Swoose Group" had never lost a group lead ship. He told

Tom that the group lead was the "safest spot in the group." On his fifth mission Tom moved up to squadron lead. Their targets were Germany, Austria, Romania, Bulgaria, Greece and Yugoslavia. The Allies bombed railroad yards, manufacturing plants and bridges. Flak from enemy antiaircraft guns was their major opposition. In nineteen missions they never saw an enemy fighter–with one exception!

The missions took place in August through October of 1944. Protection of Berlin was a major concern of the Germans at that point; but in Southern Germany, Munich was the most heavily defended target that Tom and his crew approached. It was defended by heavy antiaircraft fire, but not by enemy fighters, since they were all up north. Also, fuel was a big problem for the Germans. Enemy flak was a big problem for the Allies, and they lost an aircraft on almost every mission flying into those target zones.

On his nineteenth mission, Tom was group leader pilot of the 774th Squadron, 463rd Bomb Group; and because the weather had grounded them for several days, all crew members were rather anxious to get airborne. It was early morning November 16, 1944, and Tom realized that back home it was still the 15th of November, and it was his wife Mary's twenty-first birthday, as well as their second wedding anniversary. The target of the day was the railroad marshaling yards in Munich that the Allies dreaded, because it was a heavily defended target. Everyone knew before the raid would be completed, aircraft and crews would be lost, and bombers would return with wounded men on board. The skies were clear to the target. Tom had to get his group of airplanes into position to do the job. Their twenty-eight plane group assembled, turned northward up the Adriatic Sea and meshed in with the other groups.

The squadron commander, an Air Corps major new in the job, was in command of the group for the mission and was also acting as Tom's copilot. As commander of the group, he made the decisions in terms of the flight. It was the first time that he and Tom had flown together.

En route to Munich the radio operator heard a call that sounded like it might be a recall. It turned out to be a training plane in southern Italy, being recalled by their group because of weather conditions. But some of the other pilots in Tom's group kept radioing him thinking they were getting a recall. Tom's group commander had to make the decision. Thinking it might be a recall for them, he ordered Tom to turn the group around and head back to the base. Meanwhile, all of the other B-17 and B-24 groups in the 15th Air Force were continuing to the target. The commander then became concerned that he had made the wrong judgment, so he told Tom to turn back toward the target. By this time they had lost formation position and were trailing everyone else–and that was not a tactical way to approach Munich. At this point the commander decided they would take an alternate target, which was the railroad terminal at Innsbruck, Austria. The terminal was at the northern end of the Brenner Pass and was on the main line of travel between Italy and Germany–heavily defended.

They did a bombing run at Innsbruck at 30,000 feet, with seven aircraft in the group. They were the only ones who had deferred from the initial target. They dropped their bombs and, after a successful run, Tom was turning the aircraft to the right in order to lead the group back toward the base by way of the Adriatic Sea– when BAM–there was a tremendous explosion, causing the plane to rock violently. They also heard the hissing of oxygen escaping and smelled the hydraulic fluid pouring out of broken lines. They were racked into a hard right turn as the plane began dropping from the sky. The plane lost the two engines on the right side. Other aircraft in the group tried to follow Tom, since he was their leader, until they were unable to do so physically, so they peeled off to save their own aircraft. In just a few seconds, Tom's plane fell about 5,000 feet before he was able to get it under control. His commanding officer was sitting on the side of the plane where the explosion occurred and was in shock. He was unable to perform the duties of copilot, so the flight engineer had to lean in over the major's shoulder to hit the fire extinguish buttons and feather the two engines.

Reports later said that the aircraft was last seen under control, having lost altitude, and that was the last official record of them on the mission. From that point on they were on their own–able to survive or not. The task was to get across the Alps and into a safe position to abandon the aircraft. They wound and wandered through mountain passes and into valleys from 25,000 feet altitude and then dropped at about 800-900 feet per minute. At two points along the route, Tom worried that they weren't going to make it. He thought he could see no way out. He got his men in position to bail out over the mountains, which probably would have meant sudden death for all of them. It was that or plow into a mountainside. He was praying all of the way, when he finally saw a break in the mountains through a pass into another valley. Tom was able to keep the aircraft in the air for another twenty minutes, as he flew completely across the Alps. They could see the Adriatic Sea, but Tom knew they weren't going to make it any farther, so they all bailed out at 2,000 feet into an area north of Trieste, Italy.

All the men, including the two injured during the explosion, were able to evacuate the plane safely. Tom was the last man out, and as he was hanging in his parachute, a German Messerschmitt 109 came out of nowhere. Guns blazing, the ME-109 followed the descending bomber. Tom couldn't help but realize the irony of the moment; nineteen missions without seeing a German fighter, and there was his empty B-17 going down, with a German pilot having the time of his life shooting it to pieces. Tom was floating down in his chute, when all of a sudden he realized that the German was "making a pass at him!" He made a dramatic imitation of someone dying in his parachute. Tom didn't know how effective it was, but at that moment it seemed rather humorous.

About that time Tom hit the ground in a soft cornfield, turning his ankle a bit, but he was safely on the ground. He gathered up his chute as the fighter was flying overhead, buried the orders of the day in the cornfield, and jumped to his feet. He was approached by two Italian soldiers with submachine guns, who ordered him to put his hands in the air. Tom knew a little Italian and asked them if they were "good Italians." One replied, "For you, not so good." Off to one side Tom had noticed an Italian civilian who had been running toward him, but who had turned and run the other way upon seeing the armed soldiers. Tom assumed the civilian was probably a partisan, and if he had arrived first, Tom might not have been captured. Tom learned later that four of his crew members were not captured, but were picked up by partisans and spent the balance of the war fighting with them in the mountains of Italy. It had been a tough time physically and emotionally for them. The two men who were injured before they bailed out were captured because they were unable to move when they hit the ground. Both were transported to a German hospital and spent the rest of the war recovering. Four of the men were captured, and Tom's commanding officer was picked up by partisans; but he was hustled back to his group in Foggia, because of his rank of major.

HIT THE GROUND AND CAPTURED! NOW WHAT?

The young Italian soldiers marched Tom out of the cornfield and perhaps he was somewhat naïve, but he began to feel like he was taking part in a B-grade Hollywood movie. He couldn't remember being afraid or apprehensive, just that he had no idea what was ahead, and he felt no sense of fear. As he was led by the soldiers into town, some Italian women on the roadside were weeping and drying their eyes on their aprons. Tom wondered what it meant. Was he going to be shot? The entire little town had heard about the captured American. When the Italian soldiers led him into the garrison where the Germans had set up operations, he was turned over to them; but at no time did he feel threatened or abused. Whatever they pointed at, he did. He turned over his personal possessions; including his pocket knife, testament and personal pictures he had in his pocket.

There was much excitement on the part of the soldiers, and they all came to see the prisoner. Suddenly, the excitement intensified, as a car pulled up and a German major stepped out. Once again Tom thought it was just like a movie. The German wore tight, cropped trousers, a short-billed cap, a tight tunic with ribbons across his chest, and he carried a little riding crop. He walked up to Tom, and Tom saluted him, just as he had been told to do if captured. The major said something to Tom that sounded like a phrase from an English school book. It had nothing to do with the situation, but it was English and he impressed his fellow soldiers. Tom didn't remember exactly what the German said to him that day, but he remembered not knowing how to reply, and that it was humorous at the time.

With his parachute in his lap, Tom was put in the major's car. The major got in, stood in the front with one foot on the seat and his elbow on the windshield, and off they went to tour the town–the major with his captured American. The tour did not take long, and Tom was again turned over to the Italians.

The Italians were not warriors. From Tom's experience, it seemed like a day-camp situation with them. They walked him into the dining hall and sat him down at a big table. Tom didn't have his flight jacket, and it was a cold November, so they let him go back up to the kitchen to warm his feet. A couple of Italian soldiers hauled in a 50-caliber machine gun, apparently from Tom's aircraft. The Italian lieutenant showed him a card trick, but Tom knew it from childhood and caught him at it. The soldier laughed. Tom remembered thinking that things weren't going to be bad at all. He ate with the Italians and then they took him upstairs and put him in a storage room. There was a bed with two small mattresses, but no blankets. He slept between the mattresses, trying all night to keep warm.

The next morning he was back with the German major, did some paperwork and then was back in the major's car, touring all over Northern Italy, as the German tried to find someone to accept him as a prisoner. Late in the day they got to an air force base manned by Germans, and there Tom was reunited with the navigator and radio officer from his crew. They had been captured in another part of the country and had eventually ended up there. They were all taken to an internment spot at the base of Brenner Pass in Trieste. They stayed the night and were interrogated. Tom was asked basic questions, under the cover that it was information that the American Red Cross needed:

Where do you live?

What are your parents' names?

What was your group?

How many aircraft in your group?

The next day, the three of them boarded a train and were accompanied by two German guards. They were taken up to the lower part of Brenner Pass and had to wait in the darkness for another train to arrive. While they waited, the soldiers hid the Americans' personal belongings. Later they indicated by "sign" language and gesturing that someone had found and stolen items from the prisoners' knapsacks. The stolen items included Tom's wedding ring, his little testament and some other personal items. The soldiers seemed very regretful, and Tom felt like they were being honest. He said they were always considerate. The prisoners finally got on a train and traveled right back through the territory that Tom and his crew had bombed. The damaged rail lines had been repaired and they went on through to Munich. They changed trains and went to Frankfurt, which was the main reception area for all captured Allied flyers.

They were put in individual cells for five days and interrogated on a couple of occasions–not abused, but not comfortable. The food was okay and mainly soup–beans and cabbage–and water was available, when needed. They were also accompanied to the toilet, as needed. They were then transported by train to a dulag, (abbreviation of durchgangslager) which was a transit camp through which all POWs passed for processing and distribution to a more permanent place. They arrived on Thanksgiving Day 1944. The POWs were assembled for roll call and Tom saw a friend of his from his hometown. Tom remembered that his friend's parents owned a bakery, where Tom's friends gathered at lunch time when they were in college.

Each POW was able to write two postcards. When Tom wrote one to his mother, he put a note on the bottom of the card saying that his friend Leyton McLoren was in the camp with him. Several weeks later the postcard reached the hometown post office, one-half block from the bakery. The postman read it and immediately ran down the street to the bakery, yelling at the top of his lungs, that Leyton was alive. Prior to that time his parents had never known what his status was. Leyton's mother called Tom's mother and told her that Leyton was alive. Tom's mother asked her how she knew, and she said that Tom had "told" her! Eventually Tom's mother received his postcard from the postman.

The POWs went by train to Stalag Luft III in East Germany, near the town of Sagan, about 100 miles SE of Berlin. Tom said 10,000 Allied prisoners were in that premier German camp, from 150 different U.S. states and countries. There were five compounds separated by barbed wire, with no contact between the areas, and each held about 2,000 prisoners. Tom was mostly with other Americans, but there were also men from Britain, Canada, Australia and New Zealand encamped there.

The camp was under command of the German Luftwaffe, which was considered to be the elite of the German military forces. They were mostly respectful of others of their rank and treated

Tom and the other POWs with a great deal of respect. There were isolated stories of atrocities, but for the most part, they were treated with great fairness, according to the terms of the Geneva Convention. Prisoners were pretty much in control of their own circumstances. They had their own commander. Their ranking officer was a general and he issued orders under which they lived. They all had certain assignments to do. The only thing requested from the Germans was that they be at the morning and afternoon roll call. The prisoners had a library with books shipped in from the YMCA. Their food was supplemented by the American Red Cross. They built a theater and performed skits and musicals. They had a chaplain and Tom attended church every Sunday. They even had an ice rink and skates. Tom felt that generally it wasn't too bad–he was just usually a bit cold and a bit hungry.

Tom tried early on to find things to keep himself occupied. Prior to going into the military he had worked as an artist's assistant, and he had a knack for cartooning. He began to sketch whenever he could find a piece of paper. He sketched drawings of his roommates and fellow prisoners. He eventually earned the job of illustrator for the camp newsletter. One copy was posted on the wall of the cookhouse. The Germans gave the editors an old typewriter, and they would leave spaces between the lines of text so Tom could illustrate. He had access to pens, inks and colors. One of his roommates gave him a diary book and he started drawing in it and swapping with other artists; so he came out of the POW camp with bits and pieces of artwork. It meant a lot to him and helped him to keep a sense of humor and a healthy perspective.

The prisoners began to hear rumors that the Russians were moving in from the east and there was a lot of excited discussion about what would happen. The Germans didn't have the answers and told the men they had to wait until they heard from their leadership. The prisoners got orders from their own camp commanders to walk laps every day to keep physically strong. They began to make backpacks from blankets.

Orders came on January 26, 1945, that they were going to march out of the camp to a rail junction. The railroad nearest Sagan was already knocked out by the Russians, so they had to walk to Spremburg. They marched for three days with the temperature down below freezing and heavy snow on the ground. They started with 10,000 Allied prisoners, and the German guards really had no way of handling the situation. As they marched through villages some German civilians came out to watch, and the men would trade some of their Red Cross cigarettes, soap or chocolate for bread or vegetables. The German civilians were forbidden by their leaders to accept coffee offered in trade, but the prisoners found out that a little container of instant coffee would trade for several loaves of bread.

Many of the prisoners were exhausted, and those who could no longer march dropped out of line. Tom's best friend in the camp (who had given him the diary) stayed behind and was never seen again. Tom hoped that his friend was picked up by the horse-drawn wagon the Germans used for those who couldn't keep up. They slept in barns the first night, and in a French labor camp the second night. The French laborers gave up their bunks for the prisoners and shared some of their homemade beer with them. Although Tom was never a beer drinker, he thought that it was certainly good! Finally, on the third day, they arrived at the railhead in Spremburg and were loaded into boxcars–forty men and five guards per car. They were so crowded they had to take turns resting on the straw. They spent three days en route, with stops as needed. They arrived at Nuremberg and were herded into camps originally built as Hitler youth camps; and there they spent two months. At night the prisoners watched the bombing of

Nuremberg by the Allied and British Mosquito Squadrons. They cheered like guys at a football game as the B-17s and B-24s dropped their bombs over their targets. They continued to watch and cheer until the Germans got angry and drove them back into the buildings.

In April they were forced to walk from Nuremberg into southern Germany, through Bavaria into Moosburg. It took them seventeen days to walk out of Nuremberg; and just to survive, the German soldiers were walking with them. They moved off the main road, interacted with villagers and found their own places to sleep. Tom and a few others knocked on a cottage door and asked if the owners had any eggs. The home belonged to a woman and her daughter, whose husband had been killed in Munich. They had practically nothing, but they came outside with eggs that they had cooked for the men, and they asked for nothing in return. They wouldn't take the coffee that Tom offered them because they knew it was forbidden. Tom left it anyway. He said that he knew that he would be going home, but after the war the Germans knew nothing of what their future would be.

It was estimated that 25,000 to 50,000 Allied prisoners held in Germany were pushed down into that area, and it was Hitler's last attempt to hold them as hostages. It was there in Moosburg, at the end of April 1945 that they were liberated by Patton's arrival; and Swiss drivers in American trucks brought American Red Cross parcels regularly. Patton's tanks rolled in and there was a big celebration. The German guards threw their guns over the fences and began to search for friends they had made in the group of Americans. Things had changed abruptly and the POWs were suddenly free! Patton came in and made a speech, but Tom didn't hear it because he was under a building scrounging for wood, so he could build a fire under the cook stove. From that point on they were free Americans again, just waiting to find a way home. The next day Tom and two of his friends hitched a ride with some GIs that were going exploring to look for war souvenirs. The GIs drove to the next town up and there they gathered war items, finding a souvenir for each man. Tom's memento was a bayonet from a German soldier.

The next day the military started flying the men out of camp. Hundreds of C-47s from all over Europe lined up nose-to-tail from one end of the airfield to the other. The men were trucked in from the makeshift camp, offloaded, and as soon as twenty-one men were aboard, each plane took off. The pilots loved escorting the men to their new liberty. They flew the planes over Paris and circled the Eiffel Tower and then delivered them to Le Havre, France, at Camp Lucky Strike. They spent a week there getting fattened up; where they found ice cream stands on every corner, food everywhere, new uniforms and hot showers. Tom sailed home on a luxury liner that had been taken over as a troop ship. The ship had white-coated waiters serving them meals. They had sixty-three British war brides with them, and there were dances every night. They ate four or five times a day, and by the time Tom got off the ship and arrived home, he weighed more than when he left for the war.

Tom was discharged from the Air Corps in September 1945. Tom felt that the proudest achievement of his life was the fact that all ten men who had bailed out of his B-17 over Italy had made it home. He returned home, GI Bill in hand, waiting for the next phase of his life to begin. In 1951 he was recalled into military service with the U.S. Air Force during the Korean War. He went back to Vance AFB in Enid, Oklahoma, where he served as an instructor, was promoted to captain, and until January of 1953, helped design and build training aids.

After his military career, Tom joined an animation and film company as an artist/animator. The company became the leading animation and film production studio in the southwestern United States. After thirty-four years Tom retired as a partner and executive vice-president.

Many years after that fateful nineteenth mission, Tom received a photo taken just after his B-17 bomber had been attacked. It was snapped by an enlisted man who happened to have a small box camera with him. He was an airman on one of the other aircraft on that doomed flight, and he recounted that he had leaned over the shoulder of his copilot and captured that moment. In the photo, the two engines of Tom's B-17 were still on fire, and very shortly after that Tom's flight engineer had been able to extinguish the fire. It was a remarkable short time frame that allowed the airman to get the photo he did. It was fifty years later that Tom happened, by a curious coincidence, to get the photo. Both Tom and the airman had responded to a request by the history editor of their bomber group's newsletter to submit information they might have about their squadron. The editor wanted WWII information for a book he was writing. Coincidently, the editor received the picture of Tom's B-17 going down from the airman, and the story of that same event from Tom, both in the same mail delivery.

The following was written in 1995 by Thomas R. Young, Jr.

We who experienced it can remember World War II with a sense of accomplishment. We did what we had to do for our country. Maybe those who are younger than we, especially those of the Vietnam age, are beginning to know that now; and are beginning to appreciate the sacrifice of life, the endurance of hardships, the putting our lives on hold that we, all of us, men and women experienced in 1941-1946. If they want to call us heroes we can live with that. As for us who lived in these times, and still survived, let us prayerfully reflect on our experiences, reverently remember our lost comrades, and tell our war stories one more time. And, in those times of celebration and commemoration, let us enjoy a moment of pride. Then let us fold our tents and quietly move on, for there are others behind us from other wars waiting for their day of glory. Heroes, too!

B-17 Squadron Taking Flak

Harry G. John
Royal Canadian Air Force
French Resistance
WWII
1942–1945

"All that had been holding me in the parachute was the weight of my body."

Harry was born in 1923 in Port Arthur, Ontario, Canada, now known as Thunder Bay. His father came over from Italy at the age of fourteen and his mother also emigrated from Italy at an early age. Harry was the youngest of seven children. In those days there were no settlements between Thunder Bay and Hudson Bay, so the family spent a lot of time hunting and fishing. Harry quit school when he was in the eleventh grade, hoping to get into the world war that had started that year (1939) in Europe. His two older brothers were already in the Royal Canadian Air Force (RCAF) and Canadian Army. During the war, there was no draft requirement in Canada–all were volunteers. Harry first joined the RCAF in 1940, but the military found out he was under age, so he had to wait until June of 1941 to rejoin. In the mean time, Harry contracted the mumps, so he was deferred until January of 1942.

Harry went through pilot training, but the Canadian Air Force needed navigator/observers, so they convinced him to become an observer. The observers were placed in medium bombers and were fully qualified as navigators, bombardiers and aerial gunners. The Mitchell B-25 medium bombers carried only four crew members, unlike the American planes which carried seven. Harry acted as copilot, bombardier, navigator, and observer.

He began basic training in Edmonton, Alberta, Canada, and then went to initial training school, and eventually to flying school, where he learned to fly Tiger Moths. The navigation course was taught in St. Johns, New Brunswick. By the time the men completed training they had their designated crews. Many of them were from New Zealand and Australia. The United States had held somewhat of an isolationist reputation; but with the Japanese bombing of Pearl Harbor in 1941, they entered the conflict. The Canadians, however, were ready in 1939 to give 100 percent effort to assist their Allies in the war in Europe.

Harry related his war experiences in the following narrative.

We went over to England on the *Il de France*, a beautiful luxury liner that had been confiscated for military use before the war. We were stationed all over England for more training before being assigned to the 180 Squadron, 2nd Tactical Air Force near Guildford, just southwest of London. The 180 was an RAF (Royal Air Force) squadron. My pilot suffered from a burst appendix, so I was assigned a new pilot, who was the actual leader of the entire squadron and we became the lead crew for the entire squadron. This was just before D-Day and most of our targets were oil dumps. After D-Day we hit fortifications along the [French] coast. We flew some night missions and it was quite startling to see the antiaircraft come up [from the ground] as a big ball of flame instead of a black ball of smoke. I remember one night over France, I was in the nose of the Mitchell [and] all of a sudden there was a black thing right in front of me, and then the airplane rocked. It was one of our Mosquito airplanes on its way back to England. It missed us by inches. I wondered how many aircraft were lost due to collisions instead of antiaircraft.

Just after D-Day the allies were hung up about fifteen to twenty miles down the beach at a town named Cannes, France. The Germans were holding it at all costs. Hitler had told them they had the best SS troops in there. On this particular night raid we were going to hit the Germans so that the Canadian Army could move in the next day. We were leading the second flight of airplanes in, and we were told under no circumstances were we to bomb unless instructed to [do so]. We saw the flares we were supposed to bomb, but the commander said he couldn't see them due to so much smoke from the antiaircraft. On the third pass, we dropped below the smoke and dropped our bombs. Out of the thirty-six aircraft that night, no more than eighteen made it back to England. Many planes ditched along the beach. The next morning we got word we were going to hit it again. We were the lead plane, but when we arrived there was nothing there. The Germans had moved out during the night.

We got shot down on our twenty-fifth mission on August 6, 1944. We had already finished twenty-four missions. A tour of duty was usually somewhere between twenty to twenty-five missions. Usually after twenty-four, we would be sent back to Canada to finish our service in training commands. Two of our crew were British and had to stay on, but we two Canadians planned to leave the next morning for London and have a good time for a week; then come back and start our second voluntary tour. But the next morning there was a call for operations, so we decided to go and lead [the squadron] that day; then we [planned to] leave for London. Coming back from the mission we could see the French coast, and all of a sudden we got hit on the very first burst of antiaircraft. They hit our starboard engine and we were on fire, so there was nothing we could do but bail out. I had to jump on the escape hatch to get it to [release]. I saw three other parachutes in the air, so I assumed we all got out. Later I found out that two airplanes got shot down at the same time, and I found out my pilot did not get out and one of the [other man's] chute didn't open, so only two of us got out alive. George, the other survivor, was burned more than I was.

We had been told in training if we bailed out over enemy territory to go for the forest. So I was pulling on the shrouds to aim for the forest, but drifted right past several forests. I knew where I landed would be by the grace of God. George landed in a forest and the Germans were standing there waiting for him, so he spent the rest of the war in a prisoner of war camp. I landed in a tree in the middle of a little village. The quick release button on my buckle was gone. It must have sheared off when I jumped out of the plane. All that had been holding me in the chute was the weight of my body. There were a lot of Frenchmen around and they directed me—they pointed to a house—and I went in there. It was a beauty parlor and the beautician put some cold cream on my face and hands where I was burned, and told me to go out the back door. I found out later that, just after I walked out the back door, the Germans walked in the front door. I ran down this lane and there was an apple orchard at the end. The Frenchmen told me to jump the fence and stay there. It was a woven fence, so I could see through it. It was swampy and [I crouched down in] a tangle of bushes. I hid there and not too much later a couple of Germans came into the orchard with a dog, and they searched up in every apple tree to see if I was up there. The grass under the trees had been cut and put in piles called "stukes." They began to stick their bayonets into all of the stukes to see if I was there.

Later in the afternoon, a girl came into the orchard, and she walked along the fence slowly with a basket, and [she was] humming. I was debating what to do, so I [also] whistled, and she handed the basket over the fence and told me, "Two men will come at midnight." The basket had some bread, cheese and fruit, with a jar of liquid. I hadn't had anything to drink all day and I needed water badly, so I took a big swig—and almost died! It was Calvados, a French type of vodka—distilled applejack. About midnight I could hear noises and they [the French Resistance] whistled and I whistled back. They bandaged me up and gave me civilian clothes. They asked me for a picture of myself. We carried escape pictures just for this situation. They said they would be back at dawn to get me out of there. They bandaged my head and face so all you could see were my eyes and nose. We started out on bicycles and they told me if we came to a German checkpoint to let them do the talking. I now had identification with my photo, saying I was Jurien Labour. They told the Germans they were taking me to the dentist because I had a toothache.

They let us through and we peddled about fifteen miles to Blangy on the river. There, a woman doctor patched me up. She told me the next morning they would take me to the French underground headquarters.

The next morning I crawled into the trunk of this little car and she drove me to a little farm twenty miles away, to the head of the French Resistance. On the farm was a young Russian that had escaped from the [German] labor battalions. At this time the Allies were moving east. They [the French] told me they would take me by boat back to Britain. The French farmers had buried all of their guns before the war and they were now digging them up. You can imagine what condition they were in after being buried in gunny sacks for four years. Ivan, the Russian kid, and I were working on the guns to get them operational. They had been packed in heavy grease and all we had to clean them with was straw. We also had some [explosive] mines to assemble. After several weeks I asked when the boat was taking me to Britain and the man in charge said, "Oh, didn't we tell you? We need you here, so you are not going." So, I became their armaments officer. The Germans were moving back through our area. They pulled their armaments by beautiful horses, and it was sad that we had to set mines to blow them up. There were dead horses everywhere. We also blew up bridges. Then we got word there was going to be [an Allied] glider invasion just east of us in the grain fields. Our job was to remove the stukes of grain and stack them along the sides of the cleared areas. At dawn we would light them so the gliders knew where to land. There were several cells of the Resistance involved. We had a big meeting at the farmhouse. I was afraid that the Germans would see us, but one of the Frenchmen said they were gone.

The next night it was raining and cold, and I tried to tell them that [the Allies] couldn't fly the gliders in. But the French were so confident. We moved the stukes, then found out the invasion was cancelled, so we had to put all of the grain back. The people were so sad and disappointed. The next night it was still coming down in buckets. We went through the same procedure of moving the grain, then received word that it was cancelled again, this time for good. The poor French had thought they would be liberated that instant, and were so disappointed. I won't forget that! I was so cold and miserable trudging back to the farm.

[The French Resistance] captured some Germans and I had a devil of a time telling them they had to go by the Geneva Convention and not just shoot them. They also wanted to shoot any of the [French] girls that fraternized with the Germans. I convinced them not to do that, so what they did was shave their heads. We had a bunch of girls with shaved heads, which was not really fair, because a lot of them were getting information from the Germans and passing it on to the underground.

But eventually the Canadian Army came through our sector and liberated us. We [also] had a bunch of Polish soldiers that we handed over to them. We were liberated at the end of September, so I was there just about two months. From there the Canadian Army sent us to their headquarters outside of Paris and interviewed us. There were maybe fifteen to twenty of us airmen that had been shot down and then liberated. One had been in hiding for years. From Paris we went to England, where I was in a burn hospital just south of London. They had wanted to do skin grafting, but they thought it looked okay; so we waited, and it was not necessary. I made it to Liverpool, but found out I was [designated] a "medical case" and was being sent back on a hospital ship. I told them I didn't need that, so they put me on a troop ship back to Canada. I later found out the hospital ships were quite luxurious.

I was back in Canada on vacation selling war bonds for three months. I had the option of taking a discharge or doing anything I wanted to do in the RCAF, so I signed up for a second tour with my old squadron. When I got back to England I trained on radar. So, on the second tour I did radar work on the V-2 bombs on the ground. I did ten missions in Belgium and Germany until the war ended in May of 1945. When we heard the war was over, there was not a lot of cheering or anything. It was a bit anticlimactic. We finally decided to cook a pig, buried in a pit, and drink German wine. I can't remember if we ever ate the pig.

We were given the option of going to the Pacific. We knew if we volunteered to go, that by the time we got there and did training, the war would be over; but it would get us out of Germany. So, that is what we did. At that time I thought [as a career] I would stay in the Air Force as an attaché at an embassy. But [later] I decided I was too much of a free spirit for the formal Air Force, so I got out.

I continued my education and became an accountant, married, and we had our first two boys in Canada. My wife needed a warmer climate for her health, so we decided to move to Los Angeles, California, in 1955. In 1958 we moved to Redlands, California, but my wife died in 1975. At that time we had two girls as well. I remarried and had one more son.

Years later we wrote to the people in Blangy and said we would like to visit and meet any of the French Underground people that might still be there. When we walked into the state office in Blangy, I explained who I was and why we were there. The young girl got very excited and started yelling for the mayor. The farmer that was the head of the Underground had been killed in a motorcycle accident, but his wife and two children who had taken care of me were still there, and we had a good visit. I learned that the day after I had left the village, where I had landed in the parachute, the Germans came back and said, "We know you have an airman here." (My name was on the back of my parachute.) They took everybody out into a field and told them they would begin shooting two men at a time until they were told where I was. They shot two men. One of them was one of the brothers that had brought me to Blangy. The priest talked them out of shooting any more, saying if they did they would be tried as war criminals.

On the 50th anniversary of D-Day I went back to Blangy once again, and they had a huge parade and banquet for me. Apparently everyone in town had been part of the French Underground, because the place was packed. They gave me a royal time and the keys to the town of Blangy. From there we went to the celebrations at the beachhead in France. It was all very exciting!

Mitchell B-25 Medium Bomber

Kenny Averill
U.S. Navy
WWII
1944–1946
Navy Commendation for Life-saving

*"The living conditions were
strictly terrible!"*

Kenny was born in Nebraska and lived there until he was about ten years old, when his parents moved to Nampa, Idaho. After the Japanese bombed Pearl Harbor he attempted to get into the service, but at that time he was five-foot six and only weighed 128 pounds–two pounds less than the requirement to get into the military. He tried to stuff himself, eating bananas and other food to make the extra two pounds, but still couldn't qualify. He waited until 1943, after graduating from high school, and again tried to enlist. By that time he was up to 131 pounds and made the weight requirement. However, his eyesight did not meet the requirements for combat duty.

Because of his poor eyesight, the Navy deferred him for two months before drafting him into a special noncombat assignment. He reported for boot camp in January of 1944 and took a train to Farragut, Idaho, where he spent eight weeks in basic training. For the first few days he was very lonely, but overall he enjoyed his experience at Farragut and looked forward to his military service.

After completing basic training, Kenny was sent to Mississippi, where he spent eight weeks learning to be a diesel mechanic. He traveled to Treasure Island in San Francisco Bay and from there the Navy shipped him to the Pacific Theater. His ship took him to Pearl Harbor and several other islands before he arrived at the Solomon Islands. His base was next to a bay called Iron Bottom Bay. This name came from the fact that many ships, both Japanese and American, were sunk there during a previous battle for the Solomon Islands.

They called the base Carter City, but Kenny never knew the origin of the name. On that base were approximately 1,000 sailors and they were involved mainly in repairing machines and engines for the Navy. The men stayed in Quonset huts, and the repair shops were also Quonsets. There was nothing in sight but jungle, and when asked how the living conditions were, usually his comment was "strictly terrible!" There were still some Japanese on the island, and occasionally they would take potshots at people around the base. Several sailors were wounded, but as far as he knew no one was ever killed. In response to the snipers, patrols were sent out to investigate. He went on some of the patrols, but felt it was a waste of time, because when the men entered the dense jungle, there was no way they could find the enemy. Kenny spent a year and a half on this base rebuilding diesel engines.

There was very little recreation at Carter City, mainly playing poker or shooting dice. One time when Bob Hope and his USO tour were appearing on an island not far away, several people, including Kenny, were selected to go watch the show. They traveled on a landing craft, but when they arrived they were not allowed to go ashore, so they watched the show about 500 yards from the stage area. Another of his memories of his time on the island was when a typhoon came barreling toward them. The sailors watched as the waterspout (the same thing as a tornado funnel, but only on the water) came close to the island. Eventually it hit the beach and tore up some of the docks and equipment. The storm then spun back out to sea and dissipated. Kenny remembered it was a very awesome thing to watch, but he also had a helpless feeling, as there was nothing any of them could do to protect themselves.

As the American forces advanced toward Japan, Kenny's work crew also moved. Their first move was to Christmas Island. He remembered that the movie star Betty Hutton had donated her yacht to the Navy to be used as a patrol boat. Kenny was one of the people assigned to work on her yacht. However, he doubted it ever did any patrol work, since it was used by officers for transportation. He was on Christmas Island only a short time before they were moved to the Philippines. There they were closer to several cities. This allowed them some recreational opportunities, including some of the things that sailors wanted, such as "bars and women." His time there was enjoyable compared to his time at Carter City.

One day while sailing on a landing craft, two sailors fell in the water but, unfortunately, neither of them could swim. Kenny jumped in the water and pulled one of them to safety; but he was unable to find the second one, who drowned. For his actions he was given a commendation for saving a life.

While at this base he was also charged with helping unload incoming supplies. His crew often sampled various supplies– especially when they included steaks or fresh eggs. It saddened his outfit when they learned of President Roosevelt's death, as they considered him a Navy man. In August of 1945, Kenny was watching a movie when the news broke out that the Japanese had surrendered. Immediately, everyone at the movie ran down to the docks and jumped on a boat for the nearby city. It was quite a celebration, and he and his friends were soon in the custody of the shore patrol.

After the war, Kenny stayed in the Philippines for a few months. Some of the U.S. contractors that had built engines and landing craft had an agreement with the government that none of the equipment would be returned back to the United States. So, some of the boats were used for target practice and the rest were just abandoned.

Kenny was mustered out of the Navy in May 1946. He had thought about re-enlisting, but after attending a presentation given by an officer on that subject, he decided he didn't want to stay in the service. After returning to Idaho, he had a hard time finding a job and eventually took off on a quest to see the United States. For the next fifteen years he wandered around the country working in either restaurants or construction jobs. In 1955 he met a waitress at one of the places he was working, and they ended up getting married. For the next five years they continued to travel the country before coming back to Idaho. Kenny went into a construction business venture and remained in Caldwell, Idaho. He stated that he never again wanted to do what he did in the military. But on the other hand, he wouldn't take a million dollars for the experiences that he had there.

Quonset Huts – Photo Courtesy of Kenny Averill

Charles (Chuck) Barrow
U.S. Navy
WWII
1944–1945

*"Chow consisted of lots of Spam
and dehydrated spuds."*

Charles Barrow was born in Newark, New Jersey, in October of 1926. "Chuck" tried to enlist in the Navy in June of 1944, following his father's advice: "Don't sleep in the mud!" Eventually Chuck was able to join the Navy in September 1944, and was sent to boot camp in New York and then transferred to Rhode Island to train for PT (patrol torpedo) boats. He trained for every position on the boat. In February of 1945 he transferred with his crew to California for additional training. On April 8, 1945, they left the United States for the Philippines.

The PT boats were eighty feet long with 50-caliber machine guns, a 49mm cannon, 37mm rockets, four torpedoes, and several mortars. A typical mission was to go out searching for enemy barges or resupply vessels. They patrolled all night and made two sorties each week. The boats were equipped with three engines and made thirty-five knots. Most had two rudders, but some had three. The PT boats used aviation gasoline with a capacity of 3,000 gallons, giving them a range of about 500 miles. The crew consisted of two officers and twelve men. The officers had a "stateroom" and the crew quarters were also used as the "day room." The boat drew five and three-quarter feet of water. Their squadron, the 25th, consisted of twelve boats. While in port the PT crews lived in tents, and Chuck remembered that it rained every night. Chow consisted of "lots of Spam and dehydrated spuds."

When the Philippines were liberated and the boats were no longer needed, they stripped them of all valuable items (including the engines), and then tied them together and burned them.

Chuck returned to the States, landing in San Francisco, California. He trained in Long Island, New York, and boasted of membership in the "52-20 Club." In other words, he worked fifty-two weeks at $20 a week.

WWII PT Boats
Photo Courtesy of Chuck Barrow

William Dunbar
U.S. Navy
WWII
1943-1946

*They chased the submarine for
two days before they finally
discovered it was a whale.*

Bill was born and raised in
Boise, Idaho, and graduated from
Boise High School in 1943. He wanted to join the Navy but, since
he was only seventeen years old, his parents would have had to
give him their permission. So, as soon as his senior year was over,
he joined the Navy and shipped out. In fact, he even missed his
graduation ceremony.

While in training, Bill passed a test that allowed him to go to
an electronic school. He was then sent to Michigan City, Indiana,
for training in electronics, which included radar, sonar and
navigation equipment. This training lasted for eleven months, after
which he was sent to Seattle for another month of intensive
training.

Bill was assigned to a minesweeper ship and sent to the Pacific.
His initial duty was installing top-secret equipment that he said no
one else could help work on because of the particular wiring that
was involved. He was the only one on the ship who was trained
for that job. His ship was intended to be the lead ship in a convoy
headed for the Marshall Islands. As the lead ship, their navigation
was crucial, since all the other vessels would have to follow them.
They also had antisubmarine duties because of the sonar they had
onboard. Bill remembered one day they thought they had an
enemy submarine on their sonar, and they chased it for two days
before they finally discovered it was a whale.

One night the radar stopped functioning during the time the convoy was participating in a blackout. This was a very critical situation, since they couldn't determine where they were, much less where the ships they were leading were located. Bill determined that the equipment on the top of the mast was not working properly, and it needed to be replaced. This required him, with his parts and tools, to make numerous trips, climbing up to the top of the mast and back down again. He remembered that the sea was extremely rough, causing the ship to roll. Looking over the side, he found himself alternately over the water and then pulled up in the opposite direction. He became very seasick. All of this was happening while he was attempting to fix the radar. It took him almost two hours to complete the job. For the next two days the captain repeatedly thanked him for getting them out of a difficult situation.

Because Bill was the only person on the ship responsible for the electrical jobs, he enjoyed some good benefits, such as being excused from standing watch. On the other hand, he had to be available twenty-four hours a day, seven days a week, to fix any problems that arose. Sometimes he had considerable free time, so he was given a variety of other duties. He learned to cut other seamen's hair, took care of the ship library, and was also responsible for the projection room where movies were shown.

During Bill's war assignment in the Pacific, his ship swept many mine fields in enemy territory: the Philippine Sea, the Yellow Sea, and the South China Sea; as well as sweeping the area around Iwo Jima and Okinawa, before the Allied invasion of those two islands. The minesweepers were the first ships to go to both Iwo Jima and Okinawa to sweep for mines before the main fleet arrived. They detonated several mines in those waters where they had been planted by the Japanese. During these battles, the Japanese not only attacked Allied shipping with suicide planes, but they also sent suicide boats, and even swimmers who attempted to swim out to the ships to kill sailors. While sweeping at Okinawa, Bill's ship encountered a suicide boat that raced toward them and discharged two torpedoes. Fortunately, the torpedoes ran underneath their ship and their vessel escaped unharmed. They also had two kamikazes dive straight at them, but the threatening planes were destroyed before they could hit their intended target. The minesweeper had a 3-inch cannon, and the gunnery crew tried to hit onshore Japanese gun emplacements that were shooting at them, but with little effect. He described this battle as a giant fireworks display, with shells passing over them from both sides.

Bill witnessed a momentous event during the war, as he saw the Marines raising the American flag on Iwo Jima. That event, captured by a famous photograph, became the symbol of WWII in the Pacific.

After the war ended, Bill's fleet was sent to sweep the various bays and inlets around the islands of Japan. He recalled that this assignment was scary because they often had Japanese seamen on destroyers working with them, as well as Japanese sailors telling them where to sweep. (Right after the war there was not a lot of trust between these two former enemies.) Eventually they were able to satisfactorily coordinate the work, and they spent about six months sweeping around Japan. During his war experience, Bill spent almost his entire time on ship. When his ship was in dry dock for repairs, he was on land for only short rest periods.

Bill returned to the United States, was discharged in Washington, and then traveled home to Idaho. He decided to use the GI Bill to go to college. He wanted to continue his electronics education, so he pursued a degree in electrical engineering. However, he found that with his military training, he was far ahead of the other students. The courses became boring, so he changed to mechanical engineering. While on summer break he helped build a house, and he became so interested in construction work that he never returned to college, but spent the rest of his career as a builder in the Boise area.

Bill related that since the end of WWII, the sailors from his ship had met together for thirty-six reunions. Bill was very appreciative of the education the Navy offered him and the maturing he was able to do while in the military. Those war experiences helped him throughout his life.

Admiral Class Minesweeper

Ray Emory
U.S. Navy
WWII
1940–1946

"Never a day goes by I don't think about December 7, 1941."

Ray Emory was born and raised in Illinois. He remembered it had been very rough times during the Great Depression. His dad had an accident that resulted in having his leg removed, which made life very difficult for the family. Ray graduated from high school in 1938 and worked in a local grocery store for a few years. As the war in Europe continued to escalate, he thought it would be better to enlist than to get drafted, so in 1940 he made the decision to join the Navy.

Ray didn't have far to go for boot camp, because he was sent to Camp Great Lakes in northern Illinois. He was only there for seven weeks when, because of other military priorities, his boot camp experience was cut short, and he was transferred to the West Coast. He reported to the cruiser *USS Helena* and they sailed to Pearl Harbor in Hawaii. He was then transferred to the *USS Savannah*, also a cruiser, where he served as a deckhand. The *Savannah* sailed on a goodwill tour to the South Pacific islands, and when it returned he was assigned to go to machine gun school. While he was still attending school, the *USS Savannah* sailed without him–he was left behind to finish his training.

Ray was then assigned to the *USS Honolulu*. He was on that ship at Pearl Harbor on December 7, 1941. He remembered sitting on the bottom bunk reading the Sunday paper when, all of a sudden, the alarm went off for General Quarters. When he reached the deck he could hear the rattle of machine guns. His station was on the side facing the dock, opposite battleship row. There was a lot of shooting, and he really wasn't sure what was happening until he saw a low-flying plane drop a torpedo. He ran where he could see where the torpedo was going and watched it hit the *USS Oklahoma*. Ray saw another plane come overhead which clearly showed the red ball insignia of the Japanese Navy. He immediately tried to pry open the nearby locked ammo box with a wrench. One of his gun mates showed up and asked what he thought he was doing, and Ray replied, "We are being attacked by the Japanese!" The sailor looked at him like he was crazy, and about that time another Japanese plane flew over the ship. They were able to get their gun operational, and whenever they could see Japanese aircraft, they took some shots at them. He saw one Japanese plane break up in flames and go down into the water. The funny thing, he recalled, was the propeller stayed in the air and just kept going, even though it was no longer attached to the plane.

Ray remained at his battle station until he was relieved on the morning of December 8. During the battle, one bomb hit the dock next to the *USS Honolulu*, ricocheted and exploded, causing extensive damage below the waterline of his ship. The crew had to flood some of the compartments, but the ship was never in danger of sinking. Ray was not allowed to leave his ship until the next week.

Because of the sneak attack on Pearl Harbor, Ray and his fellow sailors maintained hostile feelings toward the Japanese. But, in his opinion, the attack on Pearl Harbor was not quite the disaster that it appeared to be. Most of the damage was done to battleships, which he felt were too slow anyway for the fleet operations of the modern Navy. Additionally, most of the ships that suffered damage, including the *USS Honolulu,* were soon restored and put back into action.

After being repaired in dry dock, the *USS Honolulu* returned to the United States and spent time between there and Australia, transporting Marines. Later the *USS Honolulu* was ordered back to

Pearl Harbor. When the ship reached there, Ray knew something was about to happen, because there was all kinds of activity going on at the port. The *USS Honolulu* escorted an aircraft carrier to nearby Midway Island. However, before the Battle of Midway, his ship was ordered to the Aleutian Islands. While in the Aleutians, they bombarded some of the Japanese-occupied islands as part of the ongoing invasion in that area. During this time Ray spent twenty-nine straight days at sea.

Ray's ship returned to the United States to pick up more troops and was then sent to Guadalcanal. Here the *USS Honolulu* engaged in a major sea battle, where several other cruisers were either sunk or suffered extensive damage. Fortunately, the *Honolulu* came out of the battle unscathed.

After Guadalcanal, Ray received a promotion to chief boatswain's mate, so he was transferred to another ship. He was stationed on a troop transport that carried Marines from the United States to Australia and several other places. His ship participated in landings on Guam, Saipan and numerous other small islands, and finally Iwo Jima. He and his shipmates returned to the United States to train for the invasion of Japan; but then the war ended. He stated that he was glad that the U.S. did not have to go through with that invasion.

Ray still had time left on his enlistment, so he sailed with a convoy to Bikini Island, where the atomic bomb was being tested. His ship carried a small herd of goats that one of the universities had donated. The goats were left on the island after the bomb was exploded. While he didn't know for sure, he assumed this had something to do with measuring the long-term effects of radiation.

While in the United States, Ray had applied to go to college at Bradley University in Peoria, Illinois. After his duty on the Bikini Island bomb test site, he requested an early release from the Navy so he could start college, and his request was granted. Ray attended Bradley for two years, then transferred to the University of Washington where he obtained a degree in architecture. He remained in the Seattle area, working for twenty years until his retirement. He then moved to Honolulu, Hawaii.

While in Hawaii, Ray became very active in the Pearl Harbor Survivors Association, serving as historian. He did extensive studies dealing with the attack on Pearl Harbor. At his Veterans History Project interview in 2005, more than sixty years after the event, he was able to name by memory one hundred and fifty ships that were at Pearl Harbor on December 7, 1941. Earlier, in 1968, he made a scale model of Pearl Harbor and identified all the ships and where they were located when the Japanese attacked. Of the 150 ships at Pearl Harbor on that fateful day, his research showed that only eighteen sustained damage.

As the fiftieth anniversary of the attack on Pearl Harbor was approaching, Ray came up with an idea to give special recognition to sailors who died there on December 7, 1941. He wanted to place flags on their graves at the National Memorial Cemetery of the Pacific at Honolulu. In talking to caretakers at the cemetery, he inquired where those killed on December 7th were buried, and found out they were scattered throughout the grounds. Researching the records of the ships' casualties, he was able to document what ship each man was on and when he was killed. He then battled with military officials to get tombstones marked with the name of each ship these men were on when they were killed. (This was the U.S. Navy's normal procedure.) This bureaucratic battle went on for two or three years. He continually received letters from the military, stating that they were following regulations, and that they could not do anything regarding his request. But Ray was able to show that, in fact, they had not followed proper procedures for identifying the graves of sailors. Finally, Ray received a letter from a military official basically telling him they refused to honor his request.

Ray started working with a senator from Hawaii who was very sympathetic to his cause, trying to get the military to cooperate. She wrote two letters to naval officials, but never received a reply concerning her correspondence. Determined to help Ray, she used her position to get a rider on a Congressional bill for the Navy budget that required them to identify, on each sailor's tombstone, the ship he was on when he was killed during the attack on Pearl Harbor.

Ray's efforts didn't stop there. For example, he found that on the wall in the cemetery, one of the sailors' names was misspelled. In fact, members of his family who had come to Hawaii noticed the misspelling and had tried, unsuccessfully, to get the military to correct it. Ray helped the family, and after a year they finally got the name changed to the correct spelling.

Over 600 sailors killed at Pearl Harbor were buried in graves marked only as "unknown." Some of the graves contained the body parts of multiple sailors. One grave alone contained the remains of more than twenty sailors. After the attack, many "unknowns" were buried in a private cemetery on the island, and in 1949, were moved to the military cemetery in Honolulu. When each was disinterred, the dental records of the "unknowns" were documented. Ray undertook the project of trying to identify some of the dead, primarily from their dental records. Armed with this information, Ray went back and found the names of people missing in action and was able to obtain their Navy dental records. He painstakingly went through those records, trying to match them up with the records of unknown sailors. When he was able to make a dental record match, he attempted to locate family members to pass on that information. Through Ray's efforts, in 2003 the military was convinced they should exhume one of the unknown service men's caskets. Using DNA testing, the remains of five sailors were identified and turned over to their families.

USS Honolulu – Before & After It Was Torpedoed

Robert R. Haga
U.S. Navy
WWII
1944–1945

"Shells were getting close as hell, and we made a turn at flank speed and got out of there."

Robert (Bob) Haga was born in 1926 in Roanoke, Virginia. He enlisted in the U.S. Navy on January 26, 1944. Two of his buddies joined with him, and they were all sent to Bainbridge, Maryland, for boot camp. Two months later Bob found himself in the back of a truck going down to the docks in Norfolk Naval Shipyard. The truck stopped and let out sailors alongside various warships. Then the chief petty officer called out the names of specific sailors and told them to board the ship next to where they had been dropped. Bob was the last guy in the truck when the chief remarked to him that he was the luckiest "swabby" in the Navy. He was being assigned to the *USS Chickadee*, AM-59, a minesweeper with a crew of 220 officers and men. It had two 3-inch guns; two 50-caliber guns, depth charges and hedgehogs for armaments. (A hedgehog was an antisubmarine weapon. It fired a number of small spigot mortar bombs from spiked fittings. Rather than using a timer or a depth fuse, these bombs exploded on contact.) After a shakedown cruise in April of 1944, the *Chickadee* steamed for Europe in a convoy of fifty ships, heading for Plymouth, England.

The following narrative summarizes excerpts and includes direct quotes from Bob Haga's diary, where he made entries most days while shipboard, until his return to Norfolk Naval Base.

In early April Bob's ship set underway to Bermuda and then to the Azores in the North Atlantic; along with minesweepers *USS Pheasant, Nuthatch,* and *Swerve* and other ships. On April 18, they had one submarine contact but saw no action. However, on the 20th they had reports of another sub in the area and on the 21st they dropped fourteen depth charges on a contact and saw oil and debris on the surface, as well as air bubbles, but made no other sightings. On the 22nd the *Chickadee* sounded GQ (General Quarters) and dropped nine depth charges and fired forty-eight rounds of hedgehogs at a suspected submarine target, but saw no results.

On April 29 the ships passed the halfway point crossing the Atlantic Ocean and had to "pay homage" to King Neptune. Bob and the other new recruits had their hair cut to the scalp; they were made to crawl through garbage, given an egg shampoo with a salt water rinse and a face wash; and their bodies were painted, stripped and shocked with a few volts of electricity. Now he was a sailor!

In May the fleet anchored on the east coastline of England at Torquay, where they saw firsthand the destruction to that city caused by recent German bombing. Each morning during the next several days, Bob's ship went to sea, where they practiced mine sweeping techniques. Toward the end of May they were resupplied, in readiness for the invasion of Europe, and then proceeded southwest to Plymouth, England. They soon received word that Torquay had been bombed again right after they left. Since minesweepers had been the only ships in the harbor, they assumed that they must have been the intended targets. The Germans "reported" all ships were sunk.

On May 30 the *Chickadee* returned to Torquay and began sweeping for "acoustic" mines while the *USS Threat* swept for "O" type mines. Most nights, because of the foggy weather, the minesweepers anchored outside the harbor. At this time the captain met with the entire crew and informed them of the invasion plans, also telling them that the *Chickadee* would be involved in the pending invasion of Europe.

On June 5 the fleet of minesweepers sailed from Torquay, steaming for the coast of France. The D-Day invasion was scheduled for the next day. They, and other minesweepers, went in first to sweep a channel clear for the amphibious crafts, supply ships, troop ships and other warships of every description. One of the sweepers, the *USS Osprey,* hit a mine. Bob recorded, "We went alongside and took on the wounded, burned and otherwise. I happened to see it when it got hit–it went up in flames sky high. Four enlisted men and one officer were killed. It was extremely lucky that all the men amidship didn't get killed. Most all of them were burned badly. Something I will never forget!" After pulling survivors aboard, Bob watched as the *Osprey* sank that afternoon.

Bob wrote in his diary:

> We continued sweeping, awaiting attacks from many sources, but nothing happened. At 2200 hours we were approximately ten miles off of the Cherbourg Peninsula, leading the invasion force, expecting the worst at any moment. At 2400 we streamed our sweep gear and started operating. We were the second ship in–distance now two or three miles from land. We were just hoping those 1-inch Nazi shore batteries wouldn't let us have it, and God was with us that time. The Allied Air Force was coming back and forth all the while, some flying low. There were thousands of planes–a good sight. The Germans didn't offer any air opposition so far.

During the early morning of June 6, the *Chickadee* continued sweeping for mines. They stopped sweeping when the sky was suddenly lit with enemy flares, and battle action was hot all around. The sailors on the *Chickadee* could see, by the light of the enemy flares, the Allied paratroopers as they floated down toward their dark landings.

Our big-boys (battlewagons) are really giving out, too, and it's one hell of a mess out here. We dropped anchor at 0330 about a mile off Cherbourg to stop any [German] subs or E-boats that may stream out. We really got the hell scared out of us around 1600. The troops in landing crafts started to invade and the battlewagons and shore batteries really got hot. They silenced some of the shore batteries, but the shells and flares are really thick all around [us] by now. They [our battleships] are still bombarding them [the Germans] continuously from off shore about four miles. During this time we went to look for pilots who were shot down by enemy fire while they were strafing and laying smoke screens. We saw a bunch of planes [that had been shot down] near and over the beach–a sad feeling for us all. We went alongside an LST hospital ship and transferred the wounded and survivors of the *Osprey*. Then we continued operations, patrolling and dodging the enemy. We later got word that our squadron of sweepers swept up fifteen mines.

From the 7th through the 11th of June, Bob's minesweeper continued to sweep and pick up German-laid mines off the Normandy shores.

Another one of our squadron, the *USS Tide,* was sunk while trying to help a sinking destroyer. That makes two gone of the eleven sweeps. Nine left:

the *Auk, Broadbill, Nuthatch, Pheasant, Raven, Staff, Swift, Threat* and *Chickadee*. We anchored again to stop [enemy] E-boats and subs from getting out.

On June 11 the *Chickadee* reversed direction toward the Bay of Biscay along the [southwestern] French coast. The *Chickadee, Auk,* and *Staff* fired on German gun positions on the beach. Fire was returned by the German guns. The ships were about two miles off shore when the Germans had the range of the American ships bracketed. Shells were getting close as hell and we made a turn and at flank speed got out of there. We had forty-seven shrapnel holes around the bulkheads, sides and decks. Two of my buddies were hit, but weren't injured very badly. My battle station was at the 3-inch/50mm cannon on the focsle, and we started firing back at the beach. We had one gun shooting at them, and they had about a dozen shooting at us. I received a pretty bad cut on the hand, but it's okay now.

For the next three days the American sweepers continued operations, trading shells with the enemy; but the German rounds did not come close again. On the 15th of June, on the *Chickadee*'s return voyage to Portsmouth, Bob's diary entry stated:

We met up with a convoy of LSTs headed for France. One had been hit by a mine and was sinking slowly. We headed full speed to assist in rescue work. We tied up alongside. She had the whole fantail blown off and a number of sailors and soldiers were lost, with many wounded. We took off the wounded and turned around to take her in

tow toward France. She was the LST 133. We
turned the towing over to a tug about 1300 hours
and headed back to Portsmouth, where we offloaded
the wounded–thirty in all. One man died on the
way into port.

On the 25th of June, ten miles off Cherbourg, the *Chickadee*
again sounded GQ and began sweeping operations. Two
battleships and four destroyers arrived on the scene and started
bombarding Cherbourg, so that the American troops could take the
town. The battleships were astern of the *Chickadee*, so Bob's ship
was now between the guns of the American destroyers and the
German shore batteries. When the battleships opened up with
shells going landward over the *Chickadee,* the German shells were
going seaward over Bob's ship in the opposite direction.

> You could hear the shells whistle and whine
> over our heads while we are just hoping and praying
> those Germans don't drop any of theirs on us. A
> few were close [resulting in] more shrapnel holes
> around, but no one was hurt. One battleship and a
> flush-deck (new) destroyer got damaged. The
> destroyer was abeam of us and we saw her get hit
> between the stacks and the bridge, and one shell
> knocked a big hole in her port side…. We were
> somewhat relieved to get out of there.

The *Chickadee* had started back for England, when they heard
a newscast on the BBC that reported on their Naval Task Force
shelling the city of Cherbourg earlier that day.

Bob's journal summarized the actions of the *Chickadee.* "We
were involved in two major operations in June–the D-Day
Normandy landings and establishing a beachhead for Cherbourg."

On the 29th of June, while heading for the River Seine estuary area, Bob's ship came upon a torpedoed merchant ship, and accompanied the damaged ship while it was towed by a tug and another minesweeper, the *Raven*, back to Portsmouth. They rejoined their squadron and during the first three days of July they swept for mines all along the invasion beaches and then anchored off shore about one-quarter mile out.

On the Fourth of July, the ships continued to sweep for mines. This time the Germans gave them a hot reception–but luckily their range was bad. "That night German bombers came over and one bomb landed between us and the battleship *Texas* while I was on watch."

Bob wrote that on July 20 their ship returned to Plymouth, England, for supplies and new sweep gear. With three of his buddies (Medek, Geezel and Red), Bob got a forty-eight hour pass and went by train to Torquay. They were able to billet at the Red Cross, where they swam, danced and took in some movies.

After leaving anchorage at Torquay, they received orders to sail for Oran, Africa. During the trip to Oran they drilled at GQ and practiced antiaircraft fire. "Saw two continents on this day– Europe (Spain) and Africa; then went through the Strait of Gibraltar." It was extremely hot in Oran. There were few ships in port aside from their squadron. "[We] enjoyed a couple of liberties for the next few days. [I] sold a carton of cigarettes for $10 to Arabs."

From the 10th through the 12th of August they sailed toward Naples, Italy. They saw the Isle of Capri and Mt. Vesuvius. The next day they immediately got under way to help sweep mines in preparation for the invasion of southern France. While not sweeping, they tied up to harbor buoys and went swimming off the sides of the ship.

"On August 27, shortly after midnight, an E-boat tried to make an attack on some battlewagons and they also had attacks by air, but there was no damage. This routine of sweep, patrol, anchor, liberty, movies and maintenance lasted almost a month."

In late October, while patrolling with a French cruiser and two destroyers, Bob's ship came upon a one-man human torpedo. They also captured two Germans who were paddling themselves toward the beach. "We took them aboard and stripped them of their possessions. They said they started out last night to attack us, but the rough water prevented it. There were thirty of them when they started."

The *Chickadee* continued on assignments in the Mediterranean off the coast of Italy. On Thanksgiving Day of 1944, the men "had a really good dinner; went to the Leaning Tower of Pisa and St. Maria Cathedral in Pisa–beautiful and untouched by war." Upon return to the ship, Bob discovered he had made the rank of 3rd class yeoman.

The *Chickadee* went into dry dock for repairs at Palermo, Sicily, and then sailed to the island of Sardinia, where it was able to locate and destroy many mines. The crew spent Christmas day in Palermo, but it was rainy and cold. In January of 1945, Bob wrote that they were sweeping along the coast near Monaco into German-held territory.

Today we got the hell shelled out of us by German shore batteries, until we could get turned around and away from the firing. The *Auk* was hit during the shelling with considerable damage done to the sides and fantail. All of us laid a heavy smoke screen for protection. Operations continued out of Nice and then Cannes, France, and on the 20th we headed back to Sardinia and then Palermo; alone this time and for repairs.

Near Leghorn (Livorno), Italy, there was an enemy air raid with flares and mines dropping all night. There continued to be numerous air raids and sweeping operations over the next several days, with good success in locating and destroying mines by the whole squadron. A month later, Bob's ship returned to Palermo, Sicily, and resumed sweeping duties along Italian and southern French coasts.

On May 7, 1945, Bob recorded: "THE WAR ENDED TODAY!" They sailed to Leghorn on May 8 with full lights on. They pulled into Leghorn and then returned to Marseille. Bob's diary entry was, "Beautiful weather and smooth water."

On the first of June the *Chickadee* sailed back through the Strait of Gibraltar, ending ten months in the Mediterranean. Traveling at twelve knots, they passed the Azores–it had only been a year since they had passed the Azores going the other direction to assist in the Allied invasion of Europe. They experienced rough seas for several days, but it calmed on the 11th of June, and they pulled into Bermuda on the 12th for refueling. On June 15, 1945, Bob and his crewmates arrived stateside at Norfolk, Virginia.

"Went home!"

A Hedgehog – a 24 Barreled Antisubmarine Mortar
Mounted on the Forecastle of *HMS Westcott.*
(*Wikipedia*)

Shirley Law
U.S. Navy WAVE
WWII
1944–1946

I*t was very difficult for fourteen women to share one bathroom.*

Shirley was born in Caldwell, Idaho, and graduated from Homedale High School. She was a senior when she heard on the radio about the Japanese bombing Pearl Harbor. The next day at school they had an assembly where they listened to President Roosevelt on the radio declaring war on Japan. She remembered that there was a Japanese girl in her class who felt ostracized because of what happened, and for the rest of the war the family kept to themselves.

After high school Shirley got a job in Boise at the statehouse working in the basement doing administrative duties, which included issuing drivers licenses. She and a friend of hers discussed becoming involved in the war effort by joining the U.S. Navy WAVES (Women Accepted for Volunteer Emergency Service). She enlisted in September 1944. Shirley was sent by train to New York City where she was trained at Hunter College. A typical day entailed getting up at 5 a.m., when they marched to breakfast, and then to their different classes. One of her memories of the training was that there were fourteen girls in each room, and they only had one bathroom. She lamented that it was very difficult for fourteen women to share one bathroom.

Shirley's boot camp lasted six weeks. Upon graduating she was sent to Cedar Falls, Iowa, for more training. Shirley was already a very accomplished typist, but stated that the Navy had a particular way they wanted things done, so she spent approximately two months at this school. One experience she remembered was that they always had to march to classes. It was in the winter time and many of the local school kids would throw snowballs at them as they passed by. One day her section leader got tired of it, and told the whole section to throw snowballs back at the kids–which they did. After that she stated that no one threw snowballs at them again.

Her first assignment was in Norfolk, Virginia, and then a Navy airbase in North Carolina. While there, she worked in the recreational department where they had a movie theater, swimming pool, and other facilities to entertain the sailors.

Shirley was then sent back to Norfolk, Virginia, where she again worked in an office until the war was over. She remembered the day it was announced that President Roosevelt had died and how upset all the WAVES were. One of the women in her section was very distressed because she thought that the United States would now surely lose the war. At that time most young people had never known any another president, and it was a scary time for them. When the *USS Missouri* docked at the base, Shirley was allowed to tour it and see the plaque that designated the place on the ship where the Japanese signed the surrender documents.

After the war she returned to Idaho, and because she was a veteran, Shirley would have been eligible for the GI Bill, but she stated she never did use it. She used her veteran's status to help get a job with the Veterans Employment Agency and later transferred to a job with the Federal Housing Authority. She eventually married, and because her husband's job moved him to various locations, she raised the family as they moved from place to place.

In recalling her memories of her service, Shirley stated she was just a small-town girl, who was amazed at how big the United States was and how much was going on in our country. She enjoyed her time in the WAVES, and helping her country in wartime.

USS Missouri in Action

Len Mallea
U.S. Navy
WWII
1943–1946
Navy Commendation for Life-saving

*The whole ship shook violently as the
kamikaze hit.*

Len was born in Idaho and spent a
lot of his younger days in Silver City.
His father was from the Spanish Basque country and he was very
proud of his Basque heritage. He went to Nampa High School,
where he graduated in 1943. He was working in a local pharmacy
on Sunday, December 7, 1944, and learned of the attack on Pearl
Harbor when he came home. At that time he had no idea where
Pearl Harbor was, nor why the Japanese were bombing it. Being a
young man, he had a strong feeling he would be pulled into the
conflict. He hoped to become a pharmacist and wanted to join the
Navy, which he was able to do when he was drafted. He didn't
have a long drive from his home to the Navy boot camp at
Farragut, Idaho, where he completed eight weeks of basic training.

Afterward Len was assigned to go to Hospital Apprentice
School, which was also at Farragut, Idaho. He was trained in the
basic fundamentals of hospital work and later went to Seattle,
Washington, then on to Portland, Oregon, where he was assigned
to the *USS Alpine* and worked in the sick bay as a hospital
apprentice. His was the first crew assigned to this brand-new ship
and he was fortunate to spend his entire Navy career on this same
vessel.

The *USS Alpine* was an assault craft with a crew of 500 men.
They spent several months in California training and breaking in
the ship for combat duty. On Len's ship they had several Higgins

boats, which were landing craft that the troops used for amphibious landings. After his California training, the ship set out for Pearl Harbor and they picked up a variety of equipment, fuel, supplies and troops. His convoy sailed to the island of Guam, where the entire crew was kept busy preparing for the upcoming invasion. It took several days after the initial landing to clear the ship of all the supplies needed for the soldiers on the beach. After landing the troops, the *Alpine* crew brought wounded soldiers back to the ship for treatment. Len's duties included helping in the sick bay. His unit had many American medical personnel assigned, including a large number of doctors, who worked in a large sick bay on the ship. Some of the medics in his unit were assigned to accompany the troops to the beach. These men gave initial aid to the wounded and then selected soldiers they thought had the best chance of survival. Those chosen were the first transported back to the ship for medical treatment.

After completing their mission at Guam, the *Alpine* was assigned as part of the invasion of Leyte in the Philippine Islands. At that time there were over 100 assault ships as part of the convoy to land the troops. They were stationed there approximately seven days and had their first experience with attacks from Japanese kamikazes (suicide planes). He saw a kamikaze dive into one of the small aircraft carriers. Len was amazed at the damage that these suicide bombers caused to a ship. After the initial Leyte invasion, his ship transported other troops to the beachhead. The last time his ship withdrew from the island, two sailors on the *Alpine* were killed when a kamikaze hit them. They still had troops on board and a lot of flammable equipment. All the men on the ship quickly started throwing the flammable items, particularly gasoline, into the ocean. As the Japanese attack on their ship had caused considerable damage, they were forced to leave for repairs, going to the island of New Guinea where a dry dock was located. It took ten days, working day and night, for the crew to make the ship operational. They returned just in time to land troops in Luzon Bay, where they participated in the last battle to eradicate the Japanese from the Philippines.

After the invasion of Luzon, Len's ship joined a large convoy that was headed to help with the invasion of Okinawa. He remembered looking out across the ocean and seeing every type of Navy ship imaginable. Prior to the invasion, many of the ships started pounding the island with explosive shells. As the battle continued, Len was working on the second deck. He heard other ships open up with antiaircraft fire and realized the shooting was getting closer and closer. When he could hear his own ship firing, he knew they were under attack. Shortly thereafter, a kamikaze dove into the main deck of his ship. He recalled that the ship shook violently. He rushed to the top deck to check the damage and could not believe the carnage that he saw there. One of the things he has never forgotten was seeing the burning flesh of many men onboard his ship. Later the crew found the engine of the kamikaze had penetrated all the way to the third deck. It took almost four hours for the fire crews to get the fires under control.

Len and another sailor searched several rooms where fires were burning, and pulled soldiers and sailors out to safety. They were awarded the Navy Commendation for Lifesaving because of their actions that day. The *Alpine* was so badly damaged it had to sail back to Seattle for repairs. All crew members got some time off and Len was able to return to Idaho for his leave. When the repaired ship started back for the Philippines, rumors circulated that they were headed for the invasion of Japan. They knew it would be a terrible battle. Shortly thereafter they were notified that atomic bombs had been dropped on Japan and within a day the Japanese surrendered. Len was personally grateful that President Harry Truman authorized the dropping of the atomic bombs, because it saved many thousands of American lives.

On his voyage back to the U.S. Len experienced what he believed was the worst incident of his naval service. His ship sailed right into the middle of a typhoon and endured twenty-four hours of horrendous winds and waves. He declared that it was scarier than any of the time he had spent under enemy fire.

Len was released from the Navy and returned home to Idaho, where he used the GI Bill to attend college and fulfill his dream to become a pharmacist. Eventually he opened a pharmacy in Caldwell, Idaho, where he worked for many years until his retirement.

Kamikaze Crashing into *USS Missouri* -
Battle of Okinawa

William A. Norman
U.S. Navy
WWII
1941–1946

The damaged rudder was stuck in place, so the ship was steaming around in circles.

William "Bill" A. Norman was schooled in Wilder, Idaho, graduating in the spring of 1940. He worked at various jobs and he and a friend enlisted in the Navy in February of 1941. They were put on a train to Salt Lake City where they were sworn in and put on another train bound for about thirteen weeks of boot camp in San Diego–or so he thought. The Navy had a couple of programs available for enlistees. One would have guaranteed him college after his time in training, and the other was an option to be regular Navy. He thought one of those programs was the old V-3 program. At any rate, he liked the idea of regular Navy so he chose to do that.

In May of 1941 Bill was consigned to the *USS Enterprise* (a carrier) and assigned to the quartermaster division. For a time his ship went to sea out of San Diego to train pilots for carrier landings and operations. Back in port they craned seventy-five P-40 aircraft aboard ship and headed for Hawaii, where their cargo of airplanes flew off to Kaneohe Naval Station. The men enjoyed liberty in Honolulu and, after boarding more airplanes and pilots, they headed for Wake Island, carrying the replacement equipment and men. Late in the evening of December 6, they returned to Pearl Harbor and stayed at sea until daylight because it would take too long for the whole convoy of four heavy cruisers and eight destroyers assigned to their task force to get into the harbor. It was too dangerous to attempt it at night.

Of course, on the morning of December 7 the Japanese attacked Pearl Harbor, and Bill's task force was ordered to stay out of sight and range until it could be determined just what was happening. After the enemy attack, they all went into port for refueling and ammunition and back out to sea as quickly as possible, so they could avoid any repeat attack, should there be one.

The task force was ordered to steam about the Pacific, going south then north to make the Japanese think there were multiple aircraft carriers, cruisers and destroyers available to the U.S. Navy. In reality, they were about the only remaining capital ships left to wage war. The ships steamed to the Mariana Islands in early February of 1942 and back to Pearl; then sailed over to Wake Island, which the Japanese had captured in late February of 1942. Their ships bombarded Wake and turned and steamed south of the equator, then turned back and sailed north up to the 38th parallel. The weather was extremely cold, and they were ill-prepared for the freezing temperatures. During this time they also bombarded Marcos Island and then joined the *USS Hornet,* which was carrying about sixteen of Jimmy Doolittle's B-25 bombers.

Bill and the *Enterprise* witnessed St. Elmo's Fire (an electrically charged atmospheric phenomenon appearing like fire on ship masts and on aircraft wings). Often in wartime these spectacular displays caused all sorts of concern, until some seasoned sailors identified just what was happening.

The *Enterprise* would typically stay at sea from thirty to sixty days at a time. The longest stay Bill recalled was 115 days. During one of these encounters with other ships and planes at sea, they received a message that read, "Sighted enemy, sank same; fired 175 rounds." Following the launch of the Doolittle bombers they returned to Pearl. The U.S. Navy by this time had two task forces with two carriers in each. Admiral Halsey was task force commander on the *Enterprise*. Admiral Spruance was the other task force commander. The *USS Yorktown* was one of the carriers. Both units were trying to locate and engage the Japanese fleet. Once the enemy fleet was found, the *Yorktown* launched torpedo planes. All of the planes were lost–not one returned to the ship– but the combined fleets sank four Japanese aircraft carriers.

Bill also recalled that he and the *Enterprise* sailed to Guadalcanal and the Solomon Islands. They were in the company of troop ships designated for landing operations. The Japanese sank four of the troop ships traveling with them.

The Japanese were commanded by Admiral Yamamoto. With the assistance of American code breakers, the Allies found out that Yamamoto was flying to some distant island. Then the U.S. decided to try to shoot down his plane. They succeeded! The impact of this victory against the Japanese war effort was significant. About this time the *Enterprise* was hit with a 500-pound, armor-piercing bomb that went through five decks and killed about seventy-five sailors. Bill and others hurried down to the engine room, and as they descended amongst the smoke and damage, they strung rope rails. This lifeline made it possible for the engine crew to return safely to the deck. The damaged rudder was stuck in place, so the ship was steaming around in circles. With the aid of engine and rudder repairs, they steamed to an accessible island where they induced a 35-degree list of the ship, which exposed a hole in the hull. After a steel plate was welded in place over the hole, the *Enterprise* returned to Pearl Harbor.

It was here at Pearl Harbor that Bill left the *Enterprise* and boarded a freighter for San Diego, and as a non-support staff member, he reported to an APC (U.S. Navy auxiliary ship). The ship was 100 feet long and twenty feet wide with three officers and seventeen enlisted men. Bill functioned as the sole navigation and signals staff. Their speed was a slow 10.5 knots. They cruised to Pearl Harbor, Samoa, and Rendova Island with the purpose of supplying forward radio contact for fighter aircraft. They also re-charted an island's port entrance by taking soundings and sightings, as well as redrawing the sea bottom contours. Bill remained aboard the APC for about eighteen months and while en route from one assignment to another spent some of his time fishing for "meat." (Food supplied by the Navy wasn't the best, so whatever fish the men caught was their major source of meat.) At one point they anchored off Guadalcanal and the ship's chief "scrounger" went ashore and "borrowed" a truck and some food from the Marines. Bill made First Class Quartermaster while he was aboard the APC.

In early 1944 he was reassigned to the PA 59 *USS Audrian*–a troop ship. The chief petty officer received a transfer about the time Bill went aboard, and he was allowed to take the test that promoted him to the chief quartermaster. His crew consisted of about thirty-five men, who were responsible for quartermaster, radio, radar and signal duties. They went to Manus Island to resupply and pick up about 3,500 troops for the Philippine invasion. They took the first troops into Leyte Gulf, then went to Saipan for more troops and returned back to Lingayen Gulf. While in Saipan, a squadron of bombers flew over the port in formation, spelling "USN" in the sky–quite a sight!

Then they began loading for Okinawa and anchored near the town of Naha. Clustered there were thousands of ships, and many of them were being attacked by the newest Japanese weapon, the kamikaze suicide planes. The big battleships were shooting over those ships that were inshore of them. Bill recalled that a kamikaze headed straight for his troop ship, when an LST (landing ship tank) hit it and blew off one wing. The enemy airplane turned on its side and crashed about fifty feet from the ship. They rescued the Japanese pilot.

Their assignment was then to furnish replacement troops to the various islands and take off the wounded for transport to hospitals.

They and about thirty ships carrying supplies went into Nagasaki Harbor shortly after the "Atomic Bomb" was detonated. It was utter and total devastation! There, Japanese citizens were contracted to unload the ships.

Bill's ship returned to Swan Island at Portland, Oregon, for refitting. It was with a buddy on their liberty that Bill double-dated and met his future wife. The date was December 14, 1945. He was scheduled to leave the ship, since his enlistment was supposed to be up in a short time. But his skipper said he couldn't cross the Pacific without a navigator, so Bill had to stay onboard. They were ordered to strip the ship of all useful items, because the ship was to be a target in the Bikini Atoll nuclear bomb testing program. He left for the atoll on Christmas Day of 1945 and finally made it back to Portland to be discharged May 27, 1946.

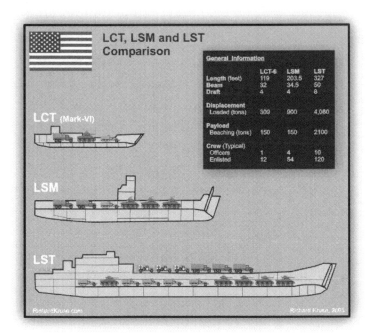

Landing Craft Comparisons

Maxine Randall
U.S. Navy WAVE
WWII
1943-1945

"Maxine, that never happened!"

Maxine grew up in Nampa, Idaho, and had what she described as a wonderful young life. "It was the best of times and we were carefree." She graduated from high school in 1938 and because of her positive attitude, love of helping people, and being an all around good citizen, in her senior year she was selected to represent Idaho at a meeting of the Daughters of the American Revolution in Washington, D.C. The high school band came to the station to send her off. She traveled cross-country by train and met up with other young women from all over the United States, where they attended events for a week and were invited to the White House to have tea with Eleanor Roosevelt. She also was able to sit directly behind President Roosevelt at an evening performance.

She enrolled at the College of Idaho after high school and completed two years of premed. She then went on to Johns Hopkins Hospital in Baltimore, Maryland, to pursue her dream of becoming a nurse. After eight months there she had to withdraw as she had developed a skin condition. She was heartbroken, since all she had ever wanted to be was a nurse. She returned home, and was trying to decide what she would do for the next chapter of her life, when Pearl Harbor was attacked in December of 1941. Maxine wanted to do something to help her country, and eventually she heard about a new organization being formed by the Navy called the WAVES (Women's Auxiliary in Voluntary Emergency Service). She took the tests, passed them, and soon was on a train going cross-country again, this time to New York. Women in the WAVES were being organized and trained at Hunter College in New York City. Training was somewhat rudimentary and the conditions weren't the best. Maxine didn't like the loss of privacy during training, but she stuck with it and graduated near the top among her peers. This gave her the option to choose what might be the best jobs for her. She wanted to be a control tower operator, but got her second choice of being a "Link Trainer" instructor.

The Link Trainer was a boxy mockup of a small airplane. It had a complete cockpit with controls and would respond to operative actions from the pilot, who sat inside the closed-in cockpit. The Link Trainer sat on top of an arrangement of bellows and levers, so that it moved and assumed different attitudes in response to the pilot's maneuvering of the controls. The pilot was given a route to fly, and the hood was closed so that he couldn't see out. His course was plotted by a moving device with a pen, which was on an adjoining table. He had to correct for simulated cross winds and weather events, and had to rely entirely on instruments in the cockpit. After each session the pilot would get out and his flight track would be reviewed with the instructor.

Maxine was sent to Atlanta, Georgia, for her Link training. It was summer and as yet the WAVES hadn't received anything other than their winter-blue uniforms. This made things next to unbearable in the summer heat of Georgia, but somehow they got through it. Eventually they received their summer uniforms and life got better.

Maxine was responsible not only for training the pilots, but she also had to make mechanical repairs to the Link if something wasn't working correctly. Initially, she wasn't the best at this, as she had never before held a screwdriver; but over time, as her confidence grew, she was able to master the required skills.

After training Maxine was sent to an airfield in Livermore, California, for her first duty assignment. There she was welcomed into a small group of Link instructors who worked around the clock to provide training to a senior group of instructor pilots, none of whom had ever received navigation training for flying in bad weather or poor visibility. Most of them had always flown by the seat of their pants and disliked the Link Trainer apparatus. They had a hard time adapting to flying when they couldn't see their surroundings and had to rely on instruments. Several of them came in at night for extra training. According to Maxine, after they exited the Link Trainer, some of these experienced pilots would be a "ball of sweat!" "They all had to have a cigarette to relax after a session." Later on, when some of these pilots had been given other assignments, Maxine got letters from them saying that the training they had received in the Link had saved their lives, when they had been in situations where their knowledge of the new skills had been put to the test.

Maxine became friendly with several of the pilots, and they would invite her to go along on training and weather observation flights. Sometimes the pilots would perform aerobatics with the open cockpit biplanes that they flew. In a way, this was their method of letting off steam and getting even with Maxine for putting them through the rigors of the Link. But this turned out to be a lot of fun for Maxine and she never got airsick. One day, a favorite pilot was flying her over the San Francisco Bay when she noticed they were getting very close to the Golden Gate Bridge. Before Maxine knew it, they had flown "under" the bridge. When they came back and landed, the pilot said to her, "Maxine, that never happened." She responded, "My lips are sealed." She recalled that two weeks later another flier was court-martialed for doing the same thing.

After fourteen months at Livermore, Maxine was sent to her next assignment at Daytona Beach, Florida. The day that Maxine reported for duty was the day that the air station at Daytona Beach had received their first group of WAVES. Maxine's reception was very cool, almost bordering on insolence, from her new chief. Some people, including her new chief, had just not adjusted to having women in the military. Maxine, although feeling very hurt, dug deep inside herself and remembered some advice two of her brothers had given her about how she could survive life in the military. She had been told to "just give it some time, do your very best, and show that person that you are capable of replacing them someday." This strategy worked, and over time Maxine proved herself, showing what a great asset she was to her group. She was eventually promoted to petty officer first class and became friends with her chief. She was allowed to move off base, where she and a couple of her friends rented a house close to the beach. This became the "bath house" for her group of Link training friends, and they all came there to change before going to the beach.

Maxine's chief had wanted to go overseas to be an aircraft mechanic and get in the fight, so when he finally got orders to do that, he chose her to backfill his position. This put her in charge of fifteen Link Trainers. It also made Maxine responsible for all maintenance of the equipment. That responsibility made her very nervous, but her chief spent many nights working with her, writing down all the things that could go wrong and having her practice fixing them. After she had taken over, Maxine was still very anxious whenever she got a repair call, but said a little prayer on the way to correct the problem. She was always able to find and fix the trouble.

Maxine was offered the opportunity to go to Officer Candidate School. She was told that after graduation she would probably become a recruiter. Maxine really loved her Link training job and the tight knit group she worked with, because she felt that she was really doing something important. So, after giving it a lot of thought, she turned down the offer.

When the war ended about fourteen months later, Maxine returned to Idaho. In 1946 she re-enrolled at the College of Idaho and graduated in 1947. She then married and moved with her husband to Albuquerque, New Mexico. She worked for Sandia National Laboratories, at Los Alamos. Even though she had a degree, Maxine had to start at a lower-level job as a technical typist. She soon became supervisor of seventy-five technical typists, and matched them up with various PhDs in the top-secret research environment. She did this for eight years and then moved into staff jobs in personnel, medical and security.

In 1976 after twenty-one years in New Mexico, Maxine took early retirement and returned to Idaho. She worked for a couple of years as a secretary for the First Presbyterian Church and later became an ordained elder and deacon in the church. In 1990, at the age of seventy, she took the competitive state exam and was hired by the Idaho Industrial Commission for two years. She received many awards and was recognized for her volunteerism, philanthropy, and as an outstanding graduate of the College of Idaho. Maxine attributed her time spent in the WAVES to making her more tolerant and more appreciative of other people's views, as well as making her appreciate the hardships that members of the military had endured.

WWII-Era Link Trainers

F. Willard (Robbie) Robinson
U. S. Navy
WWII
1941–1946

"How I got out, I don't know. There was nothing left of the plane, the crew or anything."

Born in 1918 in Long Beach, California, Robbie attended his entire public schooling there, graduating from Long Beach Polytechnic High School, the same school his father had also graduated from in 1905. The family had a cattle ranch in NW Los Angeles County, where Robbie spent his time as a child.

Robbie attended the University of Southern California (USC) on a national competitive scholarship, but at the end of two years, he wanted broader experience than sitting in the classroom every day. His adventures began in 1938 when he rode a three-speed bicycle from Detroit to Los Angeles in fourteen days and three hours. The following year he took his bike into what is now the Escalante National Monument. There were no roads back then, and he did not see any other people for thirty days. In 1939 Robbie and a friend obtained a sailboat and sailed to Alaska. When they arrived they only had $7.50 between them. Then he traveled on to Fairbanks and met with the president of the University of Alaska. Robbie explained to him that he would like to finish his college education there, but that he didn't have any money. The school gave him a little cabin to sleep in and a job cleaning blackboards and sweeping the halls.

Sometime later an armed services recruiting officer flew into Fairbanks in his Waco airplane. He explained that the government was recruiting twenty men to train as pilots. In January of 1940

Robbie was selected and eventually soloed in a J-3 Cub on skis in temperatures as low as -57 degrees Fahrenheit. He became the first government trained pilot in the territory of Alaska. After receiving his commercial certificate, he flew many trips into the bush that following summer. To make additional money, he drove a dump truck and helped build Ladd Field, which was used as a staging base to ferry military planes to Russia, a later American ally. Robbie volunteered to go into the Eagle Squadron, a group of American pilots that flew with the British RAF. These pilots enlisted before the U.S. entered WWII and helped fight the Germans, who were waging an offensive air bombardment against Britain. He received a letter from the RAF confirming that he was on their waiting list, so he went back to USC to finish up his final year of college. He was scheduled to graduate in February of 1942, but Pearl Harbor was attacked by the Japanese on December 7, 1941. The day after, he went down to a local recruiting station and enlisted in the Navy. He was inducted two weeks before he was to graduate, but the university awarded his diploma without him taking his final exams.

Robbie went through elimination training at Long Beach Naval Air Station and then was sent on to Corpus Christi, Texas, for primary training in the Stearman N3N open cockpit planes. He did instrument training there as well.

In June of 1942 the Navy needed more torpedo plane pilots. His group was called to the main hangar and the commander asked for thirty men to volunteer, so Robbie volunteered. (Earlier in the war, in the Battle of Midway, the U.S. flew Avengers, which did not have any flaps on their wings, so the steepness of their dives was limited to sixty degrees. These planes had to fly low at 200 miles per hour to release the torpedoes. It was very dangerous, because they were likely to be hit by antiaircraft fire. Only one U.S. torpedo plane survived the Battle of Midway.)

Robbie completed his advanced training in Texas and earned his wings in the summer of 1942. His parents drove out from Long Beach and his mother proudly pinned his wings on him. From there, he went to Opa Locka, Florida, for operational training and he did torpedo training in the old Douglas Devastators, followed by carrier training in Norfolk, Virginia. The group lost three pilots in accidents in one day of carrier training. And that day, when he returned back to the base, Robbie was met by the chaplain who asked him to inform one of the pilot's wives of her husband's death. Robbie escorted her back to her parents' home in Nebraska. From there he returned to California and was assigned to a composite squadron in North Island, San Diego.

While he was in Southern California, Robbie decided to look up a girl he had dated in high school. It had been two years since she had seen him, but when he asked her to marry him, she accepted and bravely took a train to Sand Point, Idaho, where they were married. Their marriage lasted more than sixty years.

Robbie's squadron was the first to be trained in night attacks carried out over the Salton Sea. Robbie recalled that he and another fellow flew out to a top secret place named Goldstone Lake, where they were introduced to a rocketeer. There they had rockets installed on their planes. In December of 1943, they flew to Inyokern, California, to meet with a team from CalTech to test the rockets. The pilots drove out to what is now China Lake to look at the targets. (At this point in the war, the armed forces still had primitive radar for night work.) It worked pretty well, as Robbie was able to hit his designated target. (Note: These were the same rockets designed by CalTech and installed in ground Jeep launchers used against Rommel in the North African campaign. But they weren't terribly accurate when launched from the ground.)

Robbie's squadron went to Pearl Harbor and traveled to Midway on the *Manila Bay* aircraft carrier. The first week the rockets were used was February of 1944, when they supported the landing of troops on the island of Kwajalein. Robbie was loaded in a TBM3 and catapulted from the carrier deck, but his plane was only able to hold altitude just above the water for one quarter mile. When coming back to the carrier, the plane shuddered, flipped over on its back, and dove straight into the sea and exploded. It blew debris 1,000 feet in the air.

In his own words Robbie retold his harrowing experience.

How I got out, I don't know. There was nothing left of the plane, the crew or anything. I was picked up by the *USS Caldwell*. I remember thinking about going in....my canopy was open, and I was out of my chute, which we weren't supposed to be below 500 feet. My hand was on the lever but I didn't want to release it because we were going straight in; but I didn't want to go down with the plane. I think what happened was that I hit the release and I was blown free from the airplane. My head hit the bar above it in the cockpit and I still don't have feeling there to this day. I remember seeing the explosion and I got one side of my Mae West inflated. They [the rescue team] threw a life preserver out and I latched on to it. The props pulled me under, but somehow the guys pulled me out and I got aboard. The captain's name was Abraham Lincoln–kind of amazing. I was in bad shape because the concussions had broken all of the capillaries in my body and my left leg was pretty well torn off. After a week, I was transferred to a U.S. relief hospital ship, where I spent a month. I eventually made it to Pearl Harbor. It was a hard time and I was in a lot of pain. I wrote a letter to my wife and told her I would be home when I could walk. So, about four to five months later I took my first steps. I was in the hospital in Long Beach and I was still having problems with my legs, but [the Navy] still needed pilots. So that September I was sent out again. It was really tough. I didn't know where I was going. We went to San Francisco and they put me on an old refrigerator ship and they told me I was going to the Admiralty Islands north of New Guinea. I was to report for flying duty. The doctor said I could fly the planes okay, but I had problems getting up and down the ladders. They put me in the hospital in the Admiralty Islands and that's where they found out I had a problem in my knee. I was sent home and did test flying on a lot of different airplanes in the desert near Yuma.

I was still doing flight test work when the war ended. My wife and I had driven to San Diego and were staying in a small hotel when we heard a lot of sirens going off and horns honking. Joan said, "What is all that?" Joking, I said, "I guess the war is over!" Actually it was! That was a big relief to a lot of people because a lot of carnage would have happened if we had landed in Japan. So it was a great day of celebration that the war was over.

Robbie went back to USC, earned a war emergency teaching credential and became a fifth-grade teacher in California at the Northridge Elementary School. He then taught at Canoga Park High School while he continued taking classes to obtain his doctorate at USC. Eventually he became the principal of Beverly Hills High School and built one of the finest programs in the country, developing the very first SAT exams. At the end of seventeen years he took an early retirement and went to work for Family Foundations in Texas, the largest family-owned grocery chain in the United States at that time.

Robbie and Joan had three children. They retired to Idaho to be close to their son, and Robbie stayed active in politics and education. He was the author of several books, including *Beverly Hills Principal* and *Navy Wings of Gold*.

The following is an excerpt from *Navy Wings of Gold*.

The writing of *Navy Wings of Gold* began nine years ago. Now as I put down my pen, we are in the fourth year of a new century and I am eighty-five years of age. During this time Joan and I have established a new life in Idaho. On occasion I stroll the nature trail along the banks of the Boise River. I listen to the movement of the water as it has for centuries rolled along the river rock. I watch the Canada geese foil their wings and drop with grace through the cottonwoods to the sanctuaries below. There is awe. Life is a gift and a great mystery. I lift my hands in wonder and thanksgiving for the assured hope of eternal adventure.

Grumman TBF/TBM
Avenger

Charles O'Leary Roe
U.S. Navy
WWII & Korea
1940–1960

"Many a good pilot was lost that day."

Charles "Chuck" O'Leary Roe grew up on a farm in rural Idaho where his family raised Hereford bulls. After a few years they moved to Cambridge, Idaho, and Chuck went to school in Weiser, Idaho. In his junior year of high school several of his seventeen-year old friends joined the Navy. Following suit, he left school his junior year as well, enlisting in the Navy in December 1940.

San Diego was his first stop for basic training. He had already served a year in the Navy when Pearl Harbor was attacked. He was assigned to an air squadron on North Island, San Diego. He had been to Hawaii the July before the attack, and he never dreamed that the Japanese would attack the U.S. Naval Fleet stationed at the islands. Assigned to the newly repaired *USS Saratoga*, he was supposed to have been in Pearl Harbor on the day it was attacked; but due to the repairs to the ship, their deployment had been delayed. Chuck didn't arrive there until December 13 and witnessed some of the ships still burning in the harbor.

Chuck was trained as a bombardier on a TBD (a torpedo plane). He received advanced training on the Norden Bombsight before joining his ship. The *Saratoga* was sent out toward Wake Island to scout for Japanese ships. His ship took a torpedo hit on January 10, 1942. Chuck was washing his dungarees and got lifted about ten feet in the air, suffering many bruises and bumps. The ship had to limp back to Pearl Harbor. The crew was left at a facility outside of Honolulu to do some training until the end of May, then they were transferred to the *USS Yorktown*. They were onboard the *Yorktown* a week before the Battle of Midway. The U.S. fleet was outnumbered five to one, but they were told the Japanese had been drawn to Midway with falsely transmitted information. The Navy was playing a guessing game, attempting to find the Japanese fleet. Torpedo planes flew out and drew the Japanese Zeros, who were the air coverage for the Japanese Navy. While the air fight took place, U.S. dive bombers went in below and sank three Japanese carriers. The Navy lost three squadrons of TBDs that day. Only two aircraft (piloted by enlisted pilots) came back, and they were so damaged they had to ditch instead of landing on the ship. Chuck said, "Many a good pilot was lost that day." Chuck stayed on board ship that day and did not fly because the TBDs were carrying torpedoes. Late that afternoon the *Yorktown* took two torpedoes in the port side and three bomb hits as well. The ship listed thirty-five degrees to port. After trying to unsuccessfully stabilize the vessel, the captain called an "abandon ship" order and the sailors went over from the starboard side. The *USS Hammann* (a destroyer) came along side the *Yorktown* to put a salvage crew on it. The *Hammann* had depth charges aboard that were armed, and a Japanese submarine put a torpedo into it and sunk it. As it sank, the depth charges exploded and blew the bottom out of the *Yorktown*. This attack took place on June 5, 1942. Sailors were panicking and drowning each other as they fought to get into the lifeboats. Chuck took off swimming. Unfortunately he couldn't get his air bottles inflated on his Mae West life vest. He swam for about an hour and forty-five minutes. Finally a destroyer (*USS Bulge*) came along side him, and he was in the process of reaching up for the netting they had hung over the side for him to grab just as Japanese bombers came upon them, and the destroyer had to pull away. So Chuck swam around for another half hour before they came back and finally rescued him from the sea. He was taken to an aviation seaplane tender and then back to Pearl Harbor. The survivors were placed in a vacated CCC (Civilian Conservation Corps) camp, so they couldn't tell anyone the *Yorktown* had sunk. He had been on the "Mighty Y" (*Yorktown*) for only a week before it was destroyed.

Next up for Chuck was an assignment on the *USS Enterprise* for a trip to Guadalcanal. Given new aircraft on August 7, 1942, his squadron flew air coverage for the battle. As they left the area after taking Guadalcanal, they were bombed by the Japanese. They had flown off the *Enterprise* when they were told to vacate the area, because the Japanese were attacking the ship. Chuck's plane was caught in the air. To save the plane, which was loaded with torpedoes, the crew flew into the night and landed back on a badly damaged *Enterprise* hours later. Chuck recalled that he saw the bodies of men lying by the gun turrets. They had been cut in half by the strafing and bombs of the battle. Two days later, Chuck's plane took off overloaded and flopped off the end of the ship. While waiting in the water to be rescued, Chuck saw a shark fin between his plane and the ship. The men on the ship starting firing at the shark, and Chuck was sure that he and his chief were going to be hit by the live gunfire. A destroyer finally picked his chief and him out of the water and they made their way back to Hawaii once again.

By now the old *USS Saratoga* had come out of repair and Chuck was reassigned to that ship. He was sent back to the Guadalcanal area and engaged in several battles, including the battle for Stuart Island. He spent five months on Guadalcanal before returning stateside in 1943. He was reassigned to pilot training. He went to several schools for the training, but didn't complete it, because the military was downsizing and didn't need as many pilots. Back on a carrier, he worked in the ordinance room for a while and then it sailed back to Hawaii. After a few months there he was sent to Treasure Island, San Francisco,

California, to work in transportation until his group was sent back to aviation. The Korean War was breaking out, so he returned to work on carriers, where he was an aviation ordinance man, loading bombs eighteen hours a day on planes that were providing air coverage for the Marines coming out of the Chosin Reservoir battle. He spent six months on a carrier off of Korea and then six months at Moffett Field, California, and then back again to another carrier. After Korea Chuck was assigned to a fighter squadron with deployments at sea and then back to Moffett Field. He did this for a year and a half before he retired as a chief petty officer in 1960.

USS Yorktown

Francis Lester Thompson
U.S. Navy
WWII & Korea
1936–1957

"I spent the night sleeping underneath torpedo tubes."

"Tommy" Thompson was born in Medicine Lodge, Kansas. His family eventually moved to Chicago, Illinois, but Tommy wanted to continue living in Kansas. He was allowed to go back to live part-time with his grandparents and go to school there. He went back and forth from Kansas to Chicago during grammar school, but returned to Chicago to attend and graduate from high school. After his graduation, he went back to Kansas for the summer to work and then on to Oklahoma, where he attended college for two years.

Because of the Great Depression, Tommy found it difficult to get more money for college, so in October 1936 he decided to join the Navy. He was sent to Norfolk, Virginia, for his basic training. He then spent two years in Washington, D.C., attending the United States Navy School of Music, where he studied the trumpet and guitar as well as music theory and history. In 1938 he was assigned to be a member of the Admiral's Band on the *USS Saratoga*, which was based in Long Beach, California. After three months the band was transferred to the *USS Lexington*. In 1939 the fleet went to the East Coast for battle maneuvers and then back to the West Coast. His primary duty was as a member of the band, but he had cleaning duties as well. At this time, Hitler had invaded Poland and Admiral Halsey took command of the *Lexington*. The admiral decided he wanted to move to the newer ship, the *USS Yorktown*. So, in the summer of 1939, Tommy's band moved with the admiral to San Diego and the "Mighty Y." This was his home

235

base, although they traveled to Washington State, Hawaii and then back to California.

In the spring of 1941 the *Yorktown* was in Hawaii, when they were told, on secret orders, to report to the East Coast. During the night they went through the Panama Canal with their ship's name obscured, so it couldn't be identified. They made their way to Newfoundland, and then Nova Scotia, and provided convoy protection for U.S. vessels sailing back and forth across the Atlantic. In November 1941 they needed to take the ship in for an overhaul, and were headed to the Norfolk Navy Yard when Pearl Harbor was attacked. After quick repairs, the *Yorktown* was assigned back to the West Coast; but after leaving the Panama Canal, they diverted from their intended course and headed instead to the area of the Solomon Islands in the Pacific. The *Yorktown* participated in several raids in that area. Then the ship went back to Pearl Harbor to replenish supplies before heading back to the Coral Sea. The *Yorktown* spent several months there, and in May of 1942 they engaged in the Battle of the Coral Sea. It was there that the *USS Lexington* was sunk and the *Yorktown* took three hits. The admiral wanted to head to Australia to get his ship repaired, but the Japanese were heavily manned in that area, so the ship went on to Tonga. Subsequently, Admiral Nimitz called them back to Pearl Harbor to dry dock. But four days later they were sailing toward Midway, even though Nimitz knew they had sustained a lot of damage.

The American fleet knew the Japanese were coming (code breakers in Hawaii had broken the Japanese codes), so scout planes were being sent out daily to look for the enemy. The *Yorktown* searched for the Japanese fleet, and found it a couple of days later. At the same time, the Japanese were searching for the American fleet, but the *Yorktown* was the only ship they found. The *Enterprise* and the *Hornet* were also in the area, but since the Japanese couldn't find them, they threw all of their might against the *Yorktown*. The ship sustained two torpedo hits and some bombing, as well. Then two more torpedoes found their mark, and the ship started to list. At that point the decision was made to abandon ship. Tommy didn't make it to a lifeboat because his battle station was three decks down. By the time he got on deck, all of the lifeboats were full and already in the water. He swam out to the closest lifeboat and hung onto the rope that was wound around the side. Before the men in the water could be rescued, the word came that Japanese planes were returning, so the rescue operation was temporarily halted. It turned out that the planes that were spotted were actually U.S. planes returning from a mission. Tommy estimated that he was in the water maybe two or three hours, before being picked up by the *USS Benham*. He spent the night "sleeping underneath torpedo tubes," because there were three or four hundred survivors onboard and not enough room below deck for everyone. After changing ships twice, the survivors finally made land in Hawaii. Tommy's band lost two men during the battle.

The men from the *Yorktown* were bivouacked in an abandoned camp in the Hawaiian hills. The Navy kept them isolated there so that no one would know about the *Yorktown*'s sinking. Also included at this camp were the men known as "Carlson's Raiders," an elite U.S. Marine force using the camp as a training base. These Marines made raids on various Pacific islands. They helped make the enforced-stay of the *Yorktown* sailors more palatable. After two weeks in the camp, Tommy was sent back to Pearl Harbor for work detail. His assignment was with a grave-digging detail at the newly-developed Punchbowl Cemetery. When the time came to be reassigned, the surviving band members were sent back to Treasure Island, California. They were given leave time, and then they were transported to Florida to help sell war bonds around that state. The band would play at various venues and functions that were being held and encouraged audiences to purchase war bonds. That was how Tommy spent the rest of the war.

After the war Tommy realized that he wanted to stay in the Navy. However, he wished to change his job classification. He decided to become an electronics technician. To switch jobs in the Navy, Tommy was required to be discharged from the service, and then re-enlist. After re-enlisting, he was required to go back to basic training. Then he went to school for advanced electronics training, after which he was assigned to the U.S. Naval Academy in Annapolis, Maryland, as an instructor. After his eighteen-month assignment he was transferred twice before he was promoted to warrant officer and moved again. He applied for and was sent to guided missile school and then assigned to the world's first guided missile cruiser, the *USS Boston*, spending time in many states and ports. He became eligible for shore duty; so he was assigned to a base in California. When he arrived there, he found out that there were no missiles ready for him to work with and no other job assignment for him. Tommy decided it was time to retire. In 1957 he retired after a long career of service to his country.

USS *Yorktown*
Dead in the Water
& Burning
4 June 1942

USS *Yorktown*
Being Abandoned
4 June 1942

USS *Yorktown*
At Bottom of the Sea
(*National Geographic* Photo)

Donald Vaughn
U.S. Navy
WWII
1943–1945

"We killed some of our own troops today while firing! Some of it was carelessness and some couldn't be helped."

Don was born in Texas in December of 1924. He was seventeen years old when the Japanese attacked Pearl Harbor. His recollection of that day was quite vivid, but he didn't join the rush to enlist. He received his draft notice in May 1943 and went down to the Navy recruiter and joined up. In June of that year he was sent to San Diego, California, for boot camp. From there he went to Treasure Island at San Francisco for training as a seaman, where he also learned how to handle fuel lines aboard ship. He then reported to the Battleship *USS Idaho*.

While in the service, Don kept an extensive journal. Many of his thoughts and feelings are quoted in the following wartime experiences he lived through.

In October of 1943 Don's ship left the United States, sailing into the Pacific Theater. During the next year the *USS Idaho* participated in bombardment duties during the Allied island-hopping strategy as it continued to advance toward Japan. It steamed with its assigned fleet to bombard the Pacific islands of New Ireland and Rabaul, then on to Guadalcanal, Saipan and Guam. Don recalled, "There were a lot of air attacks against the fleet at Saipan and Guam, and a battleship–I think it was the *USS Maryland*–was hit by a plane-launched torpedo." At Palau Island they blasted away for three days and lost several small craft in the battle, but few seamen. During this time Don was promoted to seaman and then later to coxswain.

September 15, 1944, was a big day for Don. He had been aboard the *USS Idaho* for one year and back home it was his sweetheart's birthday. He wrote her, "We are all hoping and praying we will be back in the states soon. I wonder?"

After mail call on Sept 25th, as the ship was leaving Palau, Don received a "Dear John" letter from his girlfriend. Don wrote in his journal:

> I met her on December 24, 1942. I thought the world of her, and still do. It's very hard to give up something you think of every day for as long as I have. If I had been home I believe it would have been different, but this war has caused lots of grief and heartaches, and I'm sorry it happened this way; we just weren't given a chance. I hope you get a man who can offer you a home and security and all the happiness in the world. Good bye, Sarah, and God bless you.

In September the ship traveled back to the States for refitting, where it was equipped with more and better antiaircraft guns, and the main armament was serviced. While the ship was berthed in Long Beach, California, Don seriously contemplated "going over the hill." He was genuinely tempted, but a new love interest was in the picture by then, and besides he didn't relish the probable consequences of going AWOL.

On the 20th of January 1945, the *USS Idaho* again left the States for renewed action in the Pacific. Don recorded, "I know it will be a long time before we see the States again; I am hoping and praying that Jackie waits for me."

At this time the U.S. 3rd Fleet was proceeding to hit Tokyo. The attack on Tokyo was intended to keep the Japanese military busy and away from Iwo Jima, which was 670 miles from Japan's capital city. As part of the 5th Fleet, the *USS Idaho*'s assignment was assisting in the pre-invasion barrage of Iwo Jima. The fleet started bombarding on the 16th of February; the range for their ships was as close as 1,500 yards. "That makes us ducks if they have 6- or 8-inch guns," Don recorded. However most of the first day of fire on the island was from a distance of 12,000 yards. The "tin cans" (destroyers) went in a lot closer, and they did draw a little return fire.

The enemy planes had quite a time; they were waiting for us to come in closer. If the Japanese shot shore batteries at us they would probably miss, since we're so far out. If and when we go in closer, and they fire at us, we can locate their guns placements and take them out. The battleships' planes made contact with a Zero and he took a couple of shots at us, but nothing happened.

On February 17, GQ [General Quarters/battle stations] went off at 0515 and didn't secure until 1830. ___, was everybody tired; at 1330 I came out of the turret to help bring onboard a wounded man that was on an LCI (landing craft) when she was sunk. He was hit in several places by shrapnel from a shell. He was bleeding a lot–sure made me nervous.... He died that same day. Pitts, our bosun, told me to get a helmet on. He said, "Did you see that shell that hit back there–pieces of steel were flying all over." He didn't have to tell me a second time.

Then one of our planes got hit by a 40mm shell– it shot between the pilot and the observer, but they were able to land the damaged plane okay. But the Marine observer was wounded in two or three places and he bled a lot. They buried a man at sea on the *USS Nevada* today between 0530 and 0600. We had two [tin] cans and a cruiser hit today, two LCIs and a minelayer sunk. The cruiser, *USS Pensacola*, was hit twice–once topside and once below the water. The executive and the first lieutenant were killed, and I don't know how many enlisted men died. We went in close today (about 3,000 yards), but just wait until tomorrow….

At the conclusion of each diary entry, Don wrote a prayer for his folks and loved ones back home.

February 18 was the third day of bombardment with GQ at 0505 and secured at 1830, and again Don went to stand a watch. He was relieved and went down to chow–had just seated himself when GQ sounded again–surface contact. But it lasted less than an hour, so he finally got some chow. He debated whether to go to bed or get a shower, decided on bed and GQ went off again. He jumped up, grabbed his shoes and pants, and ran to his battle station. As he ran, a plane went right over the ship, really close, but it didn't hit them. It was a Japanese suicide plane, and it hit the *USS Hamilton*–a mine sweeper. "God has been with us so far. Tomorrow is Dog Day–there will be a lot of our men killed tomorrow." The *Idaho* went in to 2,600 yards firing its 20- and 40mm guns. On the 19th they again manned battle stations. The troop landing was scheduled at 0900 hours. "They are sure having a hard time. We killed some of our own troops today while firing! Some of it was carelessness and some couldn't be helped."

After GQ the sailors did some topside cleaning and then went to the head to get themselves cleaned up. Don stood in line, took off his clothes, and GQ went off again. After GQ, Don finally got his shower and his clothes washed. There were over 800 ships involved in the Iwo Jima operation. "It's 2330 now and reveille sounds at 0410, so I might get four hours of sleep if those ___ so-and-sos don't come back around."

On February 20 Don wrote, "I am sick tonight; haven't had any rest or very much to eat for five days now." On the 28th the *Idaho* was still standing by at Iwo Jima for back-up or "call fire." The troops on Iwo Jima were still having a very tough time of it.

The *USS Idaho* left Iwo Jima on March 7 and headed for bombardment action at the island of Okinawa. "They are expecting a lot of action here. They had Navy brass all over the place here on the *Idaho:* seven captains, two admirals, and sky-control." Okinawa was hundreds of miles from either Tokyo or Formosa. The island was sixty-eight miles long and twenty-five miles wide. It had a garrison of 50,000 Japanese soldiers, between 20,000 and 25,000 civilian population, and six big air fields. There were more islands around the area that had Japanese airfields, from which they could launch flights against the Allied ships. The fleet could also be attacked from China, Japan, Formosa or other islands in the vicinity. The Allied attack force was in easy range of PT boats, submarines or anything else the Japanese had to throw at them. "We are sending out a decoy to try and bring the Jap fleet out. The new battleships will be behind us, instead of in front this time. So if the fleet comes out, they will attack us; the new ships will surround us and them, and we will be in the center, fighting them. The admiral aboard the *Idaho* will be in charge of the sea battle, if there is one...."

The plan was to take two small islands first, with the Allied ammunition ships hiding out, so the fleet wouldn't have to retreat 600 or 700 miles away to resupply with ammunition. "We bombard from the 25th of March to the 1st of April. We will land seven divisions of Army and Marines the first day. That's 140,000 men, five more divisions than at Iwo Jima." This first phase of the operation was expected to last four or five months. It would be the biggest operation the Navy had ever undertaken. "The fleet had two British battleships with them–[one was] the 5th Class *King George*; four big carriers, four cruisers, and four destroyers of the 57th Task Force." The *Idaho* was part of the 54th Task Force; included also was the *Tennessee,* the cruiser *Pensacola,* and two new DD class destroyers. There were more ships with the task force, but the foregoing ships led the others. On March 25 the *USS New Mexico* and *Nevada* went in and fired while the *Idaho* was refueling a destroyer. March 26 saw some more action– bombarding, as well as enemy air and submarine contacts. On the 27th the 5-inchers started firing and knocked one Japanese plane down and damaged another. The *Nevada* had an enemy plane crash-dive into turret number three. The *Idaho* had a submarine come to the surface nearby and then it rolled over–dead in the water.

On the 28th of March the Army took two smaller islands. From that base they could shoot their 150mm guns onto Okinawa, and the fleet could also get its ammunition from those islands. On the 29th and 30th there were more air attacks and the Navy flew over the towns, dropping pamphlets; then the bombardment restarted. "The place is awfully pretty; it's a shame to destroy property, some nice highways and some big cities, some pretty good-sized factories, too." While at anchorage and resupplying, the ships set guards on deck and all around the sides to ward off any Japanese suicide swimmers. At crucial times like this, the ships were on ten-minute notice to get underway.

April first was not only April Fool's Day, but also Easter Sunday and D-Day for Okinawa. The ships defended against air attacks of up to thirty planes at a time. An LST landing craft shot down one plane; the *Idaho* helped in shooting down two more. There were so many ships there; the sailors couldn't see the end of them. "We had a kamikaze come at us but shot him down 1,500 yards off our port bow. Another dropped a bomb–missed us by a 1,000 yards. The troops landed at 0830 this morning without opposition. The *West Virginia* was hit by a suicide plane this morning. ___, he just barely got over us…. [We have had] air attacks twice a day; [but currently] the ship [is] at *condition one-easy*."

In the ensuing days the ships guarded against air attacks. "When one task force quit firing on the island, then the next one took over. The enemy air attacks were wave after wave of suicide planes. We had a DD Class destroyer get hit, along with two transports and the heavy cruiser *Portland*. Six American Corsair fighters were shot down. Several ships will probably be scuttled. One was sunk along with both transports. I…could see ships all around burning and men jumping overboard." Allied Task Forces 54 and 58 shot down 151 enemy planes in about three and a half hours.

On the 8[th,] of April, Don witnessed a suicide plane hit a DD and another made the attempt, but just missed.

> "How they can and do get in so close before we can pick them up on our radar, I don't know; but they are on us before we know it. I just knew we were going to be hit, because here comes a plane in at us, coming right on in; we tried to hide under the gun turret. The 40mm hit the plane, and then our five-incher hit him and knocked him down. He hit the water about 100 feet from the ship and his gas tank landed on the quarterdeck–too damn close!"

That afternoon the task force got word that the Japanese fleet was out. The Allied ships steamed out to attack them.

> Task Force 58 was behind them pushing them into us. The *USS Idaho* was in command of any surface battle. The battleships *Idaho, Tennessee, New Mexico,*

Colorado, and *Maryland* were all lined up in battle formation–in a straight line. [We had] five heavy DDs off the *Idaho's* port bow, six heavy DDs off the port quarter, five heavy cruisers off the port bow and six heavy cruisers off the port quarter; similar numbers and kinds of [Allied] ships off the starboard side as well. Sure is pretty; now this is a Battle Fleet! We were heading north and anticipated to attack to the west, but we are two or three hundred miles from Japan.

Anticipating the coming battle, Don again turned to prayer for all those who would be involved in the conflict and finally all those families at home. On April 9 the planes from the U.S. fleet found the enemy ships and attacked. They sustained heavy casualties (lost numerous planes) but were very successful in inflicting damage on the Japanese fleet.

Today [April 12] was the day I knew was coming– six enemy planes coming straight for us. We shot five down and the sixth "suicided" us. It hit the blister about twenty-five feet from my battle station; although I am still in the turret. [There is] lots of armor around me; none too much to suit me. The plane parts flew all over the ship; pieces of the pilot [were found] all over the topside. It blasted a hole in the blister, blew rivets out, [made a] hole in the flag box, cut pipes in two, broke up all sorts of equipment and structure. Casualties included one man with two holes in his side– part of his little finger blown off–and two more sailors sustained scratches. We were mighty lucky! [There was] another air attack by bombers later in the evening. They dropped bombs and flares but [we] never got hit.... To our credit we have been involved in seven landings, nine planes shot down, and thirteen islands [bombarded].

In his diary Don recounted the death of President Franklin Roosevelt. Don lauded the President's dedication, perseverance and patriotism. "Our peace and welfare were in his hands. God bless President Truman and may God guide him and our people onward to victory." On April 20 the *Idaho* left Okinawa waters for Guam and headed into dry dock for repairs. They arrived there on the 27th of April. Don went ashore on the 30th. He had been aboard ship for ninety-four days. Meanwhile, the Navy was taking the biggest beating it had taken so far during WWII. The Japanese were diving into ships every day. Eight or nine battle ships had taken hits, about 150 tin cans, and so on. There were thousands of lives lost. "...I sure hate to go back up there."

The *Idaho* arrived back off Okinawa on the 21st of May prepared to help with more bombardment of the island. Don marveled at the number of vessels that had been hit, damaged and sunk. His ship continued duties around Okinawa until June 20. After eighty-two days of fighting, the Allies finally took Okinawa. The *Idaho* then went back into dry dock for repairs of "old hurts."

On the Fourth of July, Don wrote his sweetheart (apparently in response to another "Dear John" letter), telling her to "give my ring to my mother." On August 10 the crew was watching a movie, when searchlights went on all over the place–including the beach and all the anchored ships. Everyone started to run to battle stations, but soon found out the lights were celebrating in response to the news that the war was over. Star shells, fireworks and horns sounded; the band assembled and played "California Here We Come" and "Anchors Aweigh." The Japanese had accepted the Allied peace terms! On September 2, 1945 (V-J DAY), they signed the surrender terms aboard the *USS Missouri*.

Don documented that he was present and witnessed McArthur and Hirohito sign the peace agreement, and he later received a certificate of attendance. More particularly, he said he was somewhat disappointed that a battleship which saw little or no action in the war was chosen as the "signing vessel," instead of his ship, the *USS Idaho,* that participated in so many military actions– all in the Pacific Islands.

The *Idaho* left Tokyo Bay September 6, stopped at Okinawa and Pearl Harbor; and then sailed through the Panama Canal, arriving in Norfolk, Virginia, on October 16, 1945. Don was discharged on the East Coast, flown to Chicago, took a bus into town, and then hitchhiked back home to Texas. He eventually used his GI Bill benefits to buy a house.

USS Idaho during Battle Practice,
circa 1930

Darwin Dodds
Civilian, Morrison Knudsen
WWII
1941–1945
POW

The Japanese pounded the atoll day after day.

Wake Island is 2,500 miles to the west of Hawaii and is across the International Date Line. It is a tiny dot on the map in the middle of the Pacific Ocean and consists of three islands: Wake, Wilkes and Peale, which make up an atoll almost ten miles around. The highest point on the island is fourteen feet above sea level.

When the Japanese bombed Pearl Harbor in Hawaii on the morning of December 7, 1941, it was already December 8 on Wake Island. There were 450 marines, 68 Navy personnel, and 1,221 civilian workers stationed on the Island. They had been sent to construct an airfield and docking facilities for submarines, as well as support buildings and barracks, as part of the overall defensive perimeter of Naval air bases in the western Pacific. It was hoped that having these facilities in place would discourage the Japanese from thinking about expanding eastward. The island also supported a Pan Am Clipper operation. Forty-five Chamorro islanders worked for Pan Am.

The morning of December 8 on Wake Island, Darwin Dodds was one of the men who heard the news that the Japanese had attacked the U.S. Naval Fleet at Hawaii. He and his friends became very concerned about their own welfare. They didn't initially realize the extent of the attack at Pearl Harbor and thought that the U.S Navy would keep Wake Island secure. The Marine and Navy personnel understood the gravity of the situation and immediately began to take measures to make sure defenses were as ready as they could be. Civilian workers were told to go to their normal assignments and keep working, as this was considered the best way to disperse those men in case of attack.

* * *

Darwin was born in 1919 and had grown up in the small town of Meridian, Idaho, a few miles west of Boise. Meridian had a population of about 1,000 at that time and the main street was a dirt road. Its main activity was agricultural, and Darwin gathered magpie eggs after school. He received two cents per egg because the magpies were such a menace to the farmers. He often jumped over the fence near his house and went shooting quail. Darwin's father was president of the local bank and this afforded his family, consisting of Darwin, his mother and two older sisters, a comfortable life. In the 1930s, when the United States went off the gold standard and times got tougher, his father moved the family to Boise, where he took up new employment as a realtor. Darwin transferred to Boise High School for the last two years of his education. He ran track and lettered in that sport. When he graduated in 1937 at the age of eighteen, he took advantage of his deep sonorous voice and was hired as a radio announcer at KIDO, the only radio station in Boise at that time. He was paid $20 per week. This was a vocation he would pursue off and on for the next forty years.

In early 1941, he heard about the opportunities with Morrison Knudson, a large local construction company that was working on several projects for the Navy in the Pacific. The money being offered sounded fantastic; but workers had to sign a contract for at least nine months and had no control over where they would be sent. Through his father's friendship with Harry Morrison, one of the principals of the company, Darwin was able to get hired as one of the first group of forty-six men who were sent from Boise. He would be paid the princely sum of $460 per month, with the possibility of a bonus at six months, if work was completed ahead of schedule. By this time, Darwin was twenty-one years old and was married. He looked upon the contract with Morrison Knudson as a way to get ahead and save enough money to really do something with his life. There were also opportunities, on future assignments, when competent workers could move up within the company.

On April 13, 1941, Darwin and forty-five other men from Boise traveled to Alameda in northern California where they boarded a ship, the *USS Horton*, and with several other groups of men, sailed to Honolulu, Hawaii. After a couple of days in Honolulu, they boarded another ship, the *Regulus*, which then took them west to Wake Island. His first glimpse of Wake revealed that it was very flat, lonely, covered with seabirds, and seemed to be at the end of the earth. The men got right to work, moving soil and coral. One of the first tasks was to build a ramp for submarines so that they could be pulled out of the water enough to be serviced. Work was difficult and required long hours on the job. Once cement was poured for the ramp, the work was continuous and had to be completed before the cement hardened. Darwin's job was that of head timekeeper. He kept track of all the men's hours spent on the job, so that the government could be billed for the work and the men could be paid. The Morrison Knudson Company did their best to make the workers happy. They constructed a soda fountain, showed movies and provided the best food that they could. A steady stream of supply ships brought building materials and supplies to the island. Several months before Darwin arrived, a runway construction had been underway on one of the longer parts of the island. It was built to accommodate large four-engine aircraft. The runway was completed after eighteen months of work, and soon after that, twelve F4F Wildcat fighters flew in and began flying operations. Several buildings were constructed, along with barracks and bachelor officer quarters.

Upon hearing what had happened at Pearl Harbor, the Marine and Naval personnel quickly set about shoring up their gun emplacements, distributing ammunition and supplies, and doing whatever they could to provide protection to their most exposed positions. The civilians helped in this effort; but many were told it would be better if they dispersed to some of their job sites, so they would be less vulnerable. Some of the food and critical supplies were buried in order to better protect them. Major Devereux, the Marine commander, and Winfield Cunningham, base commander, showed good leadership in readying the island for the coming conflict.

Later that morning, the first sign of trouble came when thirty-six planes were spotted, approaching from the north. One of the men remarked that it looked like the airplanes were dropping their wheels off, until they realized they were actually seeing falling bombs, and then they witnessed the explosions on the ground as the planes flew overhead. It was then that they were able to see the large orange roundels of the Japanese Air Force on the planes. These planes were mainly bombers and had taken off from Roi-Namur in the Marshall Islands and flown to Wake in a coordinated attack. They were joined by several other planes that had taken off from several approaching Japanese aircraft carriers.

The Japanese pounded the atoll day after day. Before each attack, a dwindling number of American Wildcat fighters rose to meet them. At 3 a.m. on December 11, a Japanese invasion task force, commanded by Rear Admiral Sadamichi Kajioka and consisting of a light cruiser, six destroyers, two troop carriers and two armed merchantmen, confidently approached Wake's beaches. Marine gunners let the enemy ships close to within 4,500 yards before their 5-inch guns opened fire. Their patience was rewarded with the sinking of one Japanese destroyer and damaging the cruiser and three additional destroyers. Admiral Kajioka withdrew, now knowing that Wake would not be taken without a fight. This retreat was the first major defeat of the war for the Japanese and was a huge embarrassment to them.

By the 21st of December, the last of the Wildcats had been destroyed in dogfights over the atoll. With nothing left to fly, the Marine aviators were assigned duty as riflemen. Japanese airplanes now flew over the island at will, pounding American positions in preparation for a renewed attempt to seize the atoll.

On the morning of the 23rd of December the Japanese again attempted to invade the island. They came ashore in rubber boats at several locations. In all, eighty-two ships surrounded Wake. Seventy of the defenders were killed, about half of them civilians. And even though Major Devereux and his men displayed great courage, they were eventually overwhelmed, and word went out to surrender in order to save as many lives as possible. Darwin and a group of several others walked out to surrender. As they approached a Japanese soldier, it looked like he was waving them away, so they turned around and began to walk back. It was then they realized they had misunderstood his hand-signal, because he began to fire over their heads. All the prisoners were rounded up and their hands were tied behind their backs with telephone wire. The prisoners were then jammed into two suffocating concrete ammunition bunkers. Later they were herded to the airstrip and made to sit, naked, on the blistering hot concrete. When the Japanese set up machine guns nearby, most of the prisoners expected to be executed. That night, bone-chilling winds replaced the heat. The prisoners sat there, still waiting for food, water and medical treatment. The men remained sitting on the airstrip for two days, until finally they were given food—much of it spoiled by the heat. The water was contaminated from being placed in unclean gasoline cans. The prisoners were eventually herded into a barbed wire compound where they were forced to shelter and sleep under the barracks.

The Japanese had paid a heavy price for their victory. The fight for Wake Island had cost them the sinking of two destroyers and one submarine, seven additional ships damaged, twenty-one aircraft shot down and almost 1,000 of their men killed. On the 10th of January, 750 American prisoners were put on a Japanese ship, the *Nitta Maru*. They were herded below deck, where they languished in squalid, inhumane conditions while they sailed to Wusong, China. They received very little food and water and had to sleep, with just one blanket each, on the metal floor of the hold. As many as fifty men died on this voyage due to the conditions and cruel treatment by the Japanese. In January, upon their arrival, the men had to kneel outside in the freezing cold in a tub of disinfectant. They were put to work on what was to be a rifle range made to look like Mt. Fuji. This involved using baskets to move a mountain of dirt and rocks, all by hand. Five hundred men worked on this project for a year.

Through humor, the men did their best to keep their morale up. They called the Japanese colonel in charge of the camp "Mickey Mouse," since he was very short and strutted about. They told one of the Japanese guards he resembled a movie star. He really warmed to this idea, until he found out who "Mortimer Snerd" was. The men were issued three Chinese cigarettes a day. One of the guards had a shaving mirror and he would, for two cigarettes, let each man look at himself for thirty seconds. The men had not seen their own reflections for over six months. At this time, each man was allowed to write a letter home. The first letters they received from home came after about a year. Darwin recalled the Japanese would often hold an unopened letter up and burn it in front of the intended recipient.

In June of 1944, Darwin was sent to a new camp in greater Tokyo. Due to his past experience, he was selected to be an announcer on the radio. Each day he was transported into central Tokyo where he would make announcements to and for war prisoners on JOA shortwave radio. A typical announcement would consist of one prisoner talking to others, announcing what camp he was in and his state of well-being. The Japanese reasoned that this was a good propaganda tool.

When Darwin was being taken into central Tokyo, he often saw mass raids of B-29s dropping fire bombs. It got very scary when the tactic of dropping these bombs from high altitude was changed to dropping them at low altitude. The raids were very accurate, and Darwin feared he might be an unlucky victim. When the atomic bomb was dropped August 6, 1945, his captors interrogated him about this devastating weapon. He obviously knew nothing about it; but he thought it might be similar to the 2000-pound blockbusters that had been dropped in Europe. Soon afterward, his captors started to treat all the prisoners better. They brought them care packages that had been dropped by the American planes. If a package fell outside the prison camp enclosure, the Japanese still brought them to the Americans. Eventually the guards ran away. Darwin and his fellow prisoners felt it would be safer to remain within the camp until they were rescued. They didn't realize that the war had ended until they were finally rescued two weeks later on the 23rd of August. Darwin now weighed ninety-five pounds and had yellow jaundice. He was taken to a hospital ship, where he was only able to consume fruit juice. He was then transported to a hospital camp in Manila.

Finally, Darwin was able to wire home to his parents, telling them he was all right and would be coming home. They wired back that they would come to Seattle to meet him; but his wife would not be coming with them. She had heard that Darwin had been beheaded by the Japanese and so had divorced him and remarried. She had also sold off all his belongings, including his car, clothes, and even his shoes. Darwin arrived home in October 1945. He was twenty-six years old. He began to pick up the pieces of his life and was able to get back into radio announcing.

He and a partner did the 6 a.m. KIDO morning show, which became very popular. So popular in fact, that at one time it was higher rated than the Arthur Godfrey show. In Boise, for three days beginning on December 6, a big reunion of Wake Island survivors was celebrated by 300 people. It was quite a party!

The Wake civilians were not treated like military personnel when it came to receiving veteran benefits. They felt cheated, since they had fought side by side with the military and many of them were killed. In 1978 Darwin wrote to Jimmy Carter asking for help in recognizing the Morrison Knudsen workers and requesting the same benefits that the military veterans received. He soon got several calls from Washington, D.C. One was from a Captain Pruitt, who thought that the time might be right to get DD-214 forms issued to Wake civilian veterans. She asked that Darwin get the Morrison Knudsen civilians organized to write "buddy letters" to each other, describing how they had each helped to defend Wake Island from the Japanese. The DD-214s were issued by Christmas, entitling each MK survivor to full military benefits.

Darwin remarried in 1946 and three children were born from that long and happy marriage. He returned to Wake Island twice, and the experience was better than he had hoped. He was able to push aside the memories of being a prisoner and remember the earlier good times on Wake; when he was treated well, paid well and life was an adventure. He made a long-playing record called "The Wake Island Story" and was able to get the voice of Major Devereux, the Marine commander, on the record.

Aerial Photo of Wake Island

Wake Island Civilian Contractors
Marching in Captivity

John O. (J.O.) Young, Jr.
Civilian, Morrison Knudsen
WWII
1941–1945
POW

*"When Old Glory doesn't fly,
there is no freedom!"*

J.O. was born in Nampa,
Idaho, in the old Mercy Hospital
on 16th Avenue South. He grew up primarily in Idaho, although
the family sometimes lived all over the western states, as his father
was a superintendent at Morrison Knudsen for thirty years. He
graduated from Nampa High in 1940, and it was in high school
that he met his future wife, Pearl.

At age nineteen, J.O. worked in a Nampa grocery store earning
$15.00 per week. But in 1941, as a journeyman carpenter, he left
the store and went to work for his dad at Morrison Knudsen. He
worked on building projects at Gowen Field in Boise, and began
earning top carpenter wages of $1.12 and ½ cents per hour.

J.O. was one of about 1,200 working on Wake Island in 1941
when WWII started. At that time there were only 450 Marines on
the island. Two days before the war began, J.O. was given the
assignment of truck driver and helped unload a ship bringing
supplies to the island. At 6 a.m. that morning the workers received
word that Pearl Harbor had been bombed. They didn't know what
was happening. At noon, J.O. was at the canteen and heard planes
coming in. Everyone assumed they were U.S. planes, and they all
ran out onto the grounds to see them. All of a sudden the airstrip
went up in flames, because the Japanese were bombing the airport.
As the planes got closer, those on the ground could hear a "tut-tut-
tut," and realized they were being machine gunned. J.O. made a

100-yard dash to the lagoon and lay down behind some coral. The planes bombed the Pan American hotel, destroying it.

After the bombing subsided, a group of the men gathered inside a large concrete tube to discuss what they should do. A couple of hours later they walked down to the landing where a China clipper had been hit. The pilot asked if they wanted to get aboard and get out of there, but the men replied, "No. Uncle Sam will be here to get us soon, and we will be fine." J.O. decided not to get on board the plane because his uncle, Forest Reed, was on the island with him, and he had not seen him since the bombing and wanted to find him. None of the men got on the plane to evacuate. Instead, they helped the Marines load an ammunition truck and then went over to Wilkes Island, where they stayed and fought alongside the Marines for the sixteen days that the Japanese bombarded the islands. On the third day, the 11th of December, the Japanese came in to take over the island. The Marines had 5-inch guns and a set of antiaircraft guns on each island. J.O. started off helping on the 5-inch guns, but the second day a bomb hit close by and knocked the sights off the gun. One of the Japanese ships came in and got within 4,500 yards of the island. The Americans fired on the ship with 5-inch and 3-inch guns. It sank in four and a half minutes. They weren't sure which gun had hit it, but they had won the first battle of the war on the island. In all, two or three Japanese ships were sunk that day.

The Japanese continued bombing fourteen out of sixteen days– until the 23rd of December. They landed on the island in the early morning around 4 a.m. and shot out the two search lights, making everything pitch black. Then seventy-two Japanese soldiers landed on Wilkes Island. There were about sixteen Marines there, eight of whom were killed. However, seventy of the Japanese were killed. The Americans hid under a drag line and waited until dawn, when they searched for some rifles in order to continue fighting as long as possible. J.O. secured a rifle and gun belt, and his group headed down the channel that separated the two islands. There they encountered a group of Japanese, along with one of the U.S. majors, who was carrying a white flag. J.O. quickly disposed of his rifle and the shirt with corporal strips he was wearing. If the Japanese had known that the civilians had been guerrilla fighters they would have shot them immediately. The Americans were marched to the airport and spent all day there, lined up with machine guns pointed at them. The men assumed they would be shot and discussed among themselves whether they should try to rush the Japanese, or just lay down. J.O. recalled vividly their situation. "I suppose there was some fear; but the thing was, you were there and there was nothing you could do, so you just had to try and figure out what the best thing *was* to do!" Some of the enemy officers were walking around, polishing their swords, and the Americans figured that might be part of the show, but then realized the Japanese were just wiping the salt water off of their swords. They spent the day there and then later that night the Japanese crammed 1,000 of them into a hangar that would typically hold 500, causing some of the men in the back to pass out due to lack of air. Being so tightly wedged in, all the men could do was stand there throughout the night. The next day they were herded back to the barracks.

On the morning of the attack, J.O. remembered seeing the flag with the stars and stripes flying over the compound. Not long after, a white bed sheet was hoisted, and by the end of the day, a Japanese flag with the rising sun took its place. With tears in his eyes, J.O. described being marched past the officers' barracks and seeing the American flag wadded up in a fish net, being used as a door stop. He said the thing he realized was that, "When Old Glory doesn't fly, there is no freedom!"

The captives were put to work as Japanese slave laborers, unloading sacks of rice. On the 12th of January they were forced onto a ship which sailed toward China. The further north they went, the colder it got. The men were each given a blanket, so four of them decided if they huddled together they could use all four blankets to cover themselves to keep warm. The Japanese guards screamed at them, and they had to break apart and spent a miserably cold night. In the morning and also at night they received a little bowl, usually containing a tablespoon of barley and a daikon (a type of radish), along with one cup of water per day. For fourteen days they never left the hold of the ship, using five-gallon cans for latrines, which were emptied once per day. It was a deplorable situation. They stopped in Yokahama for two days, still held captive in the hold. While there, one of the Japanese commanders forced five Marines up on deck, where they were beheaded. Four days later they arrived in China and were marched to Wusong, the first of John's prisoner of war camps. There were thirty-six men to a section. J.O. was in barracks 3, section 6. The prisoners were each issued an eighteen-inch mattress, six feet long, with a sawdust pillow and a blanket. There was no fire and it was miserably cold. For their food ration they were each served one bowl of rice in the morning and one at night.

J.O. worked as a camp carpenter for the first six months, building coffins and repairing barracks. Most of the other prisoners were building "Mt. Fujiyama," as they named it, piling dirt twenty-one meters high. (It was destined to become a rifle range.) It was very excruciating work, and the prisoners did what they could to be sent to the hospital for some sort of rest. A group of them decided they would get circumcised, because they could then spend fifteen days in the hospital (which they painfully regretted later). J.O. recalled that the Japanese doctor was a wonderful, humane man, who did everything he could for the prisoners. In 1942 J.O. had an appendicitis attack. The camp had no anesthetics; so while he was awake, they shot a local around his abdomen and cut him open to remove the appendix. He recovered okay–thankful for fairly good hospital conditions.   Additional particulars about POW life, J.O. recounted in his own words.

There was very little humor, but we got along. I used to whistle and it bothered the Japanese. Some humor helped us to survive. We finally got some Red Cross boxes with a can of powdered milk, two cigarettes, cocoa, butter, sardines, etc. I traded three cigarettes for three fish heads, which turned out to be rotten. I was so sick I thought I was going to die–but I didn't!

Most of the Japanese guards were okay to be around, but as they gained authority it was not good. I was the first one to be beat up when we got to Shanghai. The only fortunate thing was they didn't use a fist head on, but hit from the side on the head, and it was not as bad as a blow that would have been head on. Someone was always getting beat for something. If one man did something, everyone was guilty. It wasn't the best of years. We were living on 600-800 calories per day. One of the guys from Homedale starved to death because he traded all of his rice for cigarettes. His brother came home and committed suicide not too long after we all came home. While there, we had a hard time being optimistic all the time, and didn't want to be pessimistic, so I coined the term "hopetimistic." We hoped that good things were going to happen.

I was working in a steel mill, where we were lined up ready to go to work, when they told us "no work"– and the war was over. The guards quit beating us and pretty quickly they were all gone. Some Navy planes flew over and wiggled their wings. Several days later they came over and dropped duffle bags with supplies and clothes. On the way home we landed in Guam and nobody told us what to eat, so we ate so much rich food in large amounts that we were all sick. I gained sixty pounds in thirty days on the way home–eating so much. We landed in San Francisco in October of 1945. Pearl and my mother came to greet me. We [had planned] to be married in October of 1941, but [before we could get married] I was hired by Morrison Knudsen and was [instead] sent to Wake Island in September 1941.

The greatest thing that ever happened was dropping those two bombs on Japan. It saved millions of lives!

When we got home, I knew I was coming home to marry my girl. I got busy and went to work and we began our family of nine children. I really didn't think about the war or hating the Japanese. A lot of the guys still to this day can't stand the Japanese. I never even thought about them. I guess it just depends on what attitude you choose to have.

Thirty-six years after WWII, the U.S. Congress granted the status of Navy E4 to the civilians who fought with the U.S. Marines on Wake Island.

J.O. Young's POW ID Card

Robert Hedeman
U.S. Air Force
Korea
1949-1952

*The body of a Chinese soldier
was at the bottom of the creek!*

Bob was born in Chicago,
Illinois, and raised in that area. In
1949, when he was only fifteen years old, he convinced his parents
to sign for him so he could quit high school and join the Air Force.
He was very excited because he had never been away from home
before. He was sent to North Carolina for training, where he
volunteered to become part of a crash team; this is what would be
considered a firefighter position in the civilian world. In 1950 as
the Korean War was heating up, his training was cut short and his
unit was sent to Korea.

Bob did not enjoy the boat trip to Korea. In the fourteen days
the troops were at sea, they sailed through three typhoons, making
for an extremely unpleasant journey. They were supposed to go to
Seoul, South Korea, but when they got there, the Chinese had
entered the war and had overrun that city. His unit was instead
sent to an airbase in Japan. He stated that it was an airbase in
name only, since there were few structures or buildings there. His
unit had to construct their own fire station, which they did with the
help of Japanese laborers. To augment his crew, some of these
Japanese men were also trained to be firefighters. So they would
have a short response time to any emergencies, their fire station
was set up next to the airstrip. The base was primarily for cargo
planes since the runway was too short for jets. However, the
airbase was a stopover for airplanes that were shot up, low on gas
or had other problems. Those planes could land there instead of
trying to fly to their home bases, which were farther away. Bob

remembered that one of the things he hated about that airbase was typhoons seemed to hit and damage it every few weeks.

Bob related the following story: He had a brother-in-law that was in the Army and stationed in Korea close to the thirty-eighth parallel. Bob had some time off coming, so he got the idea that he would go visit his brother-in-law. He did not have permission, nor any of the forms needed to leave his station, but he decided to go anyway. He knew a pilot who flew one of the C-46s that was headed for Korea, and the pilot let Bob stow away on his plane. Once he got to the airbase and got off the plane, Bob started walking down a road. A while later, a Korean truck came by and stopped. The driver couldn't believe an American airman was out in the middle of nowhere, so he gave him a ride. Bob sat up on top of the truck and soon he fell asleep. Later the driver woke him and told him that he had to get off because the driver was headed in a different direction. Bob started walking back down the road, hoping another truck would come by, but there was virtually no traffic. It was getting dark, so when he saw a pile of rocks, he thought he would lie down by them and rest. Behind the rocks was a small stream, and he spied something shiny in the water. When he looked closer, he discovered it was a Chinese rifle. Then he got an even bigger surprise, when he realized that the body of a dead Chinese soldier was also at the bottom of the creek!

Bob returned to the road, where eventually he was picked up by another Korean truck driver. This time Bob was taken directly to his brother-in-law's camp. There he located his relative, who was completely shocked to see him, but even more shocked when Bob told him the story of how he got there. He stayed overnight, and his brother-in-law was able to arrange transportation to get Bob back to the nearest airbase. After reaching the airbase, he tried to hitch a ride with some of the pilots, but none of them would accommodate him, saying that new regulations forbade them to take on any passengers.

Not knowing what to do next, Bob decided to contact a chaplain on the airbase to see if he would be able to help him. He related his story to the Catholic priest, who found it difficult to believe him. However, the priest made a long-distant call to his captain, who was also amazed that Bob was AWOL in Korea. The chaplain was able to arrange transportation back to his airbase in Japan. Bob said, "They [his supervisors] were waiting for me." However, he stated that although he wasn't severely disciplined over the incident, everyone was amazed at what he had done.

After the Korean Armistice Agreement was signed, the Air Force rotated his unit back to the United States. He again had to sail back over the ocean in a ship. Luckily this time, they didn't experience any typhoons. Once he was back in the United States the Air Force encouraged him to re-enlist, but he had decided against it and returned home to Chicago. He had not been home once during the two and a half years he was in the service, and he was very excited to see all his friends and relatives. Bob tried to get a job as a fireman, but since he was not yet twenty-one years old (which was a requirement at the time), he decided to become a tool maker. He stayed in that profession for many years, until he retired.

Arnold Bahr
U.S. Army
Korea
1952–1954

*One of the biggest needs was
replacing uniforms after they
wore out.*

Arnold was born in Gooding, Idaho, where he was raised and graduated from high school in 1949. After high school he went to the University of Idaho, where he studied engineering. In September 1952 he was called up to the Army and reported to Fort Lewis, Washington. From there he took a train to Fort Ord, California, where he completed six weeks of basic training. He stayed on at Fort Ord for four weeks of additional training, operating diesel equipment. After that training, his next assignment was to take a troop ship to Japan.

On the trip over, the ship was hit by a typhoon and for twenty-four hours all they could do was stay in their bunks and hold on tight. In his unit, a soldier who had suicidal tendencies jumped overboard. The ship stopped and the crew spent two or three hours trying to locate him, but with no luck. Another incident he remembered happened when he was going in to eat at the Navy mess hall. Each soldier had to have a meal card, but when Arnold reached into his pocket, he found out that someone had slit it and taken not only his wallet, but his money and the meal card as well.

The ship took Arnold to Camp Drake in Japan, where he stayed for a short time before being transferred to Korea. His first assignment in Korea was at Pusan, where he arrived in February 1953. That first night they had no heat in their hut, and they had to wear all the clothes they owned just to get through the bitter cold.

In Korea Arnold was assigned to the Signal Corps, and his first job was riding a train between Pusan and Seoul delivering orders. The trip took two days, and he had to do it two times a week. After doing this job for about a month, he was assigned to be the company clerk. One of his duties was to type up commendations for different awards and medals that were awarded to soldiers in Korea. He found this task very interesting–reading the stories of what the soldiers had done to merit their awards.

By this time Arnold had been promoted to sergeant and had been transferred to a communications company in Seoul, Korea. His unit had many Korean laborers that worked in their camp, and in 1953 when the Armistice was signed, they threw a huge party for all of them. While stationed at this camp one of the biggest needs was replacing uniforms after they wore out. A Marine base was nearby and the Marines always wanted liquor. Arnold's unit had access to liquor, so they traded liquor for Marine fatigues. They wore the fatigues on duty, until one day they had an inspection; and when the captain realized what they were wearing, he saw to it that they got new army fatigues.

Arnold and the men in his unit adopted two Korean youngsters (a boy and a girl) and they made efforts to raise them and get them in school. The girl, whom they called Joy, had "unbelievably" good grades. One day a couple of the men decided to talk with her teacher. After locating the teacher, they realized she was very nervous. They found out that Joy had told her teacher that if she didn't get good grades the GIs would be very upset with the teacher. So feeling intimidated, the teacher had given Joy inflated scores. As they were getting ready to leave Korea, Arnold heard that the company commander was making efforts to adopt Joy; however, he never found out what happened to her after he left. One day at the camp, a Korean man showed up to find his son. It turned out, he was the young boy who the soldiers thought was an orphan. Actually, his parents were living in the immediate vicinity of the camp the entire time the soldiers were doing their best to care for the boy.

After the Armistice, the men were given some time off to go to Japan. On the way back to their base, an engine in the plane they were flying in caught on fire. Fortunately they had an experienced pilot, and he did a great job of landing the plane without anyone getting hurt.

In 1954 Arnold was sent to Fort Lewis, Washington, where he was mustered out of the Army. He returned to Gooding, Idaho, where he married his fiancée and used the GI Bill to complete his engineering degree at the University of Idaho. He worked as an engineer for Idaho Power for thirty-five years before retiring. He stayed in touch with a few of his Army buddies and joined the VFW. While he said that he had no use for his time spent in Korea, he did have good memories of his time in the military.

Korean War Memorial – Washington, D.C.

Korean War Images - *National Archives/Wikipedia*

Clockwise from top: U.S. Marines move through Chinese lines; U.N. landing at Incheon harbor; Korean refugees in front of an American M26 Pershing tank; U.S. Marines landing at Incheon; U.S. F-86 Sabre fighter aircraft.

271

Freddie Callison
U.S. Marine Corps
Korea
1952-1954

"Sergeant, get that man some food!"

Freddie was born in 1934 in Oklahoma. He remembered how hard his parents worked. His mother often spent fourteen-hour days working in the local cotton mill, and his dad was a local barber. They later moved to California, and Freddie remembered listening to the radio, when President Roosevelt talked about the declared war on Japan.

Many families during the Second World War experienced the heartache of losing more than one son. The most well-known example was the five Sullivan brothers who joined the Navy and were all killed when the Japanese attacked their ship. The Callison family experienced a similar tragedy.

Before WWII, two of Freddie's brothers were already in the Marines, and at some point all five of the brothers, including Freddie, made a pact that they would join the Marines; and none of them would get married until they were at least twenty-one years of age. Billy Callison was the first to see combat, serving at Guadalcanal and Tarawa, where he was wounded. He was later killed when fighting on the island of Saipan. Freddie's brother Tommy was fighting on the island of Bougainville when he got malaria and was sent back to recover in the States. When the Korean War started Tommy was sent over there. He took part in the invasion of Inchon and was killed during that battle.

Freddie's brother Bobby was also in the Marines and was stationed at Camp Pendleton in California. One day he was training new recruits, when one of the men accidentally pulled the pin on a hand grenade. The recruit froze and in his panic refused to throw the grenade. Bobby grabbed it from him and threw it. But it exploded nearby, and killed Bobby. His heroic actions saved the lives of other Marines who were part of the training exercise.

Bobby's body was returned to Idaho for his funeral. The family set up a private and a public ceremony. A two-star general contacted the family and asked permission to be at the private ceremony. When he arrived he had several other officers with him and, as they visited with the family, a major asked Freddie if he was bitter about losing his brothers. The general become very upset with the major and explained that this was a Marine family and his comments were inappropriate.

Freddie joined the Marines in 1952 and was trained at Camp Pendleton in California. He recalled that during his eleven weeks of basic training, one of the drill instructors was extremely hard on him. When they were almost done with training he decided to discuss his ill treatment with the drill instructor. During his interview, Freddie became very emotional when he recalled this conversation, because the drill instructor told him he knew his two brothers that were killed in combat, and he was being hard on Freddie in hopes that the same fate wouldn't happen to him. After completing his basic training, the Marines would not assign him to Korea because of the death of his brothers; however, he continued to request a Korean deployment, until the Marine Corps finally complied, and he was sent to Korea and assigned to a headquarters company.

Freddie's job was driving for various Marine officers. This assignment not only allowed him to see a lot of the country, where he had many experiences he never forgot; but he also garnered first-hand knowledge of the stories about the abuses American prisoners of war suffered at the hands of the Chinese and North Koreans. He was also present in the city where dignitaries held peace talks for the Korean War. One experience Freddie remembered was as a driver for a lieutenant colonel who was an artillery expert. He drove him all over the countryside, where the colonel helped both the Marines and the Army set up firing ranges, as well as showing them where to strategically place the artillery.

Another time Freddie remembered driving an officer to an Army camp. As he was waiting for the officer to return, he noticed a chow line; and since he hadn't eaten for quite awhile, he decided to get in line. An Army sergeant noticed him and told him that it was an officer line only and that he couldn't go through it. Freddie asked if he could at least have a cup of coffee, and was told no. About that time a voice from inside a nearby tent called out, "Sergeant, get that man some food!" After he finished eating, he was ordered back to the tent; and to his amazement, the person inside was the same man that had ordered the sergeant to let him eat–Maxwell Taylor, the four-star general in charge of the Allied forces in the Korean War.

After the Korean Armistice was signed, Freddie returned to the United States and used the GI Bill to get a college degree and eventually spent twenty years as a correctional officer in California. One of his later accomplishments was to assemble a display table that exhibited all the medals that he and his brothers received during their service in the Marine Corps. In 1958 his youngest brother became the fifth Marine in the family.

Arnold Larry DeHaan
U.S. Air Force
1954–1958

*The ceiling of the Quonset hut
was black with tarantulas*!

Larry was born in August of
1936 in Chicago, Illinois, where
his dad worked for Otis Elevator Company. When Larry was an
infant the family moved to Southern California. They lived in
Santa Monica and then Pasadena, before settling in Monrovia,
California. Larry had two sisters; one four years older and one
younger. His dad worked for Aerojet General Corporation as an
engineer, and his mom had worked briefly as a telephone operator
during World War II. His dad had been an air raid warden during
the war, and Larry remembered hearing some of Roosevelt's
speeches on the radio. He was about ten years old when the war
ended, and he remembered that they could begin to get things that
they hadn't been able to get for years, such as certain food
products, tires and gasoline.

Larry went to high school in Monrovia. He was singing in
clubs at the time and playing ball, and he loved the social aspect of
school. He said it was a nonstop great time, just like the "Happy
Days" TV series. He graduated in 1954 and was accepted to
UCLA. He got his locker assignment on campus and his draft
notice in the mail. The draft meant he would be inducted into the
Army, unless he enlisted in another branch of the military within
thirty days. Eighteen good friends from high school, including
Larry, enlisted in the Air Force and went through basic training
together at Lackland Air Force Base in San Antonio, Texas.
Larry's mom wasn't thrilled that he was in the military, but his dad
was proud. Larry and his friends were all in for four years and
there was no choice in their assignments. The young men were

tested and, based upon aptitude, were each given an assignment. Larry hated math, but ended up in electronics–specifically aviation communications. They finished up their sixteen weeks in basic training. Larry's memory of boot camp in San Antonio was that of "desert, rattlesnakes, and mud!"

After completing basic training, Larry and his friends went to Keesler AFB in Biloxi, Mississippi, for electronics fundamentals training. They were there about ten months and graduated in April of 1955. Their next class was airborne electronics, and they graduated from there in July of 1955. Larry graduated top of his class and said it surprised everyone, including himself. They were trained on everything that was currently being used in the B-29s and the B-47s. The B-29 Superfortress was a four-engine, propeller-driven, heavy bomber, flown primarily by the U.S. toward the end of World War II and during the Korean War. The B-47 Stratojet was a long-range, six-engine, jet-powered bomber that flew at high subsonic speeds and high altitudes.

Larry's next assignment was Mountain Home AFB in Idaho, where he spent a little over three years. Mountain Home was the home of the Strategic Air Command's 9th Bombardment Wing. It was all B-29s when he first arrived, but the base was in the middle of phasing them out and only about half of the fleet remained. By the time he had been at the base for about eight months, the B-29s were all gone. Mountain Home was strictly a "bomb wing" at that time, and initially the B-47s were all they had. They ended up with about forty of them and within about six months they started getting C-97 Stratofreighters and KC-97s, used to refuel the B-47s. Larry and the other men on the airborne electronics team were passengers on the aircraft, and they resolved equipment problems. The men were transported back and forth to work on the C-97s and went wherever the B-47s went. The first place Larry was stationed was Guam, which was a ninety-day temporary duty station. From Guam they flew back and forth to Yokota Air Force Base in Japan.

They took the C-97s to Tokyo for maneuvers and training. It was mostly pilot training, but there was some troop training with the C-97s.

Larry's group was in Guam just nine years after World War II. He thought Guam was pretty much cleaned up after the war, but there were still areas of town where they had to use the buddy system, and they never traveled alone. The people of Guam were very friendly and even invited soldiers to their homes for dinner. Larry didn't like the climate in Guam because it was hot and humid, and he remembered a shower proved almost useless. He also remembered the two typhoons he lived through and the terrible food. The only place he found acceptable food was at the Naval hospital on Guam, where he spent a little time recovering from an eye injury.

The crews also went to Wake Island to deliver merchandise, such as motor scooters and hospital supplies for military people stationed there. At Wake Island they would offload, fuel up, and then head over to Japan. Larry saw lots of sunken barges, landing craft and emplacements off the coast of Wake Island; which gave it a very historic feeling, almost as if it were still wartime. He went there at least six times to drop off supplies.

When flying from Guam to Tokyo, the route took the aircraft over Iwo Jima. On one flight from Guam, they took off about 7 p.m., and about three hours out they lost an engine. There were eighty-nine men on board. In addition to the troops, there were B-47 engines, as well as refueling equipment. About another hundred miles along their route they lost another engine. Larry said it got pretty quiet on that airplane. Then they lost some more electrical equipment, and there wasn't a sound on that aircraft other than what was heard from the two remaining engines. Less than a hundred miles out from Iwo Jima, they lost a third engine. In the distance they could see the beacon on Mt. Suribachi. They dumped their cargo–two B-47 engines and all the equipment they could get rid of–until the only thing left were the crew members. When they finally came up on the beacon, Larry estimated that they were no more than 500 feet off of the water. They had no electronics for landing the plane, and no one was expecting them. They "sort of" landed on the runway, and fortunately there were enough runway lights on so the pilots could see the pathway. They landed with the wing scraping the ground all of the way to the stop. According to the captain, the thing that helped them land successfully was that the VHF antenna on the belly of the aircraft dug into the runway and helped guide the craft on a straight path. When they landed, it was about 3 a.m. on Iwo Jima.

Larry said there were no permanent buildings on base, just Quonset huts on the beach, six in a row. They each picked up a mattress and a blanket and sought out one of the Quonset huts. It was obvious that there hadn't been anyone in them for years. One of Larry's buddies put his mattress down right across from him. Larry saw his friend's eyes open very wide. He asked him what he was looking at and his friend, as he pointed at the ceiling, told him to look up. The entire ceiling of the Quonset hut was black with tarantulas. Everyone gaped at them, and in their skivvies, ran out into the stormy night. The only other place available to them was the base chapel, and that is where they all stayed for three days. Larry recalled that the best part of that experience was the chaplain was a terrific guy, and he had actual footage of all the battles of Iwo Jima. For three days they had the privilege of going around to all of the battle sites. They first watched the footage of the battle and then visited the actual sites. They were told that at the time they were there, some Japanese soldiers were probably still living in caves on the island.

The U.S. military maintained a very small staff on Iwo Jima. It was a ninety-day rotation off of the island. Scheduled flights delivered supplies. Once their aircraft was repaired they went on to Japan. Larry said that seeing the tarantulas was worse than losing the three engines on the plane.

Most of the flights to Japan were into Yokota, but some landed at Misawa in Northern Japan. Larry had ninety-day TDYs (temporary duty assignments) at both bases and said the Japanese people were very caring and kind to them and invited them into their homes.

Larry's crew also made some flights into Okinawa. Mostly they delivered lots of aircraft parts, engines, radar and radio equipment. Occasionally they had to fly on the B-47s so they could work on equipment problems that couldn't be resolved on the ground. The B-47 crew consisted of a pilot, copilot and bomb navigator. There was a "fourth man" position, which Larry occupied more than once. It was on the cold iron steps in the back of the B-47. While they were in flight to Grandjean, Seattle and Anchorage he had to crawl through the tunnel that housed the electrical components so he could assess problems and repair them. The only way out for him was to crawl out backwards.

After his four years were up, the military asked Larry to re-enlist, but he declined. He said that he never regretted a day of his military career and that he met some very nice people. The most perplexing time of his military experience was when he and his friends were in Biloxi, Mississippi, for training. Of the eighteen young men from Southern California that he had enlisted with, four were African American. He spoke of their first trip into town together. They ordered a cab, but when it arrived, his black friends were not allowed in the cab with him. He didn't understand it, but he knew it was a horrible experience.

Larry wished everyone could experience the military because of its focus on discipline, respect, good citizenship, work ethic, and making good choices. He felt that by working closely together in the military, with all different kinds of people, a person would become a better communicator.

After his time in the service, Larry owned and operated a total of eleven nightclubs in Idaho and California. He then spent twenty-two years in the field of education.

B-47 Stratojet

Ben A. Collins
U.S. Air Force
Medical Service Corps
Vietnam
1954–1976
Bronze Star

"I sat in my Jeep listening on my radio, while the Viet Cong killed all eighteen people!"

Born in a coal camp in Derby, Virginia, Ben Collins worked hard to get a good education and was able to earn his Associate's Degree in business. The Korean War had started and, since he had attended only a two-year college, as he was getting ready to graduate, he received his draft notice. The Monday after he received his diploma, he joined the U.S. Air Force–not wanting to go into the Army. Sampson Air Force Base was his first stop. With his degree, they pulled him out of basic training early and made him a training instructor for two years. Soon the Korean War was officially declared over, and his instructor position was made a senior NCO (noncommissioned officer) slot. All of the junior instructors were given their choice of career fields, and he chose accounting and finance, since his degree was in accounting.

For the next several years, Ben traveled back and forth across the country and to England for various assignments. Alaska (a favorite), England, Mississippi, and South Carolina were all home for a while. Promotions were tight in the Air Force, and Ben decided he really wanted to go back to college to finish his four-year degree. Five nights a week he attended classes until they moved him to Sandia, New Mexico. After a year there and, with only a year left to complete his degree, the Air Force agreed to release him to go back to school full time. He enrolled in the University of Nebraska. A month before graduation he applied for a commission in the Air Force Medical Corps and was accepted. He received his commission in 1965 and, though still on active duty, he wasn't called into service until January 1966, when he was sent to Gunner Air Force Base in Alabama for medical officer school. Since he was the top of his class, the chief of staff at Maxwell Air Force Base in Alabama decided to recruit him as his administrative assistant for student services. Ben didn't want that assignment and asked instead to be sent to Vietnam. Six months later he was on his way.

Since most of the men in the Military Assistance Command were senior officers, Ben was honored to be the first Air Force second lieutenant in that command to serve in Vietnam. He was pleased with his orders because he had an APO address in Saigon. But when he landed in Tan Son Nhut Air Base, all the military assistant officers were told to step forward. They were being sent to a compound in downtown Saigon, where in thirty days they were expected to learn at least 100 words in Vietnamese, plus the customs and courtesies of the country. The class was a multi-service group, and they were going to be sent out across the country when they were finished with their studies. In Vietnam there were twelve Military Public Health Assistance teams–four each from the Army, Navy, and Air Force. Ben's team was sent to the Four Corps area of the country, down in the Mekong Delta (the main infiltration route from Cambodia) and was assigned to the Vietnamese Army. There were also CIA, Army, Navy and the U.S. Agency for International Development personnel attached with them in Vinh Binh Province. Because it was 1966 (early in the war), there were no American combat troops south of Saigon. Ben was part of a sixteen-person, enlisted medical team which also included three doctors. Four of the medics were sent out to the rural hamlets, along with some American advisors and the South Vietnamese units. The doctors stayed in Vinh Binh because the surrounding area was unsecured, and the Army did not want to lose any of their medical teams. The bulk of the activity in Vinh Binh was against the Viet Cong and Viet Minh. Ninety-one Americans went in with the team and, at the end of the one-year tour, only thirty-five of the original team were left to leave the country.

On a normal day, Ben would take a couple of medics and supplies out to the field and give aid to the local people. Their goal was to try and win the hearts and minds of the Vietnamese. The people called Ben "bac si" (meaning doctor), even though he wasn't one. His team gave out medical supplies for malaria, scabies, TB and rashes. But no matter what medications were given out, the people would all swap them, and also take them to their families who were often Viet Cong. Ben and his men were not allowed to treat American personnel. They had to be evacuated to the hospital in Saigon. But his team could treat the local equivalent of our national guard and other forces. They could also render aid to the local people. The American doctors worked in an old French hospital. It had a surgical suite and a delivery suite. There were no windows, bathrooms, or running water. The generator ran only during the day. It was all very primitive. There was also a prison unit where Viet Cong soldiers were confined and they, too, were treated by the American medical personnel. Ben's office was also in the hospital, and his duties included going to Saigon on a monthly basis to pick up his unit's pay and any medical supplies that might be needed.

In addition to his normal duties, Ben did a lot of other things. Because of the potential danger from the enemy, by the time it was dark, all Americans had to be back in their compounds. On some nights, Ben would ride along on night air flights. One example: An Australian pilot named Rex Ramsey, training in the Mekong Delta, heard there were enemy antiaircraft guns in the area. Ben flew with Rex to drop phosphorous, which was used to illuminate target sites so F-100s could fly in to drop their bombs. When the first F-100 flew in, it took enemy fire. The F-100 pilot began yelling about being fired upon. Rex, in his best Aussie accent, radioed back to him, "What'd ya think mate, this is a war!" When the F-100s couldn't stop the enemy, a Dragon ship (C-47 airship with Gatling guns) was called in to assist. After the fire fight, Rex dropped down again to check for enemy fire and received none.

Ben's last military action took place thirty days before he left Vietnam. Navy patrol boats were blocking the river to stop the Viet Cong from leaving the area. Ben's group had made a sweep and picked up a few suspects and burned some propaganda booths–nothing exciting. It was noon and the South Vietnamese Army stopped for lunch. (They always stopped the war for lunch and a nap.) While the group was stopped, and since nothing was happening, the patrol boats decided to leave. Sixteen South Vietnamese soldiers went across the river to keep watch. After the break, the group was told to prepare to leave. Ben was in the rear of the group and, as the sixteen men started to cross back to rest of their group, 30-caliber machine guns began firing and the men were all gunned down. Then the enemy machine guns fired on the helicopters that were coming in to extricate Ben and the rest of the survivors. One helicopter went down and several men were severely injured. After his rescue, Ben decided he had experienced enough excitement (while he was in Vietnam) and didn't take any more excursions into the jungle.

Ben recalled that living conditions in the jungle were primitive. The soldiers were housed in an old French plantation house. There were forty men in the house, using two-man bunks, with no running water and no window screens. The South Vietnamese provided security, since there were too few Americans to man the posts. There was an intelligence briefing every night to keep them informed of any activity in the area. While Ben was there the town of Vinh Binh was badly damaged by a Viet Cong attack.

The day that Ben would never forget came on Easter Sunday 1967. He was assigned to go into Saigon to pick up medical supplies, and while he was waiting there for an Air America flight, he sat in his Jeep listening to the radio. It was a tactic of the Viet Cong to put up roadblocks and mines on roads that the U.S. military was using. Every night, a patrol consisting of an American advisor, a medic, and a radioman, plus South Vietnamese soldiers, went out to take the road blocks down. On this particular day there was a road block set up by the enemy outside of Vinh Binh. Later in the day an American major, a medic, and sixteen South Vietnamese soldiers headed out to take down the Viet Cong roadblock. The radio had been left on in the major's Jeep. Hidden in a school nearby, the Viet Cong lay in wait for the patrol, and when they approached the roadblock, they opened fire on them. Since the radio in the major's Jeep was on, Ben could hear on his radio everything that was happening to the men of the Vinh Binh patrol as the ambush took place. He listened helplessly, while all eighteen of the men were killed. "I sat in my Jeep listening on my radio, while the Viet Cong killed all eighteen people. There was nothing we could do!"

There was one Army medical assistance team located in the southern most part of Vietnam. According to Ben, it was the worst place on earth, because it was infested with Viet Cong. Ben was sent there to find out why the medics weren't treating any South Vietnamese patients. He found out that the Viet Cong had threatened the locals with death if any of them went to the Americans for aid. All the U.S. medical personnel could do was get through their year and hope they would get safely out. Ben recalled spending "three horrible days there."

June 1967 was a welcomed month for Ben. It was time to go home. His orders were sending him back to Elmendorf Air Force Base in Alaska, but this time with the Medical Corps. He was assigned to the hospital there which, at that time, was the second largest hospital in the U.S. Air Force with its 500-bed casualty staging unit. All the wounded came through the Elmendorf base on C-141s. If the plane had to be on the tarmac more than two hours, the wounded were brought to the hospital and stayed there eight hours before being allowed to continue their journey. Any personnel dying en route to the United States were processed there as well. Ben spent four years there before heading to Mountain Home Air Force Base, Idaho, and then back to Elmendorf for two and a half years, before he finally retired on June 30, 1976.

For his service in Vietnam, Ben was given the Bronze Star for combat. He was one of the few Medical Corps personnel to receive that honor.

Vietnam War Memorial

Sam Goodwin
U.S. Air Force
Vietnam
1957–1983

His duties included electronically jamming enemy communications over Vietnam.

Sam Goodwin was born in 1934 in Shreveport, Louisiana. He attended high school in Louisiana, where he enrolled in the Reserve Officer Training Corps (ROTC). After high school he attended Louisiana Tech University, graduating in 1957. He then entered the military and went to preflight training and navigator school at Biggs AFB in Texas. He was trained to fly B-52s. Often his missions were seven hours or more. He was then assigned to Castle AFB in California, and went on twenty-four hour missions with midair refueling, two to three times per month.

Sam participated in missile training, where he was assigned to various missile silos. Each missile site was assigned targets that were the responsibility of the two-man crew. Again, crews often did twenty-four hour shifts. Most of the sites were remote and it often required driving two or three hours to get from their living accommodations to their assigned silo.

Eventually Sam returned to B-52 duty and served as an electronic navigator. In 1966 he went to Thailand as a support staff officer for B-52 missions. His duties there included electronically jamming enemy communications over Vietnam. Their missions of four or five hours were focused on jamming ground radars, making it safer for combat aircraft to avoid detection, especially underpowered spotter planes.

Sam returned to Louisiana Tech for a master's degree in industrial engineering and was assigned to the Strategic Air

Command (SAC) in Omaha, Nebraska. His assignment was to debrief POW returnees and gather information about their capture and treatment as prisoners. Information from them was beneficial to the military training programs that focused on preparing military personnel in case they were ever captured and became prisoners of war.

Following that assignment, Sam was promoted to Lieutenant Colonel as Missile Commander in Minot, North Dakota. He had thirty two-man crews in his unit, with fifty missiles under his command. He stayed at this assignment for two years and was then transferred back to SAC as a MX Missile officer involved in missile deployment for U.S. defenses. He stayed in this assignment for four years. Lastly, Sam went to Cheyenne, Wyoming, as a full colonel and as base commander at Warren AFB. Colonel Goodwin retired from the U.S. Air Force in 1983, after serving his country for over twenty-five years.

Boeing B-52 Stratofortress

David Lee York
U.S. Air Force
Vietnam
1952–1972

*"There's always something to
learn."*

David York was born and
raised in Brownville Junction,
Maine, where his father was a
railroad engineer for the Canadian Pacific Railroad. While a junior
in high school, David turned seventeen and was unhappy in school.
He decided that, since he was now eligible to enlist in the service,
that was what he would do. He had always wanted to be a pilot,
but his poor eyesight disqualified him for that job. He still wanted
to wear Air Force blue and enlisted in April of 1952. For basic
training he was sent to Sampson Air Force Base in Geneva, New
York. In June of 1952 he was assigned to Lowry Air Force Base
in Denver, Colorado, for advanced training. Originally, he was
supposed to be in the airborne radio class. After twelve days in
that school, orders came down for ten members of the class to
report to the munitions and weapons school because, due to the
war in Korea, the Air Force was short on trained munitions
personnel. He was one of the ten chosen to be reassigned, and he
graduated as a munitions specialist in August of 1952.

Since David was one of the school's three top students, he was
allowed to choose where he would be assigned. He chose
England, because Korea was still an active war, and he didn't want
to take a chance of being shot. He went to Sandia, New Mexico, to
a special weapons school for two weeks and then to New Jersey to
be shipped out. His assignment while in England was to work with
an EOD (Explosive Ordnance Disposal) unit handling the storage

and security of nuclear weaponry being warehoused there. While David was stationed at the RAF Wethersfield Base, he was able to observe the British citizens as they prepared for the coronation of Queen Elizabeth II. He also was able to watch Roger Bannister break the four-minute mile run in 1954 at Oxford. Those two events were memorable for David. In April of 1956 he left England for his next assignment.

After four months in California, David was no longer able to avoid being assigned to Korea and was transferred to Kunsan Airbase. (The conflict had ended in July 1953.) Three months later, he was reassigned to Taegu, Korea, to help phase out a munitions storage area, where the bomb dumps were being cleared out. His job was to load the bombs and rockets on LSTs (Landing Ship Tanks) in Pusan to be taken out into the Yellow Sea and dropped into the water. After completing his one year in Korea, his next assignment, in June of 1957, was to Johnson Airbase, Japan. He spent the next three years working with nuclear weapons there as well. It was in Japan that David began his college studies with the University of Maryland. He also studied various Oriental subjects and taught a communism class at the Individual Military Training School. From Japan he was assigned to Kung Kuan Airbase in Taiwan to assist the Taiwanese Air Force in their operations to protect the Matsu Islands from mainland China. His job was to teach the Air Force personnel how to assemble Aim-9 missiles and load them onto F-86 fighters. He didn't want to leave Taiwan, but the Air Force sent him back to the States to Hill Air Force Base in Utah. There he was the NCOIC (noncommissioned officer in charge) of Inspections and Explosives Safety. Then came an assignment to Hahn Air Force Base, Germany, for three years and then back to Utah where he tested all kinds of munitions and explosives and fired Minuteman missile motors at the Great Salt Lake testing area.

In the mid 1960s the Vietnam War was heating up, and David was sent on temporary duty to Kadena, Okinawa, to load F-105s and send them off to bomb targets in Vietnam. In the summer of 1966 he was then assigned to Vietnam for a year. He was in the Cam Ranh Bay area, where they were offloading munitions and storing them. When his year's assignment was completed, he went back to California for three months. From there he was sent back for the next three years to Hahn Air Force Base as an Explosive Safety NCO. This was not where he wanted to go, since he had only been in the States for a short time. However, the Air Force had given him a choice–Germany now, or Thule, Greenland, later. He made the most of his time in Germany by hunting and becoming an honorary member of the DJV (the German hunting association). His only disappointment with the Air Force came in 1971. Hoping to get assigned back to Utah from Germany, so he could get ready for retirement, he was sent instead to Korat Air Force Base, Thailand. This was another one-year unaccompanied assignment as a munitions inspector. He returned to the U.S. on November 1, 1972, and retired on November 2, 1972!

David said he loved all of his assignments and all the traveling he was able to do while assigned to the different countries. He made friends in every country and found something to enjoy about every assignment. He felt "there's always something to learn." He also used his military munitions and safety training to find employment when he started his second career as a civilian, especially his involvement in the formation of OSHA in 1972.

Vietnam-Era Gun Boat

Mary Fran Meyer Brown
U.S. Army Nurse Corps
Vietnam
1965–1968

*"The year I spent in
Vietnam was when I lived
most intensely."*

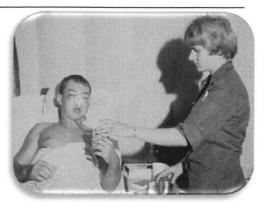

Born in St. Cloud, Minnesota, Mary Fran attended the college of St. Theresa, where she majored in nursing, with additional clinical experience at the Mayo Clinic in Rochester, New York. She graduated in 1965 just as the Vietnam War was beginning to escalate. She utilized the Army Nurse Corps nursing program, where they paid for the last two years of college in exchange for a three-year obligation in the Corps. Basic training was in San Antonio, Texas, for twelve weeks. There she learned Army nursing procedures, with specifics on how to run hospitals, how to manage patients, as well as casualty training.

Mary Fran met her future husband while stationed at Fort Ord, California, where he was in charge of the pharmacy. She returned to San Antonio to set up the 45th Surgical Hospital Unit that the Army would be taking to Vietnam. This group was the first to be deployed and was given the acronym MUST (Medical Unit Self-contained Transportable). It replaced the earlier MASH (Mobile Army Surgical Hospital) units. Instead of tents, MUST units used inflatable structures for the hospital wards. The operating rooms and pharmacies were built of metal structures. They were designed to be more portable than the MASH units. The operating rooms were planned so that each item required for a specific medical procedure was already located in that "box" or unit. Mary Fran's unit consisted of ten female nurses, five male nurses and fifteen doctors.

The hospital was located in the Parrot's Beak area in Tien Yen on the Cambodian border. Two nights before their unit was to be opened, the commanding officer and two corpsmen were killed during a mortar incident. There were several other attacks associated with their MUST unit, one in which a patient was killed.

Despite the ongoing military fighting in the area, the inflatable hospital wards were fairly quiet inside, because air was always being pumped into the structures and each had air conditioning. However, their "hooches" (thatched huts) were close to a helicopter landing area; and the take off and landings, plus the exploding mortars, were quite deafening. Also the hooches were not air conditioned. She recalled in her own words the following demanding schedule.

I worked nights, 7 p.m. to 7 a.m. The patients that remained overnight were patients that could be cared for surgically. I worked in post op primarily. Usually the patients were shipped to an evac-hospital the next day. Five or six critically ill patients that had not been able to be relocated that day would remain, and then the new patients would start coming in. They would almost always have all twenty beds filled by 5 a.m. Most surgeries were gut or chest wounds. Burn and head injury patients were usually moved to other units. Then the decision was made as to who could be moved out that day. There was constant turn over.

One of the things I always worried about was that I never remembered any of [the patients'] names, because they weren't there long enough. I thought I would have remembered a few, but I didn't–not a single name. Usually we worked six days per week, but there was one period in early 1967 where we worked thirty-two days without a day off. Most were fourteen-hour days.

During her time there, September 13, 1966, to September 8, 1967, Mary Fran was granted two R&Rs [rest and relaxation], one in Hawaii and one in Hong Kong.

> The contrast of going from a war zone to a non-war zone necessitated us having to "click things on" and "click things off;" otherwise it just didn't work. It was amazing. I flew with a few burn patients to Saigon to keep them on IV pain control in the helicopter transport. They were relocated to Fort Sam in Houston, Texas, within twenty-four hours, which was remarkable.

Mary Fran became engaged to her future husband while in Hawaii. "We did the reverse.... He wrote many letters to me and I wrote back when I could. Remember, there were no phone calls from Vietnam back then. We married two months after I returned from Vietnam, and later had three children."

After returning to the United States Mary Fran was stationed at Fort Lewis, Washington, where she treated patients from Vietnam and trained numerous corpsmen.

> The year I spent in Vietnam was when I lived most intensely. I learned about medicine and how people behave when they are stressed. I learned about teamwork. One thing I remember is that people either worked well with the team or we moved them out. How rapidly we moved some of them out was just brutal, but that's the way it worked. If a new physician or nurse came in and complained about the workload or

weren't professional, they were gone within a week or ten days.

One of the fascinating things that I have learned over the years is that I don't tell everybody that I was in Vietnam. But on occasion people find out, and about once a year someone will come up to me and say, "You know, I was in Vietnam and I was wounded." Then he tells me a story in great enormous detail about his experience and proceeds to say, "Thank you" to me. I think to myself, "But I wasn't your nurse." Later I learned that my role was to simply say, "You are welcome," because I could say that for some other nurse.

On November 11, 1993, Mary Fran attended the dedication of the Women's Vietnam Memorial in Washington D.C.

Vietnam Women's Memorial

William R. Carrol
U.S. Army
Vietnam
1969–1971
Bronze Star
Excellence in Infantry Badge

"You can't recon if they know you're there."

William was born in October of 1950 in Zanesville, Ohio. He graduated from high school in 1968 and joined the military. Since service in the Army was a family tradition, William decided to enlist in the infantry. After basic training for "jump school," he went to Fort Benning, Georgia, and then was deployed to Vietnam.

In April 1969 he was assigned to the 101st Airborne, I Corps. He was a member of the Alpha Company as a specialist 4th class at the time the U.S. troops reconnoitered Hill 937 (Hamburger Hill) as part of the Apache Snow campaign. William's company was in combat for ten days and sustained heavy losses before they finally reached the top. They had been under heavy fire from North Vietnamese forces, who were entrenched on the hill. Unfortunately, fourteen men of the American troops were killed by friendly fire from Cobra helicopters. During the fierce fighting, the troops fought with M-16s and a couple of M-60 machine guns. The men slept whenever and wherever they could and subsisted on C-rations. They had no ponchos for cover during rainy periods, because the fabric would reflect light at night if it got wet.

Charlie Company moved up the backside of Hamburger Hill, where they were resupplied by choppers. The soldiers carried their water, along with 100-pound packs that included their ammunition. After taking Hamburger Hill, they were sent to Camp Evans for three or four days. While at camp their accommodations consisted of tents that each slept thirty-five guys. It was typical to have thirty to forty days of operation with a rest period of three or four days in between. By this time William had advanced to "buck" sergeant and was the squad leader of eleven men. Their weapons included M-16s, M-60s, and M-39s. During the heavy fighting, his entire attention was focused on caring for his men and their weapons. He remembered that having clean, dry feet was essential. When a vacancy occurred, he was promoted to platoon sergeant and also acted as staff sergeant.

In April of 1970, William's one-year tour was completed and he was given a thirty-day leave. He then traveled to Germany, where he was assigned to the 3rd Infantry's Mechanized Personnel Carrier Company. The 3rd had been Audie Murphy's unit. (Murphy was a celebrated WWII hero.) At his repeated request, ten months later William was sent back to Vietnam and the 101st Airborne. He had earned his EIB (Excellence in Infantry Badge). He went to sniper school in Da Nang and then returned as a unit sniper with an M-14 (7.628mm) rifle that had a four-power scope. While in Alpha Company he participated in ambushes of the enemy by lying in wait along specific trails. He had a spotter (a radio man) with him. They would spend a week or ten days at a time in the field. William had to maintain the ranking of an "expert" shot at 500-700 meters. He was eventually wounded and transported to Pleiku to the hospital for a week's stay. After he recovered he was assigned to a "sneak-and-peak" unit, which consisted of five guys who would be dropped off by helicopter at their assigned recon area. That group consisted of a medic, a telephone man, and three riflemen. Depending on whether or not they were discovered by the enemy, they would spend up to thirty days in the field. William commented that, "You can't recon if they know you're there."

On one such sneak-and-peak mission, William rescued his lieutenant, who was bleeding severely, wounded in both legs. For his bravery, William received the Bronze Star.

In 1971 William returned to Fort Lewis, Washington, where he was discharged. He worked in construction until 1985, when he was hired by the Idaho National Guard as a full-time soldier/instructor. While in the Guard he was 1st sergeant of the Charlie and Bravo companies and performed duties as instructor, armorer, and master gunner.

M-60 Machine Gun

Colt M-16 Rifle

Jim Cornwell
U.S. Army
Vietnam
1969–1972
Bronze Star

Their mission was to find trails the Viet Cong were using through the jungle.

Jim was born in Enterprise, Oregon, in August of 1946. He attended Oregon State University 1964 through 1965, studying range management. In 1969, Jim was selected for training in the Army OCS program (Officer Candidate School) as one of several hundred candidates. For twenty-two weeks, he trained at Ft. Benning, Georgia. He was then sent to airborne school and tactical officers school in Panama and finally to Charleston, South Carolina.

In October-November of 1970 Jim's orders sent him to Vietnam. He was assigned to A Company of the 1st Cavalry Division, with duty station in Bien Hoa. While there, Jim was appointed as a platoon leader and was stationed at a firebase north of Bien Hoa. There were twenty-nine soldiers in his platoon. The platoon was made up of several squads, each having a medic and a radio man. Every man carried an M-16 (rifle) weapon. Their mission was to find trails through the jungle that the Viet Cong were using. Typically, the troops were in the field for up to fifteen days at a time. When they found a Viet Cong trail, they would booby trap it with buried Claymore mines, then move back away from the trail and lie in wait for the enemy to trip off the explosives. Once the squad heard the mines explode, they would sweep the area, looking for any survivors, and then clean up the site. Then they would move up-trail and lay more mines and traps; and the wait would start all over again.

Helicopters would resupply the squads every three to five days. Their only protection from the weather was a poncho. None of the men liked being in a "free-fire" zone, because everyone there was fair game as a target. They always patrolled with fixed bayonets, but fortunately had little hand-to-hand combat with the enemy. Their areas of operation were within eleven kilometers from the firebase. That was the effective range of the 105mm howitzers, which were standing by to support them in case of a firefight with the Viet Cong.

While actually at the firebase, the soldiers lived in "hooches" (thatched huts). The walls were made from sandbags and empty ammunition boxes. Malaria was a constant concern and the soldiers were medicated for it daily. In 1971 Jim was in the field with his platoon for about nine months. He not only confronted the enemy, but had to rescue his own men several times. Another time he was in charge of cleaning up another platoon's ambush gone bad.

Jim was eventually assigned as a firebase supply officer. His assignment included directing the firebase move to a new location. It took nearly a hundred helicopter loads to get the base moved. He was later in a motor platoon which fired 105mm and 175mm guns in direct support of Cobra gunships.

The normal tour of duty in Vietnam was twelve months and, when Jim had fulfilled that obligation, he was returned to California. He had only two months left on his enlistment, so he took an early discharge and returned to Oregon State University to finish his education. It was there that he met his wife.

Jim earned the Bronze Star for his courageous service in Vietnam. Through the years Jim attended several reunions of his OCS class.

Lorraine Diehl
U.S Army Nurse Corps
Vietnam
1968–1970

"The explosions killed several patients, and one of the nurses."

Lorraine was born in a small town in Pennsylvania. She graduated from high school in 1963 and then traveled to Philadelphia where she worked in a hospital and completed a three-year program to become a registered nurse. After graduating in 1966 she went back to her hometown, where she worked at a community hospital until she got married and moved to Florida.

Lorraine worked in a hospital in Florida until 1968 when her family decided to move back to Pennsylvania. There she was hired as a nurse at Valley Forge Army Hospital, which was near where she grew up. About that time her husband died, and many of the people at the hospital encouraged her to join the Army as a nurse. She enlisted in March of 1968, and she was sent to Texas, where she did six weeks of basic training. While there she was made a first lieutenant and then sent immediately to Vietnam.

In May 1968 Lorraine arrived in Saigon, Vietnam. Her first impression was how unbearably hot the country was. She was driven to a small trailer south of Saigon and dropped off there. Nobody else was in the trailer and she became very frightened. She was too scared to leave, even to go to the mess hall to eat. She remembered remaining there by herself for three days before someone came for her.

She was then flown to a new hospital in Quy Nhon, Vietnam. It was a very nice facility that was located on the beach. She said the food was good there and they enjoyed seaside living.

The hospital was a 350-bed facility that had ample medicine and modern equipment, but it was short of nurses. Lorraine worked twelve-hour shifts, six days a week. On her day off she often enjoyed swimming in the ocean. While she was not close to the actual battle lines, wounded soldiers were transported to her hospital. The hospital staff also cared for local Vietnamese, treating the day-to-day injuries and sicknesses among the population.

In November 1968 she was transferred to a hospital at Chu Li. Situated high on a cliff, it was not nearly as nice as her previous hospital. The weather was extremely hot, with lots of rain, making it muddy all the time. There was not much else there–just a hospital with a mess hall and a small PX.

This hospital had been set up with a special ward of fifty beds for the treatment of the Vietnamese. Since Lorraine had some previous experience helping the locals, she was put in charge of this ward. As supervisor she had four other nurses who worked for her, as well as five or six Navy corpsman. While there she saw many diseases, such as cholera and typhus–sickness that she would not normally see in the United States. The hospital hired an interpreter who worked twelve hours a day. However, when he went to bed, the night shift had to make do without an interpreter, and that made communication very difficult.

The Vietnamese patients Lorraine cared for were civilians, soldiers, and occasionally a prisoner of war. Most of the prisoners of war were badly injured, thus they were not much of an escape threat, and they caused very few problems. The hospital personnel shackled them to their beds, and there was always a military policeman (MP) on floor duty. The MPs would get bored sitting around, so Lorraine often put them to work feeding patients, as well as making beds, etc. She felt they appreciated being able to do various tasks to keep themselves busy.

Often, when a Vietnamese was a patient in the hospital, his entire family would show up to also stay. This meant that typically they might have up to 200 people in the ward. The families often slept there and, as a result, the staff had to help feed these people and find a place for them to stay. When one of the patients died, the family immediately took the body and left. Lorraine stated, the first time this happened on her watch, it was quite a shock to return to the patient's bed and find it empty.

Lorraine told the story of how many of the Vietnamese people would put tar on their feet and then step in the sand–which basically made shoes on the soles of their feet. At first she instructed the staff to remove the tar and sand because it was unsanitary; but when the nurses tried, the Vietnamese became upset, because this technique was the only protection they had for their feet. The staff ended up leaving the tar and sand in place and working around the feet as best they could.

Lorraine had a lot of empathy, particularly for the children, because even if they did get well they would continue to have a difficult life. She and her staff often wrote to people in the United States and asked them to send clothing to help the Vietnamese people, particularly the children. They received a tremendous response from both the Girl Scouts and Boy Scouts and other civic groups.

One night the North Vietnamese fired a rocket at the hospital, and it exploded in the middle of one of the Quonset huts. Because of volatile oxygen bottles, the blast set off other explosions that did considerable damage to the hospital ward. The explosions killed several patients; and one of the nurses, Sharon Lane, was also killed. She was the only nurse killed due to enemy action during the entire Vietnam War. For Lorraine, it was a very traumatic time, experiencing the loss of a fellow nurse.

One of the programs that the military had was called Med-Cap. When the medical staff had time, they went out into the villages and helped deal with minor injuries and sickness. Lorraine remembered helping many pregnant women. She specifically recalled one time they had a young person with a club foot. They were able to get this youngster to come into the hospital, where the doctors operated on his foot. That child was given a better chance for a productive life.

Lorraine became friends with several Vietnamese families, and on one occasion she was invited to one of their homes for dinner. Their house was very humble, and she stated it was amazing to see how other people survived on so little. For dinner the hostess brought out a chicken that had been cooked with its head still intact. Since the family thought she was in charge of the hospital, she was treated as their honored guest; so they gave her what they thought was a special treat–the eyeballs of the chicken! She ate the eyeballs, just to be kind to her friends, but she said they tasted terrible.

About the time Lorraine was finished with her military tour, the hospital where she worked was due to be closed. It was very sad for the staff to board everything up, especially when they knew the local Vietnamese would no longer have access to any medical facilities. Before they left they put up a plaque in remembrance of Sharon Lane, the nurse who was killed.

In August 1969, Lorraine left Vietnam and was assigned to the Valley Forge Hospital in Pennsylvania, the very hospital where she had started out as a civilian nurse prior to joining the military. While in Vietnam Lorraine had fallen in love with an Army sergeant, and they were married while on leave together in Hawaii. She considered staying in the military, but it was somewhat awkward with her husband being a noncommissioned officer. At that time she was a captain, so she decided not to re-enlist. Her husband continued his military career, and for many years she worked as a civilian in military hospitals. Lorraine was proud of her Army service and enjoyed her time in Vietnam.

U.S. Army Hospital – Vietnam
Photos Courtesy Lorraine Diehl

Donald S. Menger
U.S. Army
Vietnam, Grenada &
The Cold War
1964–1990
Bronze Star
Meritorious Service Medal
Legion of Merit

*"The military has given me focus,
attention to detail, and faith in my God
and my country."*

Don was born in January of 1946 in Tulsa, Oklahoma. As a young boy, he moved with his family to Venezuela, where Don's father worked for Standard Oil Company of New Jersey under the name of the Creole Petroleum Corporation. They lived in an oilfield camp where there were schools, dispensary and housing for the foreign workers. As a child Don learned the Spanish language and Latin American culture. The family, including five boys, later returned to the United States in time for Don to complete junior high and high school in Tulsa. In May 1964, just two days after high school, Don began drawing Army pay, since he had enlisted in the Army and took the oath to defend the Constitution of the United States of America. He initially joined as a volunteer for four years–and twenty-six years later he retired.

In Don's oral history interview, he recalled the following military experiences.

> I was put on a bus to Oklahoma City and then flew on to Missouri, where I took my basic training. I initially was trained in Morse Code and began code intercepting. I was sent to the Panama Canal, and they [the Army] found out I could speak

Spanish better than I could read Morse Code, so I was made into a voice intercept operator in the Spanish language. I spent eighteen months there and was sent back to the United States. I had wanted to go to West Point, but after spending enough time in the Army, I found out that West Point was not my forte; so I was transferred from Virginia to Florida, where I lived on Homestead Air Force base in an Army unit. We worked on a Navy installation in the Everglades. Our job was to intercept foreign communications.

I was sent to Fort Holabird in Maryland, and there I learned to be a counterintelligence agent. I spent about four months there, and it was there that I met my first wife. I was then sent to foreign language school in Washington, D.C., where, for a full school year, I spent five days a week learning the Vietnamese language. In October of 1970 I was sent to Vietnam, where I was attached to the 702 Military Intelligence Detachment, U.S. Army Headquarters, Vietnam. There we conducted counterintelligence, primarily against the Viet Cong and the North Vietnamese Army. Counterintelligence was the effort to counter espionage activities conducted against the Army and/or our nation. We were trained to catch spies and our ultimate goal was to incarcerate. One of the things I really enjoyed doing there was translating a Vietnamese propaganda film that was included in the archives of the United States Army.

The North Vietnamese Army had invaded South Vietnam, and the Viet Cong were rebels from South Vietnam who chose to rebel against the South

Vietnamese government. The Viet Cong had North Vietnamese and Chinese advisors, and we had information that they had Russian advisors, as well.

I remember vividly, on the flight over to Vietnam, wondering if I was going to be a good soldier, and worried that I may not come home to see my wife and three-month old baby son. Once I was on the ground, I learned to put away my fear and concentrate on my job and surroundings. Since I knew the Vietnamese language, I joked with [my fellow soldiers] that I knew a little sooner than they did when to get out of the area. I learned that if it was very still or quiet, or if children were not around, something was wrong, and we took measures accordingly. The only real concern we had was that the North Vietnamese would shoot their 122mm rockets with boosters at us; however, their accuracy was slim to none. In Cam Ranh Bay they were trying to hit the ships that supplied power to the military installations, [thus] interrupting our communications. One night a group of us had gone downtown to a bar and heard gunfire. We high-tailed it back to the base. But it turned out to be a bunch of AWOL GIs.

The Vietnamese were very gentle people. I enjoyed visiting with them in their language and learning their culture. I was respectful of the elders; and in our training we learned how to treat children, such as: one should never pat a child on the head, as that was a sign of insult, because that was where their spirit [resided]. Never take a photo of three people, as that was bad luck. Never sign anything in red ink, because that was a sign of death or extreme bad luck.   [Also], quite frequently I was the translator for my commander.

I took an oath to defend the Constitution of the United States, and regardless of my feelings about the war, it was my job to do the best I could, wherever I was; even though I didn't agree with how the war was being [fought]. I saw a lot of graft and corruption by Americans and the other foreign people that were in Vietnam.   I think the United States learned a great lesson by being in Vietnam, about how to handle our support personnel and contractors.   Millions [of dollars] were made by people who had no business being in Vietnam. Militarily, we had the war won in Vietnam.   The war was actually lost here in the United States with the highly vocal minority and our Congressional leaders and the Executive Branch.   There were atrocities that occurred, because our young soldiers did not have the leadership they should have had, and they were being trained very quickly.   The soldiers involved with the My Lai Massacre were prosecuted and put in prison. No one was above the law in our country.

One of the proudest things I did, as a result of the Vietnam War, was debriefing a returning U.S. Army POW, who had spent five years as a prisoner of the Viet Cong and three years at the Hanoi Hilton.   He was a crew chief on a helicopter that was shot down. The warrant officer and I debriefed him over a period of about six weeks, [concerning] the time just before he was captured to the time he was released from the Hanoi Hilton. I also had the privilege to meet and work with the man whose

POW bracelet I wore–Sergeant First Class Cardine McMurray. For about two years during the war, I [had been wearing] Cardine McMurray's bracelet. The POW/MIA association had been selling these bracelets to help support the families and to keep the POW/MIA issue before Congress, so that they would not be forgotten. We wore them in remembrance of each of the POWs and MIAs.

We took our POW [whom we had been debriefing] and Cardine into San Antonio one evening. My partner and I got into a little bit of trouble with the nursing staff at Brook Army Medical Center, because our POW friends came back slightly the worse for wear, with some severe hangovers the next morning. The nurses read us the riot act because neither one of our guys was in any condition to talk that next day.

I went from Vietnam to Fort Polk, Louisiana, where our daughter was born. I was with the 112th Military Intelligence Group. I ran background investigations and other counterintelligence activities; and security inspections throughout Louisiana, and parts of Texas, Mississippi, and Arkansas. We were still concerned with radicals on both the left and the right, who were attempting to steal weapons from the National Guard Armories. We had our efforts aimed in that direction to ensure that everybody was meeting the regulations, and that the facilities were properly [designed and constructed for security]. During that time, there was an underground anarchy movement in the United States that truly wanted to destroy our country from within. Part of that movement included the demonstrations against the war in Vietnam. So the military services, in compliance with directives from Congress and orders from the Presidential Executive Office, did what we did from the military point of view. [Our work was accomplished] in cooperation with the FBI and other agencies, in order to protect our country; just as we still do today.

I was at Fort Polk for four years and was then transferred to the Netherlands, where I was assigned to the Allied Command Europe Counterintelligence Activity. My assignment was on a NATO base. I was with Allied Forces Central Europe in the southern portion of the country, with Germany on one side and Belgium on the other. Our unit was also known as the 650th Military Intelligence Group, and our primary mission was to provide counterintelligence to the seven nations that made up the Allied Forces Central Europe. While there, I completed my college degree, and I opted to learn to speak German. I also learned to speak a little Dutch. I was divorced while there, and stayed with my two kids for another year in the Netherlands, before I was transferred back to Fort Meade, Maryland, for two years with the 902nd Military Intelligence Unit. At that time I was instructing others on inspecting, maintaining and protecting from surreptitious entry, safes and security devices that were being used to protect national classified information. While in Fort Meade, I was fortunate to meet my new wife, who became an instant mother to my two children.

In 1980 I requested and was transferred to West Berlin, Germany, with the 766th Military Intelligence Unit. My family and I often took tour buses into East Germany to shop. My family learned some German while we were there, and they would sometimes go [to East Germany] without me. The [economic & cultural] differences between West and East Berlin were like night and day. West Berlin was the Western showplace [in the heart of] of East Germany. It was capitalism in its most ostentatious form. It was "stick it in the nose of the Soviets," to show them what they were missing out on. A water tower (a large ball up in the sky) was constructed in the East German sector of the city. Some people called it divine intervention; but due to the design of the water tower, whenever the sun would shine on it, a large cross (a crucifix) would appear. The East Germans and Soviets tried to paint over it, and do whatever they could to make it disappear–without any success.

The French, Germans and Americans each had what they called a "duty train" that would transit out of East Germany into the western sector. It was quite an operation to watch, when they hooked up to an East German engine in Berlin. The Allied cars on the train were locked from the inside by the military police, and we were surrounded by East German and Soviet soldiers on the outside. The excuse (made by the communists) was to ensure that we didn't escape; but normally we only saw the backs of the Soviet Bloc soldiers, as they prevented their citizens from jumping onto the trains to escape East Berlin.

After three years we were transferred to Fort Lewis, Washington. Ninety days later I received orders that I was going to the island of Grenada. The invasion of Grenada had already occurred. Because I was a senior Army counterintelligence Spanish linguist, I was sent down with four others. We were attached to an airborne unit, where I was told to wear a red beret. I explained I was not airborne qualified and should not be wearing the beret. I was told to wear it [anyway] and try to blend in. The Eastern Caribbean Commonwealth of Nations' concern was that Cuba had taken over Grenada and was establishing a military base there. Yes, the Cubans were there. Yes, they had taken over the island of Grenada, and had the people under curfews, and controlled the harbors and airport so they could land ammunitions and weapons. We were there three weeks until our mission was completed.

I was sent back to Fort Lewis and went to Army computer security school. This was the period of time that the United States Army was beginning to take on the computer world. The Army needed people to be security conscious and to teach security awareness, and I became the division computer security expert. It was a fun time.

I and my family were then sent to Seoul, Korea, and worked in the counterintelligence unit there and had the privilege of seeing the 1988 Olympics. Our daughter learned to speak Korean while there. From there we went to Fort Monmouth, New

Jersey, with the 515th Military Brigade, where I worked in the security division.

Don retired from the military with twenty-six years in the Army. He was awarded the Bronze Star for operations against the enemy while in Vietnam. He also received the Meritorious Service Medal and the Legion of Merit award. After retiring, he worked for the federal Drug Enforcement Administration from which he retired after a twenty-one year career.

Don summed up his military experience by saying: "The military has given me focus, attention to detail, and faith in my God and my country. I have been proud to be an American."

This will remain the
land of the free only so
long as it is the home of
the brave.[3]

Elmer Davis

---

[3]Elmer Davis. (n.d.). BrainyQuote.com. Retrieved January 25, 2015, from BrainyQuote.com Web site.

Thomas Marshall Anderson
U.S. Marine Corps
Operation Iraqi Freedom
2008–2009

"If we aren't doing our job, it's a good day."

Thomas Marshall wanted to be a welder, but the welding class in his high school was full, so he took an automotive repair class, instead. This class enabled him to work at an auto dealership while in high school. After graduating from Centennial High School in Boise, Idaho, he continued his auto repair work for a few years. He then decided he wanted to become a fire fighter. Although he passed the admittance test (his was one of the top 200 scores), they weren't accepting that many into the class. He ended up working for Horizon Air for a while, trying to decide what he wanted to do with his life. A buddy had enlisted in the U.S. Marine Corps, which inspired Thomas to consider the military, and he decided he wanted to join the Air Force. Unfortunately, he wasn't accepted; so he then applied to, and was admitted, into the Marine Corps. His field of service in the Corps was crash-fire rescue.

Thomas spent the next four months at boot camp in San Diego, California. While there he was put on a weight-loss program and lost thirty-five pounds. He then headed to San Angelo, Texas, for crash-fire rescue training on Goodfellow Air Force Base. His training lasted three or four months, and he learned hazmat (hazardous materials), and aircraft and structure firefighting techniques. After finishing his training, he was told he wouldn't be deployed to Iraq. He was very unhappy about that directive, since he was really eager to go. Instead he was sent to Miramar

Naval Base, California, for an additional year of training. Upon arrival at the base, he was told he was actually assigned to the deployable side of Miramar; so he realized he would, in fact, be going to Iraq. In May 2008 he took leave to go home and marry his hometown girlfriend, and then deployed to Iraq on September 15, 2008.

The plane ride overseas was a wakeup call for Thomas. He was on a flight with a mixed group of Marines. Some had already been deployed to Iraq a few times and some, like him, were "newbies." He remembered feeling anxious, but not fearful. They flew into Amsterdam and deplaned, but the airport was on lockdown, and for a time the Marines could not leave the area. Eventually they continued on to Kuwait. Upon landing there, he was issued sixty rounds of ammunition, which he was required to count and keep with him at all times. Kuwait was just a short stopover before heading into Iraq. The flight to Iraq was a rough one because the pilot had to continually divert from his flight path to avoid enemy fire. When they finally touched down, it was eerily quiet because it was Muslim prayer time. Thomas remembered that during his deployment in Iraq, this was the only time it was quiet.

Thomas knew he was going to Fallujah, which was well known as a hot area for insurgents. The men flew with all of their gear in a CH-46 helicopter. The flight took off in the dark, carrying the pilots, two gunners and four marines. It was an uneventful landing, and as soon as they arrived they were sent to their "can" or housing. The accommodations were quite comfortable, since they were living with the civilian fire department. Two people were assigned to each room, which had air conditioning and internet connections. The civilian fire fighters were there to fight structure fires and, as a marine, Thomas would be fighting aircraft fires. He stayed there for about one and a half months. Fallujah had great chow halls and he had time to exercise without wearing his heavy battle gear. (They did have to keep their weapons on them at all times.) He saw no insurgent activity, except for one old Iraqi man, who would climb up the fence and randomly shoot off rounds. The soldiers didn't worry about him, because he couldn't hit anything and, besides, he was in a spot where they couldn't get to him.

In the first six weeks in the country, Thomas' team was split up with four firefighters, including Thomas, going on to Ramadi. Again he was flown in at night on a CH-46. His unit thought that since Fallujah wasn't hot any more, Ramadi wouldn't be either. But upon landing, they were met by the team they were replacing and told that because militant jihadists remained in the area the U.S. Abrams tanks and the AABs (Advise and Assist Brigade) were still needed there. That meant the area continued to be considered a hot area of activity. Thomas spent the next six or so months in Ramadi. There was a lot of terrorist activity there, as far as insurgents were concerned, but the crash-fire rescue people didn't see much action. Since they were there to rescue people, dead or alive, Thomas stated that, "If we were busy, things were going wrong." He experienced no major incidents–only minor injuries. There were only four crash-rescue people there for the first four months, so they were on call 24/7. The only time they enjoyed a decent amount of sleep was during the sandstorms, because during the storm, no military equipment could make it into the city. The men were always on the move. Thomas never got outside the base during calls because they were short-handed, and the military couldn't take a chance on losing one of the crash-fire crew members.

While Thomas was in Ramadi, there was only one aircraft crash. A helicopter fell out of the sky, bounced on the ground and landed in the mud. Luckily, there was no fire. By the time the crash crew dressed in their gear and reached the helicopter, the situation was resolved.

There was some hostile-weapons fire, and a few helicopters did take some damage. They had no repair facility at Ramadi, so most damaged aircraft went back to a base that had repair facilities. There were also additional medical services back at the base. The emergency services group consisted of EOD (explosive ordinance disposal), crash-fire rescue, veterinary services, and a psychologist. While Thomas was primarily crash-fire rescue, he certified as an EMT and gave medical support when needed.

When it came time for Thomas to leave the country, he tried for two weeks to secure transportation to fly out. Due to the drawdown in troop numbers, there was a lot of activity and consequently no transportation was available. They finally had to convoy out. He left Iraq on April 27, 2009, going through Germany and back to Miramar Marine Corps Air Station, California, to finish his service time. By October 22, 2009, he was due to re-enlist or be discharged. He wanted to re-enlist as a gunship door gunner or a crew chief, but his wife said, "No!" He realized that if he stayed on active duty, he would be deployed to Afghanistan, so he had to make a decision. He loved being a marine, but he wanted a family life and, even though his wife said she would stand behind him, he made the decision to leave the Marines and move back to Boise, Idaho, where he attended college.

U.S. Troops in Iraq

INDEX

Made in the USA
San Bernardino, CA
16 February 2017